Cyber Law in Sweden

Cyber Law in Sweden

Second Edition

Christine Kirchberger

This book was originally published as a monograph in the International Encyclopaedia of Laws/Cyber Law.

General Editor: Roger Blanpain
Associate General Editor: Michele Colucci
Volume Editor: Jos Dumortier

Wolters Kluwer
Law & Business

Published by:
Kluwer Law International
PO Box 316
2400 AH Alphen aan den Rijn
The Netherlands
Website: www.kluwerlaw.com

Sold and distributed in North, Central and South America by:
Aspen Publishers, Inc.
7201 McKinney Circle
Frederick, MD 21704
United States of America
Email: customer.service@aspenpublishers.com

Sold and distributed in all other countries by:
Turpin Distribution Services Ltd.
Stratton Business Park
Pegasus Drive, Biggleswade
Bedfordshire SG18 8TQ
United Kingdom
Email: kluwerlaw@turpin-distribution.com

ISBN 978-90-411-56679

This title is available on www.kluwerlawonline.com

The Author

Prof. Christine Kirchberger (editor of this monograph and main author)

Christine Kirchberger earned her Law Degree from the University of Vienna in 1997. After working as a trainee with the European Parliament and at two district courts in Austria, she obtained a Master's Degree in Law and Information Technology from the University of Stockholm in 2000.

Christine Kirchberger joined the Swedish Law and Informatics Research Institute at Stockholm University in 2001 as a junior lecturer. She has been involved in teaching legal informatics to law students as well as computer scientists, both in Stockholm and other Swedish universities as well as at King's College in London. Within IT law, her main focus areas have been data protection, electronic commerce, and intellectual property rights. She has also been teaching and publishing articles on legal information retrieval and legal informatics in general.

Since 2006, Christine Kirchberger has been writing her doctoral thesis 'Legal Information as a Tool' where she focuses on legal information retrieval, the concept of legal information within the framework of the doctrine of legal sources and also examines the information-seeking behaviour of lawyers.

She is the editor of this monograph and has written the Introduction as well as the parts on Protection of Intellectual Property in the ICT Sector (original version), Electronic Transactions, Privacy Protection, and the Conclusion. She can be found as @iinek on Twitter and at iinek.net. Together with Pam Storr she founded legalgeekgirls.com.

The Author

Co-authors

Stanley Greenstein (Part I Chapters 3 and 4)

Stanley Greenstein has a Law Degree (BA, LLB) from the University of Cape Town, South Africa as well as a Masters Degree in Law and Information Technology from the University of Stockholm. He has been a Junior Lecturer at the Swedish Law and Informatics Research Institute since 2007 and administers the International Masters Programme in Law and Information Technology offered by the Swedish Law and Informatics Research Institute at Stockholm University. His main area of interest is information security.

Ulf Isaksson (Part V)

Ulf Isaksson, partner of the law firm Danowsky & Partners, has a Law Degree from Uppsala University (1990) and an LLM from the University of Amsterdam (1993). He began his professional career as a law clerk in the Stockholm District Court (1990–1992). In 1993, he joined Danowsky & Partners, a Swedish law firm focused on corporate and commercial law and dispute resolution. The firm is considered as one of the leading Swedish law firms within media and intellectual property rights.

Ulf has represented publishers and other companies and organizations in the media industry, both as counsel and litigator. He has been assigned by the Swedish Bar Association to comment on proposed legislation regarding copyright and media. He is also the author of several articles, mainly in the field of media and intellectual property. He is a guest lecturer in the field of media law at the University of Stockholm.

Part V of this monograph was written together with Karl Hägg who is an associate at the law firm Danowsky & Partners. Karl Hägg has a Law Degree from Uppsala University (2010). He has also studied one year at the Department of Media and Communications at the same university. He had an internship at Danowsky &

?artners during the fall of 2009 and joined the firm directly after his graduation. Karl also has experience as a company lawyer during the later part of his student days.

Johan Kahn (Part III)

Johan Kahn is a partner of Advokatfirman Delphi and heads the firms TMT/Intellectual Property group. His areas of practice range from Outsourcing and ITC Contracts to data protection and IT-related IPR issues. Johan Kahn provides legal advice to Swedish and international clients and has specific experience from complex outsourcing transactions within the banking and insurance sector including BPO and off-shoring deals. Together with his colleague Agne Lindberg, he published a comprehensive guide to outsourcing deals 'IT-avtal – Särskilt om Outsourcing' (Norsteds Juridik 2009). Johan Kahn is a frequently engaged speaker and has published a large number of articles within the field of business law and specific ITC-related topics.

Part III in this volume was written together with Daniel Lundqvist who is a senior associate at Advokatfirman Delphi. Daniel Lundqvist has a Law Degree from the University of Stockholm as well as a Commercial and Business Law Degree from the University of Linköping. Since joining Advokatfirman Delphi, he has rendered legal advice in the fields of IT Law, Outsourcing, Data Protection Law, Telecommunications Law, Intellectual & Industrial Property Law, and general corporate and commercial law to a multitude of clients including several IT service providers, equipment manufacturers, broadcasting entities, producers, designers and software developers. His primary areas of expertise include IT Contracts, Outsourcing and Software Distribution issues.

Henrik Nilsson (Part I Chapters 1 and 2)

Henrik Nilsson is an Advokat at Gärde Wesslau law firm in Stockholm, Sweden He has practised Telecommunications Law since 1997 and is a frequent contributor to legal and business journals on these issues.

Henrik Nilsson advises clients on regulatory and commercial issues with a focus on the IT and telecom industries and acts on behalf of clients before government agencies and authorities, in Sweden and internationally such as with EU organizations. He has previously worked for the Swedish Competition Authority and the Swedish Post and Telecom Agency as well as international and domestic law firms. Henrik is ranked for IT & telecommunications law by Chambers & Partners 2014 and Legal500 2014.

Per Nordenson (Part I Chapter 5)

Per Nordenson has a Law Degree from the University of Stockholm and worked at the Stockholm District Court for two years after graduating. He worked at Advokatfirman Frie and subsequently at Advokatfirman Cederquist until 2004, where he was partner for the last years. He founded Nordenson Advokatbyrå in 2004 and specializes in litigation and arbitration, telecommunications and IT, including related IP- and advertising matters, mergers and acquisitions, distribution and agency matters, real estate and tenant law.

Per Nordenson is a member of the Swedish Bar Association and IBA, and has a broad experience of advising in business law, particularly as counsel in domestic and international litigation, including arbitration and dispute resolution. During the past five to six years, he acted as counsel for clients in a large number of cases and matters under the frameworks for regulation of telecommunications within EU. He has also been lecturing on procedural law at, among others, the University of Stockholm.

Pam Storr (Updates 2014 – Part I Chapters 3 and 4, Part II)

Pam Storr earned her law degree from the University of Durham, England in 2006. She has LLM degrees from Stockholm University in the fields of Law & Information Technology and Intellectual Property Law.

Pam Storr joined the Swedish Law and Informatics Research Institute at Stockholm University in 2009 as a junior lecturer. She teaches primarily within the areas of cyber law and legal informatics, both to law students and computer scientists. Since 2012, she has been course director and programme coordinator of the Master Programme in Law and Information Technology at Stockholm University.

Her main areas of interest within cyber law are intellectual property rights, privacy, e-business and social media. She is also focused on comparative law issues, legal English, along with e-learning and productivity tools for lawyers and legal academics.

Pam Storr can be found as @pamstorr on Twitter and at legalgeekgirls.com.

Co-authors

Erik O. Wennerström (Part VII)

Erik O. Wennerström has a Master's Degree in Law from the University of Uppsala in Sweden. In 1990, he joined the Ministry for Foreign Affairs of Sweden and served with its diplomatic service, until he joined the European Commission in 1996, to work *inter alia* with issues related to judicial cooperation in criminal law. For the Commission, he drafted, for example, the Framework Decision on Fraud and Counterfeiting of Non-cash Means of Payment, later adopted and made part of the EU acquis, and was instrumental in areas encompassing measures against cybercrime. Returning to Sweden, he joined the Ministry of Justice in time for the first Swedish EU Presidency in 2001. He has negotiated and rendered legal advice in the fields of Police Cooperation, Judicial Cooperation, Telecommunications Law, and Information Exchange to the Swedish Government and the cooperation mechanisms under the European Union. He has given lectures at several European universities, and is the author of numerous articles and books. After obtaining his Doctor's Degree in Law from his alma mater in 2007, he returned to the Ministry for Foreign Affairs, where he worked as the Principal Legal Adviser on International Law. He is currently the Director-General of the Swedish National Council for Crime Prevention (*Brottsförebygande rådet – Brå*).

Table of Contents

List of Abbreviations

ADR	Alternative Dispute Resolution
B2B	Business-To-Business
B2C	Business-To-Consumers
DOS	Denial of Service
ICT	Information Communication Technology
ISP	Internet/Information Service Provider
PTS	Swedish Post and Telecom Agency (*Post- och telestyrelsen*)
SKL	Swedish Association of Local Authorities and Regions – SALAR (*Sveriges Kommuner och Landsting*)
SMP	Significant Market Power
SOU	Swedish Government Official Reports (*Statens Offentliga Utredningar*)
USO	Universal Services Obligation

General Introduction

Chapter 1. General Background of the Country

§1. Geography and Demographics

1. With its 450,000 km^2, Sweden is the third largest country in Western Europe. In between Denmark and Germany in the south, the Atlantic Ocean/Nordic Sea and Norway in the west, the Baltic Sea in the east and the Polar Circle in the north, Sweden is mainly covered by forest (52%), water (9%), and agricultural land (8%).

2. The total population of about 9.3 million is spread mainly in communities with more than 2,000 residents. The three largest cities – Stockholm (the capital), Göteborg, and Malmö – locate together 1.6 million people, which is 17% of the total Swedish population. While the southern part, especially the area in between the cities Stockholm, Göteborg, and Malmö, as well as the Baltic coastline north of Stockholm are the most densely populated areas, the northern part, Norrland, is rather sparsely populated.

3. Sweden is a rather homogenous country, with about 12% of Swedish residents being foreign-born. There are two minority groups of native inhabitants, the Finnish-speaking group in the northeast, along the Finnish border (about 30,000) and the Sami (Lapp) population of about 15,000. The Sami also live in other nearby northern areas such as Norway, Finland, and Russia and are about 60,000 in total.

The national language is Swedish, a Germanic language. Other minority language include Sami (Lapp), Finnish, Meänkieli (Tornedalen Finnish), Yiddish, and Romani Chib.

§2. Economics

4. Agriculture is still an important sector of the Swedish economy, though less than 3% of Sweden's labour force works in agriculture. Also fishing and mining, though small sectors of the national economy, should be mentioned in this context.[1]

From a historical point of view, the country's rich natural resources including forests, ore deposits, and hydroelectric power, have been the basis of Sweden's industrial economy. Though the focus has shifted, indigenous raw materials such as

1. See <Sweden.se>, the official website of Sweden.

timber and metals are still of importance for the industry. Factories within the automotive and aerospace industry are situated mainly in the south of Sweden (Göteborg, Trollhättan, Linköping, Södertälje), while the electronics industry is predominantly located in Stockholm and Västerås.

Sweden also has a pharmaceutical and biotechnology industry, which is primarily connected to the universities in the central and southern parts of Sweden. With regards to the number of employees, distributive trade, transportation, administration and services comprise a large percentage of the national economy, while exports in these areas are rather small.

5. Sweden's Gross Domestic Product (GDP) in 2012 was USD 523.8 billion (ca. EUR 380 billion) and GDP per capita in 2012 was USD 55,041 (ca. EUR 40 180). High-technology exports amounted to USD 18.5 billion (ca. EUR 13.5 billion) in 2012.[2] In 2011 the revenue from telecommunications was 1.6% of the GDP, while the investment in telecommunications amounted to 13.3% of the revenue.[3] The Information Communication Technology (ICT) goods exports were 9.3% of the total good exports, while the ICT goods imports were 10.6% of the total goods imports.[4] ICT services exports amounted to 51.9% of the total service export.[5] In comparison, the UK shows 5.0% of ICT goods exports, 8.2% of ICT goods imports and 39.4% of ICT service exports.[6]

§3. Administrative Structure

I. General Democratic Framework

6. Sweden is a constitutional monarchy with a democratically elected parliament. While the monarch nowadays mainly has representative duties, the one-chamber Parliament (*Riksdagen*) is the main legislative power and approves the Prime Minister who appoints the Government (*Regeringen*) consisting of about ten ministries. According to the constitution, '[t]he Government governs the Realm', which mainly consists of drafting the national budget (which is approved later by the parliament), submitting legislative bills, administering justice, and heading government agencies.

The distribution of political power is one of a separation of function, not separation of power, as expressed in the constitution:[7]

2. The World Bank, Data, <data.worldbank.org/indicator/NY.GDP.PCAP.CD> and <data.worldbank.org/indicator/TX.VAL.TECH.CD/countries>, 5 Apr. 2014.
3. The World Bank, 'The Little Data Book on Information and Communication Technology 2013', 2013, 202; available at <www.itu.int/en/ITU-D/Statistics/Documents/publications/ldb/LDB_ICT_2013.pdf>, 5 Apr. 2014.
4. *Ibid.*
5. *Ibid.*
6. *Ibid.*, 220.
7. Laura Carlson, *The Fundamentals of Swedish Law* (Lund: Studentlitteratur AB, 2009), 25.

Chapter 1. Basic principles of the form of government
Art. 1. All public power in Sweden proceeds from the people.
Art. 4. The Riksdag is the foremost representative of the people.

7. The Parliament comprises 349 members in its single chamber.[8] Elections are generally held every four years.[9] Commonly, elections for counties and municipalities are held on the same day. Every Swedish citizen who is at least 18 years old can vote in all three elections. Non-Swedish citizens who are either citizens of another European Union (EU) Member State or a Nordic country and registered in Sweden at the time of election can vote in their county and municipality.[10] In order to achieve seats in the parliament, a party has to reach at least 4% of the votes cast nationally.[11]

8. The Swedish public administration features three levels of government: national, regional, and local. On a regional level Sweden is divided into twenty-one counties with county councils (*landsting*), while on a local level Sweden is governed by 290 municipalities (*kommuner*). The counties' areas of responsibilities range from medical care to regional traffic and transit planning, while municipalities are responsible for services such as housing, roads, schools, childcare, and fire protection.

The importance of local government is expressed in Chapter 1 Article 1 of the Instrument of Government: Swedish democracy 'shall be realized through a representative and parliamentary polity and through local self-government'. Chapter 1 section 1 of the Swedish Local Government Act (*Kommunallag (1991:900)*) furthermore states:

> Sweden is divided into municipalities and county councils. These attend to the matters indicated in this Act or in special regulations, proceeding on principles of democracy and local self-government.

Each of the twenty-one counties (*län*) is headed by a county administrative board (*länsstyrelse*) which in its turn is lead by a governor (*landshövding*).[12] The county administrative board is part of the local administration and deals with questions such as health care and regional transportation. County councils (*landsting*), however, with their county council assemblies (*landstingsfullmäktige*) are elected at the regional level.[13]

Municipalities are lead by a municipal assembly (*kommunalfullmäktige*), who are elected locally, and who in turn appoint the municipal council (*kommunstyrelse*).

In general, there is no hierarchical exercise of powers between municipalities, counties, and regions, as they all have different areas of responsibility. In some

8. Chapter 3 Art. 1 Instrument of Government (*Regeringsform (RF)*).
9. Chapter 3 Art. 3 Instrument of Government.
10. Carlson, 30.
11. Chapter 3 Art. 7 Instrument of Government.
12. See <www.lansstyrelsen.se/>, 5 Apr. 2014.
13. Chapter 1 Art. 7 Instrument of Government: 'Sweden has municipalities and county councils. The decision-making power in these local authorities is exercised by elected assemblies.'

cases, however, the Parliament or any national authority may set requirements that local authorities must follow.[14]

II. Public Agencies

9. In addition to public administration, there are around 400 public authorities with specific areas of competence in Sweden.[15] They are commonly independent and have the authority – delegated by the Government – to issue regulations within their area of responsibility.[16] A lot of day-to-day administrative work is carried out by these small or large public authorities, and they are also able to decide in specific cases regarding private subjects vis-à-vis public authorities.

10. Two specific agencies that should be mentioned here are the Parliamentary Ombudsmen (*Justitieombudsmannen*/JO) and the Chancellor of Justice (*Justitiekanslern*/JK). The Parliamentary Ombudsmen[17] are elected by the Swedish Parliament and supervise courts of law and other public authorities as well as the public officials they employ in their application of the law. The Chancellor of Justice,[18] though appointed by the Government, is an independent institution. The duties include:

- representing the State in trials and other legal disputes;
- receiving complaints and claims for damages directed to the State;
- supervising the governmental authorities and the civil servants;
- ensuring freedom of the press and other media, and acting as the only public prosecutor in cases regarding offences against the freedom of the press and other media; and
- protecting privacy in different fields.

11. Other agencies of particular interest within the ICT sector are the Swedish Post and Telecom Agency (PTS - *Post-och telestyrelsen*) and the Swedish Consumer Agency (*Konsumentverket*).

The Swedish PTS[19] is the supervisory authority with regards to electronic communications[20] and also monitors the postal sector in Sweden. PTS issues regulations within the electronic communications sector, supervises communications operators and informs the general public on issues regarding Internet security and

14. For example, regarding national standards for education. See Carlson, 33.
15. Swedish Ministry of Finance, *Styra och ställa – förslag till en effektivare statsförvaltning*, SOU 2008:118 (Stockholm: Finansdepartementet, 2006 års förvaltningskommitté, 2008), 9.
16. Chapter 8 Art. 11 Instrument of Government: 'Where, under the present Chapter, the Riksdag authorizes the Government to adopt provisions in a particular matter, the Riksdag may authorize the Government in such context to delegate the power to adopt regulations in the matter to an administrative authority or a local authority.'
17. The first was appointed in 1810. <www.jo.se>.
18. The Chancellor of Justice is not appointed for a specific term, but until retirement. The function was first introduced by King Charles XII in 1713. See <www.jk.se>.
19. <www.pts.se>.
20. The term electronic communications includes telephony, the Internet and radio.

consumer rights with regards to communication services. It reports to the Ministry of Enterprise, Energy, and Communications, and is headed by a board appointed by the Government.[21]

PTS is partly funded through charges imposed on operators and undertakings for licenses subject to PTS's supervision and is also involved in initiatives such as Surf Calmly (*Surfa Lugnt*).[22]

The Swedish Consumer Agency (*Konsumentverket*)[23] is responsible for ensuring consumer interests and is headed by the Consumer Ombudsman (*Konsumentombudsman*/KO) who can pursue consumer interests by legal action in the courts.

III. General Court Administration

12. Chapter 11 Instrument of Government regulates the courts. According to Article 2, courts are independent of other arms of government and their decisions cannot be influenced by the Parliament or any other public authority.[24]

The Swedish judicial system is built upon two pillars, the general courts and the administrative courts. In addition, there exist specialized courts with specific jurisdiction, such as the Market Court (*Marknadsdomstolen*) and the Court of Patent Appeals (*Patentbesvärsrätten*).[25] They all fall under the administration of the Ministry of Justice and its agency, the National Court Administration (*Domstolsverket*).[26]

The general courts consist of the district courts (*Tingsrätt*), Courts of Appeal (*Hovrätt*), and the Supreme Court (*Högsta domstolen*); the general administrative courts comprise county administrative courts (*Förvaltningsrätt*),[27] Administrative Courts of Appeal (*Kammarrätt*), and the Supreme Administrative Court (*Högsta förvaltningsdomstolen*).[28]

§4. Legal System

13. From a historical perspective, the Swedish legal system has been influenced mainly by German law. However, since Sweden joined the EU in 1995, harmonization on a European level has been prevailing.[29]

21. Swedish Post and Telecom Agency (PTS), 'Introducing the Swedish Post and Telecom Agency (PTS)', <www.pts.se/upload/Ovrigt/Om-PTS/infomaterial/pts-broschyr-eng-08.pdf>, 5 Apr. 2014.
22. <www.surfalugnt.se>.
23. <www.konsumentverket.se>.
24. Chapter 11 Art. 2 Instrument of Government: 'No public authority, including the Riksdag, may determine how a court of law shall adjudicate an individual case or otherwise apply a rule of law in a particular case.'
25. See the website of the Swedish Courts (Sveriges Domstolar) <www.domstol.se/templates/DV_InfoPage____2317.aspx>, 5 Apr. 2014.
26. <www.domstol.se>.
27. Earlier called *Länsrätt* in Swedish.
28. Earlier called *Regeringsrätten* in Swedish.
29. See Carlson, 35–36.

Like many other jurisdictions, the Swedish legal system is divided into private and public law, the latter including areas such as constitutional, administrative, procedural and criminal law, and the former including family law as well as the law of obligations and property.

14. The Swedish doctrine of legal sources is based upon a hierarchy of legal material, where legislative preparatory works have more importance than in other European countries. The following sources are commonly recognized in Sweden:[30]

(1) The Constitution consisting of four fundamental laws: the Instrument of Government (*Regeringsform/RF*), the Act of Succession (*Successionsordning*), the Freedom of the Press Act (*Tryckfrihetsförordning/TF*), and the Fundamental Law on Freedom of Expression (*Yttrandefrihetsgrundlag/YGL*).[31]
(2) Legislation, including parliamentary acts (*lagar*), government ordinances (*förordningar*), as well as agency regulations (*föreskrifter*).
(3) Legislative preparatory works (*förarbeten*) including governmental bills (*proposition*) as well as other governmental reports preceding the Governmental Bill, such as Swedish Government Official Reports (SOU) and Ministry Publications Series (Ds).[32]
(4) Case law, mainly including decisions by the highest courts such as the Supreme Court (*Högsta domstolen*) for civil and criminal matters, the Supreme Administrative Court (*Högsta förvaltningsdomstolen*) for administrative law, as well as some specialized courts such as the Market Court (*Marknadsdomstolen*) for matters within marketing and competition law, and the Labour Court (*Arbetsdomstolen*) for labour law related matters. To some extent decisions by the appellate courts can also have value as a legal source.
(5) Custom.
(6) Legal scholarship (*doktrin*).

15. Swedish Parliamentary Acts and Government Ordinances are published in the Swedish *Code of Statutes* (*Svensk Författningssamling*), or SFS. Each Act or Ordinance receives a unique SFS number, which consists of the year it is published and a chronological number, for example, 1998:204.[33] A statute will always keep its original SFS number, even if the law is amended. Using the SFS number of a law is a common way to refer to legislation in Sweden.

Public agencies in Sweden are in general independent and have a rather important function in the legal system, not only from an administrative, but also from a

30. Ulf Bernitz et al., *Finna rätt: juristens källmaterial och arbetsmetoder* (Stockholm: Norstedts Juridik, 2008), 28 et seq.
31. As in many other jurisdictions, constitutional law takes precedence over regular laws; hence, the hierarchy is not surprising in that respect.
32. An overview of the legislative process can be found at <www.riksdagen.se/en/How-the-Riksdag-works/>, 5 Apr. 2014.
33. Personal Data Act (*Personuppgiftslag*).

legislative point of view. Within their area of competence,[34] agencies, such as the Swedish Tax Agency (*Skatteverket*) and the PTS, can issue binding regulations.[35]

16. Legislative preparatory works have a rather important status in Sweden as a legal source. Specifically, the Government Bill (*proposition*) as well as the governmental reports preceding the Governmental Bill, which include the Swedish Government Official Reports (SOU)[36] and Ministry Publications Series (Ds),[37] often complement the rather abstract statutes by providing interpretation as well as examples of application of the law.

17. Though there is no strict obligation for courts to follow case law, such as the *stare decisis* in English law, typically the lower courts follow decisions by the higher courts. There are two highest courts in Sweden, the Supreme Court (*Högsta domstolen*) for civil and criminal matters and the Supreme Administrative Court (*Högsta förvaltningsdomstolen*) for administrative law. In addition, specialized courts exist within certain fields of law, for example, the Market Court (*Marknadsdomstolen*) and the Court of Patent Appeals (*Patentbesvärsrätten*).

These courts publish their decisions in official series. Judgments by the Supreme Court are published in the series *Nytt Juridiskt Arkiv* (NJA) and are referred to by year of publication followed by volume page number, for example, NJA 2005 section 361. The Supreme Administrative Court publishes its decision in the series *Högsta förvaltningsdomstolens årsbok (*HFD).[38] Cases are referred to by year of decision and reference number, for example, RÅ 2001 ref. 35.

34. Commonly delegated by the Government who in turn is authorized by a statutory provision enacted by the Parliament.
35. A list of some of these agencies and their regulations can be found at <www.lagrummet.se/rattsinformation/forfattningar/>.
36. Statens offentliga utredningar (SOU).
37. Departementsserien (Ds).
38. Previously *Regeringsrättens årsbok* (RÅ).

Chapter 2. Telecommunications Infrastructure

§1. General Infrastructure

18. Sweden has one of the most developed telecommunication markets in the world. The infrastructure is increasingly focused on the mobile market, while the number of fixed-line communications slowly declines. The market for mobile services has reached a penetration rate of more than 100% which is the result of consumers holding multiple subscriptions, commonly one for private and one for business purposes.[39]

The Swedish telecommunications market was liberalized in 1993 and has become very competitive in the past years. At the moment, around forty operators provide mobile services. Four of them – TeliaSonera, Tele2, Telenor (previously Vodafone), and Hi3G (Tre/3) – own mobile networks.[40]

Six different frequencies are being used for mobile telephony and mobile broadband services: 450 MHz, 800 MHz, 900 MHz, 1800 MHz, 2100 MHz, and 2600 MHz. The mobile network operators cooperate in creating and maintaining the infrastructure; the cooperation can differ depending on the frequency.[41]

At the moment there are around 45,000 base stations in Sweden, spread over 15,000 unique antenna masts. 2G and 3G voice networks cover 84% of the geographic area and more than 99% of the population area of Sweden; 1 Mbps data networks (3G) cover 39% of the geographic area and 99% of the population area of Sweden; 10 Mbps data networks (3G) cover 24% of the geographic area and 95% of the population area of Sweden, 10 Mbps data networks (4G) cover 42% of the geographic area and 98% of the population area of Sweden. The lowest coverage is for 30 Mbps data networks (4G), which cover 2% of the geographic area and 61% of the population area of Sweden.[42]

19. Sweden, unlike other European countries, did not auction licenses for the UMTS[43] services. Instead, the licenses were awarded after an application procedure where financial capacity, technical, and economic feasibility as well as access to relevant expert knowledge and experience were taken into account. In December 2000, PTS allotted UMTS licenses to Europolitan, Hi3G (Tre/3), Orange, and Tele2. These licenses were later changed and now include Hi3G (Tre/3), Telenor (previously Vodafone), and TeliaSonera/Tele 2 (SULAB).[44]

---

39. Economist Intelligence Unit, *Telecoms and Technology Report Sweden*, November 2009.
40. Swedish Post and Telecom Agency (PTS), 'The Swedish Telecommunications Market, First half year 2013', PTS-ER-2013:21, available in English at <statistik.pts.se/start_en/>; and Swedish Post and Telecom Agency (PTS), 'Rapport av uppdrag att samla in statistik om tillgången till mobila kommunikationsnät', PTS-ER-2014:11, 11.
41. The PTS report 'Rapport av uppdrag att samla in statistik om tillgången till mobila kommunikationsnät', 12–13, shows the different operators who own the networks.
42. *Ibid.*, 20, 28–38.
43. Universal Mobile Telecommunications System.
44. See <www.pts.se/sv/Telefoni/Mobil-telefoni/Mobiltelesystem/>, 5 Apr. 2014.

The operators are allocated certain radio frequencies[45] and the licenses include a condition that obliges the mobile operators to provide certain UMTS coverage throughout Sweden in accordance with their original applications. The definition of coverage concerns the amount of citizens that have to be able to access the UMTS network, not a certain amount of masts or financial investment. In accordance with PTS regulations, the companies were allowed to cooperate with regard to 70% of the radio infrastructure and up to 100% with regard to the masts.[46]

In 2010, PTS announced the winners of the auction for the fourth-generation (4G) frequencies, which will allow access speeds of more than 100 Mbits/second. In total, 758 municipal and two national licenses were awarded.[47] Among them, TeliaSonera received a license[48] for fifteen years for a cost of SEK 563 million.[49]

§2. Broadband

20. Access to broadband is provided either through wired networks – such as fixed telephone, cable television or fibre-based networks – or by wireless means. The fixed telephone network covers 98% of households and 95% of businesses,[50] while wireless 3G networks reach 99% of the population in Sweden. Cable networks and fibre-based networks are mainly available in urban areas.[51]

Providing access to broadband for households and businesses has been one of the goals of the Swedish Government.[52] While the infrastructure for broadband is mainly provided by private operators and public sector players, services for individuals and businesses are primarily offered by private operators.

§3. Operators

21. TeliaSonera is the largest telecommunications operator in Sweden and has held a virtual monopoly on traditional Public Switched Telephone Network (PSTN) subscriptions. With the rise of IP-telephony, the number of subscriptions will decline over time, possibly due to lower costs for the consumer.[53]

---

45. 2 × 15 MHz radiofrequencies in the 1920–1980 MHz band together with the 2110–2170 MHz band, as well as 5 MHz in the 1900–1920 MHz band.
46. See Swedish Post and Telecom Agency (PTS), 'Faktablad – Information om UMTS', 13 Aug. 2001, in Swedish at <www.pts.se/upload/Documents/SE/Faktablad%20UMTS.pdf>.
47. Economist Intelligence Unit, *Telecoms and Technology Report Sweden*, November 2009.
48. The license concerns four frequency blocks totalling 2 × 20 MHz in the 2.6 GHz band.
49. See Press Release by TeliaSonera, 'TeliaSonera to build 4G – next generation mobile network', 18 Nov. 2008.
50. xDSL technology is used for broadband connection.
51. Swedish Ministry of Enterprise, Energy and Communications, 'Broadband Strategy for Sweden', 6 Nov. 2009, <www.regeringen.se/sb/d/2025/a/134980>, 9–10.
52. According to the Broadband Strategy Sweden, 90% of all households and businesses shall have access to broadband at a minimum speed of 100 Mbps, by 2020.
53. Economist Intelligence Unit, *Telecoms and Technology Report Sweden*, November 2009.

The second largest operator for telecommunications as well as mobile services is Tele2. The company was formed in 1993 and offers fixed-line and mobile telephony (Comviq), as well as data network and Internet services.[54]

Telenor, a Norwegian company, is currently the third largest telecommunications operator in Sweden. It acquired Vodafone's Swedish mobile operation in January 2006, and while it provides fixed-line telecommunications in Norway, it focuses on mobile and broadband services in Sweden.[55]

Rather unique for the Swedish telecom market with regards to operators are around 200 city networks (*stadsnät*) that locally provide broadband through fibre networks. Often, these network providers are cities or municipalities, who offer the connections as open networks, which enables other market players to offer their services on top of the city network.[56]

Sweden's telecommunications industry in general is dominated by Ericsson, a manufacturer of wireless telecommunication equipment and provider of related services to mobile and fixed network operators worldwide. Ericsson is followed by TeliaSonera which is the second largest company based on net sales and employees.[57]

---

54. *Ibid.*
55. *Ibid.*
56. More information can be found in Swedish at the organization representing the city networks, <ssn-f.org>.
57. *Ibid.*

Chapter 3. The Information and Communications Technology Market

§1. Fixed Communications Market

22. In June 2013, there were 4.0 million fixed telephone subscriptions in Sweden, compared with 5.2 million in 2009. Out of the 4 million, 2.45 million were PSTN-based and 1.48 million based on IP (compared to 860,000 in 2009). IP-telephony is mainly based on xDSL and fibre or fibre LAN. ISDN is still being used in 88,000 subscriptions. In addition to traditional fixed switched telephony, the service VoIP (Voice over IP), that is, broadband telephony, is also being offered in Sweden.[58]

From these subscriptions, 6.9 billion outgoing traffic minutes were registered during the first half of 2013, compared with 11.5 billion in 2009. This means 279 minutes per subscriber per month, compared to 361 minutes in 2009.[59]

Looking at the market share in June 2013, the former state monopoly TeliaSonera had 61.1%, followed by the operators Tele2 (9.6%), Telenor (7.1%), and Comhem (which is a cable TV operator; 8.3%).[60]

In November 2013, 69% of the population in Sweden had a fixed telephone subscription in their home.[61] This number can be compared to 84% in 2009.[62]

§2. Mobile Communication Market

23. After steadily growing for several years, subscriptions (and active prepaid cards) for mobile voice services and mobile data services reached 14.0 million in June 2013. Out of these, 4.2 million were prepaid cards and 9.8 million were contract subscriptions. 3.7 million mobile subscriptions were used solely for voice services.[63]

The number of mobile broadband subscriptions amounted to 7.5 million in June 2013. Mobile broadband subscriptions as a stand-alone service (i.e., only mobile packet data and no voice traffic, e.g., dongle, plug-in card) amounted to 2.1 million, while the number for subscriptions as an add-on service (i.e., at least 1 GB of data per month is included in regular subscription) was 5.4 million.[64]

In June 2013, 811,000 subscriptions used services in 4G (LTE) networks, compared to 83,000 the same time last year, that is, an increase of 873%.[65]

---

58. Swedish Post and Telecom Agency (PTS), 'The Swedish Telecommunications Market, First half year 2013'.
59. *Ibid.*
60. *Ibid.*
61. Swedish Post and Telecom Agency (PTS), 'Swedes' use of telephony and Internet, PTS Individual survey 2013', PTS-ER-2013:20.
62. Swedish Post and Telecom Agency (PTS), 'Survey of Individuals 2009, Use of telephony and the Internet by Swedes', PTS-ER-2009:28.
63. PTS, 'The Swedish Telecommunications Market, First half year 2013'.
64. *Ibid.*
65. *Ibid.*

The number of outgoing voice minutes from mobile telephones amounted to 12.6 billion minutes in the first half of 2013 (9.6 billion in 2009), which means 176 minutes per customer and per month (159 in 2009). During the same period in 2013, around 7.5 billion text messages (SMS) were sent from mobile telephones (6.8 in 2009), averaging 105 text messages per customer per month (112 in 2009). These 7.5 billion text messages do not include messages transmitted via other services such as iMessage, Viber, and chat functions in apps. In addition, during the first half of 2013, 139 million Multimedia Messages (MMS) were sent (67 million in 2009).[66]

24. The mobile communication market is dominated by the network-owning operators TeliaSonera, Tele2, HI3G (Tre/3) and Telenor; the largest operator being TeliaSonera with a market share of 38.9% followed by Tele2/Comviq (29.3%), Telenor (17.1%), and HI3G (Tre/3) with 11.1%.

With a population of around 9.3 million and 14 million subscriptions for mobile voice and mobile data services, more than 100% of the Swedish population uses mobile services. Almost 100% uses their mobile phone for private purposes. In 2013, around 30% used a mobile subscription as their only telephony service.[67]

§3. Internet Access Market

25. The Swedish market for active Internet subscriptions reached 10.7 million in June 2013,[68] compared to 4.4 million in June 2009. Out of the total number of broadband connections in June 2013, 7.5 million are mobile connections and 3.1 million are fixed Internet connections. The majority uses mobile broadband as an add-on service (50%), followed by stand-alone mobile broadband (20%). The fixed Internet technologies xDSL[69] (12%), fibre and fibre LAN[70] (10%), and cable television (5%) amount for a smaller portion of the market.[71]

The transmission speed for broadband services is often higher for downloaded data than for uploaded data. The number of subscriptions with a high transmission rate capacity has been increasing the past years, reaching 840,000 subscriptions with a download speed of 100 Mbps or more in June 2013. The most common download speed for fixed broadband is 10–30 Mbps (1.2 million); for mobile broadband it was 30 Mbps or more (2.7 million) and 2–10 Mbps (2.2 million) in June 2013.[72]

66. *Ibid.*
67. PTS, 'Swedes' use of telephony and Internet, PTS Individual survey 2013'.
68. PTS, 'The Swedish Telecommunications Market, First half year 2013'.
69. DSL (Digital Subscriber Line) was the most common access technology in June 2009 (39%).
70. Internet access is reached via a property network, that is, a LAN (local network) usually based on Ethernet technology. The property network (commonly via optic fibre cables or copper-based cables) in its turn is linked to a public fibre network, for example, an area network.
71. PTS, 'The Swedish Telecommunications Market, First half year 2013'.
72. *Ibid.*

Data traffic in mobile networks amounted to 124,700 terabytes during the first half of 2013, compared to 11,664 terabytes in 2009. Mobile broadband as a stand-alone service was used for 83,600 terabytes, which is two-thirds of all data transferred over the mobile networks. The average use per month was therefore 6.6 GB for stand-alone services, 1.2 GB for mobile broadband as an add-on service in the first half of 2013.[73]

26. The market share is rather equal. In June 2013 TeliaSonera held 35.4%, Telenor 21.4%, Tele2 19.7%, HI3G (Tre/3) 10.8%, and Comhem 5.1%.[74]

More than 90% of the population in Sweden between the age of 16 and 75 uses the Internet, while 90% have Internet access at home.[75]

§4. Other Related Markets

27. In June 2013, the total number of television subscriptions on the Swedish market was 5.3 million. More than half (54%) of the subscriptions are distributed by digital technologies, such as the terrestrial network, digital cable television, satellite, and IPTV (fibre, fibre LAN or xDSL); the rest (46%) uses analogue cable television. Other ways of viewing television (apart from traditional television) such as video-on-demand services,[76] have not been included in the statistics but have an impact on the traditional television subscriptions.[77]

28. A market that has been very common in the past years are bundled services, where two or more services are combined as one offer with a packaged price. Most commonly this includes telephony (fixed and/or mobile), television, and Internet access. Overall, there were 1,730,000 bundled subscriptions in Sweden on 30 June 2013.

29. In 2013, Statistics Sweden presented the results of a survey on the use of IT by enterprises. According to the report, 98% of enterprises use computers, and nearly all of them have access to the Internet. Around 95% of larger Swedish companies (more than 250 employees) offer their employees mobile devices including mobile broadband. Sixty-nine per cent of larger companies in Sweden use social networks, such as Facebook and LinkedIn.[78]

In total, Swedish companies purchased computer equipment for SEK 10.7 billion and telecommunications equipment for SEK 7.3 billion in 2013.[79]

---

73. *Ibid.*
74. *Ibid.*
75. Swedish Post and Telecom Agency (PTS), 'Survey of Individuals 2009, Use of telephony and the Internet by Swedes'.
76. In Sweden both Netflix (<netflix.com>) and HBO Nordic (<hbonordic.com>) are offered.
77. PTS, 'The Swedish Telecommunications Market, First half year 2013'.
78. Statistics Sweden (SCB), 'Use of ICT in Swedish Enterprises 2013 (*Företagens användning av it 2013*', <www.scb.se/Statistik/_Publikationer/NV0116_2013A01_BR_IT02BR1401.pdf>.
79. *Ibid.*

Chapter 4. E-Commerce: Facts and Figures

§1. Internet Use

30. Sweden has a very good ranking as an IT-nation and was listed at the top of the World Economic Forum's Networked Readiness Index (NRI) in 2012 and was ranked third in 2013.[80] The index measures how well a country utilizes the benefits of ICT to promote work and entrepreneurship and covers 142 countries.[81]

In a survey from 2013, it was found that 90% of the Swedish population have access to a computer at home, 89% access to the Internet and 86% broadband access. In 2012, one in five Swedes (20%) had access to a tablet; a number that increased to one in three (31%) in 2013. Sixty-five per cent are using a smartphone to connect to the Internet.[82]

Eighty-six per cent use the Internet on a daily basis (compared to 62% in 2009 and 52% in 2007), mainly for checking email (96% on occasion), buying goods or services (84% occasionally), paying bills (79%) and logging onto the bank (84%) or posting photos (65%), status updates (48%) or commenting on others' posts (52%).[83]

Almost 50% of the population visits interest communities; 56% are a member of Facebook. Young people between the ages of 16–19 years spend about 7.6 hours a week on social networks, in the age group 20–25 years the amount is 6.6 hours, compared to 2.9 hours/week in the ages from 36–45 years.[84]

§2. E-Commerce

31. During the period April 2012 to March 2013, a total of 68% of individuals in Sweden, aged 16–85, bought or ordered goods or services over the Internet, for their private use. Twenty-five per cent of individuals have bought or ordered films or music via the Internet during the same period. Around 13% of individuals in Sweden, aged 16–85, have used the Internet for selling goods or services, for example, via auctions. Around 50% of individuals in Sweden, aged 16–85, have used the internet for services related to travel or travel related accommodation.[85]

The turnover of the Swedish online retail market increased from SEK 20.4 billion in 2008 to SEK 37 billion in 2013. In total, this amounts to 6% of the retail market in general. Electronics were sold the most online in 2013 with 20% of the

80. World Economic Forum, 'Global Information Technology Report 2013', <www.weforum.org/reports/global-information-technology-report-2013>.
81. Olle Findahl, 'Swedes and the Internet 2013,.SE (the Internet Infrastructure Foundation), <www.internetstatistik.se/rapporter/swedes-and-the-internet-2013/>.
82. *Ibid.*
83. *Ibid.*
84. *Ibid.*
85. Statistics Sweden (SCB), 'Use of Computers and the Internet by Private Persons in 2013', <www.scb.se/en_/Finding-statistics/Publishing-calendar/Show-detailed-information/?publobjid=19861+>.

total turnover in the electronics retail market.[86] According to DIBS Payment Services, the estimated e-commerce turnover in Sweden per year is SEK 75.7 billion. Regarding mobile purchases, DIBS expected 15.3 million in 2013.[87]

Business between consumers (C2C) is steadily growing; in 2010, the Swedish e-auction site Tradera[88] had around 2 million members and more than 3 million visitors every month. A normal day generated more than 900,000 active auctions on the site in 2010.[89]

32. Regarding e-commerce[90] in total, every fifth business, with more than ten employees, received orders from customers via a website in 2012. These companies are mostly active within the field of ICT (22%), retail (29%) or the hotel and restaurant sector (30%).[91]

86. PostNord i samarbete med Svensk Digital Handel och AB Handelns Utredningsinstitut (HUI), 'e-barometern, 2013 årsrapport, <www.hui.se/statistik-rapporter/index-och-barometrar/e-barometern>.
87. DIBS Annual Report on e-commerce, mobile e-commerce and payments 2013, <www.dibspayment.com/>.
88. Tradera is a part of eBay, <www.tradera.se>.
89. '1400 miljarder kronor – Så stor är den svenska e-handeln', *Internetworld*, April 2010, 16–19.
90. E-commerce in this respect includes ordering of goods and services via the internet or other computer networks, even if delivery of goods or payment is not done electronically. Neither ordering by exchange of emails nor the financial sector are, however, included.
91. Statistics Sweden (SCB), 'Use of ICT in Swedish Enterprises 2013'.

Chapter 5. E-Government Initiatives

33. During the last few years, e-government has become one of the focus areas for the Swedish Government. In 1998, the Swedish Government assigned the ICT Commission (*IT-kommissionen*)[92] as an Advisory Board in the field of Information Technology. Its task was to analyse the impact of ICT on the Swedish society and to promote the dissemination of information about the new opportunities in the information society.

Its mandate ended in May 2003 and some other committees and groupings continued some of its work. Among them were the Swedish Agency for Public Management (*Statskontoret*), 24/7 Agency Delegation (*24-timmarsdelegationen*) and E-Commission (*E-nämnden*).[93] The latter merged into Verva (The Swedish Administrative Development Agency)[94] in 2006.

34. Verva was assigned to stimulate the use of public e-services and the employment of the Swedish eID (*e-legitimation*). It published several reports on these issues and contributed greatly to the development and implementation of new e-government applications, *inter alia* through funding of new e-services. In January 2009, the authority was closed and its different departments were incorporated into the Government Offices of Sweden (*Regeringskansliet*), the Legal, Financial and Administrative Services Agency (*Kammarkollegiet*)[95] and the Delegation for e-government (*Delegation för e-förvaltning*).

35. In January 2008, the Government presented its Action Plan for e-government[96] that mentions four focus areas – regulation, technology and standards, common IT support, and contact with citizens – which should be implemented by 2010. Part of the Action Plan was a conference on e-government during the Swedish EU Presidency in 2009.[97] The Action Plan specifically emphasizes the importance of electronic identification in order to sustain the trust and dialogue between government, citizens, and businesses.

36. In this context, a Delegation for e-government (*Delegation för e-förvaltning*)[98] has been formed, consisting of representatives from sixteen key public authorities in Sweden.[99] As one of its first tasks, in September 2009, the delegation presented a strategy for public authorities regarding possible improvement

---

92. An archived version of the website is available at <www.itkommissionen.se/index-2.html>.
93. Some of the reports can still be found at <www.edelegationen.se/Publikationer/Innan-E-delegationen-bildades/>,5 Apr. 2014.
94. Verket för Förvaltningsutveckling.
95. <www.kammarkollegiet.se/kammarkollegiet>.
96. *Handlingsplan för eFörvaltning, Nya grunder för IT-baserad verksamhetsutveckling i offentlig förvaltning*, <www.regeringen.se/content/1/c6/09/65/12/4ffd1319.pdf>, 5 Apr. 2014.
97. The fifth Ministerial e-government Meeting and Conference was held in Malmö, Sweden, <www.egov2009.se/>.
98. <www.edelegationen.se/>.
99. A list with the representatives is available at <www.edelegationen.se/In-English/About-the-Delegation/Members-and-experts/>, 5 Apr. 2014.

of their e-government efforts.[100] The strategy is based on the idea that better technical and legal conditions will facilitate the development of coordinated e-services by public agencies.

The tasks of the e-Government Delegation have been extended and its main tasks are to work with e-government, social media and reuse of public sector information. The delegation is also tasked with investigating IT standards within the health care sector. Some of its projects include My Messages (*Mina Meddelanden*),[101] a public service that allows individuals or companies to receive messages from public authorities electronically instead of on paper; and e-Archive (*e-Arkiv*) and e-(*e-Diarium*)[102] dealing with digital filing by public authorities.[103]

37. Besides the official e-government initiatives, several public authorities and other organizations are involved in e-government and the promotion of new e-services. The Stockholm Chamber of Commerce (*Stockholms Handelskammare*), for example, published an e-government index in September 2009.[104] In a survey among 100 public administrations and municipalities, factors such as information security, channels of communication, electronic procurement and electronic invoices, as well as the content of the websites and technical accessibility, were evaluated and analysed. Some of the conclusions of the report included that the Swedish Tax Agency came in first place regarding public e-government; electronic public procurement was still being used on a low level though it had increased; and almost 20% of the public administrations had no information regarding data protection on their websites.

Furthermore, the Swedish Data Inspection Board (*Datainspektionen*) has published guidelines for municipalities, in particular a checklist for secure e-government.[105] The checklist includes recommendations for municipalities regarding the processing of personal data within their case management system and on their websites.

---

100. The e-Government Delegation, 'Strategy for the Government Agencies Work on E-government', Summary of SOU 2009:86, < www.edelegationen.se/In-English/Reports/Third-generation-eGovernment/>, 5 Apr. 2014.
101. See more in Swedish at <www.edelegationen.se/Nationella-utvecklingsinsatser/Forvaltningsgemensamma-tjanster/Mina-meddelanden/>, 5 Apr. 2014.
102. See more in Swedish at <www.edelegationen.se/Nationella-utvecklingsinsatser/Forvaltningsgemensamma-tjanster/E-arkiv-och-e-diarium/>, 5 Apr 2014.
103. Some of its reports are available in English at <www.edelegationen.se/In-English/Reports/>, 5 Apr. 2014.
104. Chamber of Commerce, 'Stockholms Handelskammares e-förvaltningsindex 2009', 24 Sep. 2009, <www.chamber.se/filearchive/2/28304/e-index%20rapport%202009.pdf>.
105. Swedish Data Inspection Board, 'Vägledning för kommuner: Checklista för säker e-förvaltning', 12 Apr. 2007, available in Swedish at <www.datainspektionen.se/press/nyhetsarkiv/2007/Vagledning-for-kommuner-Checklista-for-saker-e-forvaltning-/>, 15 Apr. 2010.

Part I. Regulation of the ICT Market

Chapter 1. Regulatory Framework of the Telecommunications Sector

§1. Background and Overview

38. An important milestone in the liberalization of the Swedish telecommunications sector was the introduction on 1 July 1993 of the Telecommunications Act (*Telelag (1993:597)*) and the Radio Communications Act (*Lag (1993:599) om radiokommunikation*). These two Acts were the results of the development of private interests in the telecommunications market, seeking to compete with the Government-owned incumbent as much as a part of Sweden's alignment with the then European Community.[106] When the Government at that time adopted the proposal introducing the legislation to the Parliament on 25 March 1993, Sweden had tentatively applied for membership of the Community, but the national referendum eventually approving the application had not yet been held. The legislative bill explained that the proposed regulations sought to adapt to the *acquis communautaire* as well as to a possible European Economic Area (EEA) Agreement.

39. These two Acts were replaced through the implementation of the 2002 EU Regulatory Framework for electronic communications.

The EU regulatory framework consists of five main Directives, two Regulations and several Decisions:

(a) Directive 2002/21/EC of the European Parliament and the Council of 7 March 2002 on a Common Regulatory Framework for Electronic Communications Networks and Services, as amended by the Better Regulation Directive 2009/140/EC of 25 November 2009 (hereinafter 'Framework Directive').
(b) Directive 2002/20/EC of the European Parliament and the Council of 7 March 2002 on the Authorization of Electronic Communications Networks and Services, as amended by the Better Regulation Directive 2009/140/EC of 25 November 2009 (hereinafter 'Authorization Directive').

106. Government Bill (Proposition) 1992/93:200, 'Regeringens proposition om en telelag och en förändrad verksamhetsform för Televerket, m.m.', 69.

(c) Directive 2002/19/EC of the European Parliament and the Council of 7 March 2002 on Access to, and Interconnection of, Electronic Communications Networks and Associated Facilities, as amended by the Better Regulation Directive 2009/140/EC of 25 November 2009 (hereinafter 'Access Directive').
(d) Directive 2002/22/EC of the European Parliament and the Council of 7 March 2002 Universal Service and User's Rights relating to Electronic Communications Networks and Services, as amended by the Citizens' Rights Directive 2009/136/EC of 25 November 2009 (hereinafter 'Universal Services Directive').
(e) Directive 2002/58/EC of the European Parliament and the Council of 12 July 2002 concerning the Processing of Personal Data and the Protection of Privacy in the Electronic Communications Sector, as amended by the Citizens' Rights Directive 2009/136/EC of 25 November 2009 (hereinafter 'Directive on Privacy and Electronic Communications').
(f) Regulation (EC) No 1211/2009 of the European Parliament and of the Council of 25 November 2009 establishing the Body of European Regulators for Electronic Communications (BEREC) and the Office.
(g) Regulation (EU) No 531/2012 of the European Parliament and of the Council of 13 June 2012 on roaming on public mobile communications networks within the Union.

The EU Regulatory Framework was transposed into Swedish law in 2003, primarily through the Electronic Communications Act (*Lag (2003:389) om elektronisk kommunikation*).[107] A special transitional regulation was also enacted, the Act on the Introduction of the Electronic Communications Act (*Lag (2003:390) om införande av lagen (2003:389) om elektronisk kommunikation*).[108] Telecommunications equipment is regulated separately, through the Radio- and Telecommunications Terminal Equipment Act (*Lag (2000:121) om radio- och teleterminalutrustning*). There is also a special law regulating the activities of the Swedish country top-level domain.se: the National Top-Level Domains for Sweden on the Internet Act of 1 July 2006 (*Lag (2006:24) om nationella toppdomäner för Sverige på Internet*).[109]

The Ordinances supplementing the Acts in the area of telecommunications are:

- Ordinance on Electronic Communication (*Förordning (2003:396) om elektronisk kommunikation*).
- Ordinance on the Introduction of the Electronic Communications Act (*Förordning (2003:397) om införande av lagen (2003:389) om elektronisk kommunikation*).
- Ordinance on National Top-Level Domains for Sweden on the Internet (*Förordning (2006:25) om nationella toppdomäner för Sverige på Internet*).
- Ordinance on Radio- and Telecommunications Terminal Equipment (*Förordning (2000:124) om radio- och teleterminalutrustning*).

---

107. Government Bill (Proposition) 2002/03:110, 'Lag om elektronisk kommunikation, m.m.'.
108. *Ibid.*
109. See Part II Ch. 6 *infra*, paras 207 et seq.

The above-mentioned Swedish laws and ordinances have been subject to frequent amendments.

40. The national regulatory authority, the Swedish PTS has adopted a number of binding Regulations (*föreskrifter*) and soft-law General Advice (*allmänna råd*). The Regulations and General Advice are published in the PTS Collected Regulations (*Författningssamling*), PTSFS.

§2. Scope of the Law

41. The scope of the Electronic Communications Act is set out in its Chapter 1 section 4. This section states that it applies to electronic communications networks and communications services with associated facilities and services together with other radio use. The terms 'electronic communications network', 'electronic communications services' and 'associated facilities' are defined in Chapter 1 section 7 of the Act. These definitions follow the ones given in Article 2 of the Framework Directive. Thus, the Electronic Communications Act applies to transmission systems, to switching or routing equipment, and to other resources as long as they permit the conveyance of signals. The type of information or the means used in the conveyance are irrelevant.

According to Chapter 1 section 7 Electronic Communications Act, an 'electronic communications network' is a system for transfer and, in appropriate cases, equipment for connection or routing and passive network elements and also other resources that allow the transmission of signals, via wire or radio waves, by optical means or via other electromagnetic transmission media, irrespective of what kind of information is transferred. As in the Framework Directive, the definition is function oriented and technologically neutral except in requiring the use of electromagnetism. An 'electronic communications service' is defined as a service that is normally provided for payment, and which completely or mainly comprises the transmission of signals within electronic communications networks. The term 'service' implies that the function is provided to other parties; transmission purely for the transmitter's own use falls outside of the definition. Payment to the service provider need not be in cash but purely beneficial service, for example, as only provided for charity falls outside of the scope.[110] An 'associated facility' is defined as an arrangement, function or something else that does not constitute, but is related to an electronic communications service or an electronic communications network, and which facilitates or supports that service or provision of services via that network. Very few regulations of the Electronic Communications Act are directly applicable to associated facilities.

42. Chapter 1 section 4 states explicitly that the Act is not applicable to content that is transferred in electronic communications networks with the aid of electronic

110. Government Bill (Proposition) 2002/03:110, 358. An example could be a company which only provides the service for its own in house use but also to external users without charge, *pro bono*.

communications services. The intention behind the exemption is to except the provision of services that do not completely or mainly consist in the transferring of signals from the application of the Electronic Communications Act. Primary examples of such services are the provision of content in radio- and television programmes, and via the Internet.[111] Chapter 1 section 6 points to the Radio and Television Act (*Radio-och TV-lag (2010:696)*), and its provisions concerning broadcasting of sound radio and television programmes that are intended for the public and intended to be received with technical aids. Section 6 also points out that there are provisions concerning equipment in the Radio and Telecommunications Terminal Equipment Act.

43. It follows from Chapter 1 section 5 Electronic Communications Act that the provisions of the Act do not replace the regulations for consideration under other Acts. Decisions based on the Electronic Communications Act do not substitute for decisions required by other legislation, such as regarding Right of Way in the Utility Easements Act (*Ledningsrättslag (1973:1144)*) or under the Expropriations Act (*Expropriationslag (1972:719)*). It should also be noted that as regulated in the Chapter 10 section 17 sub-paragraph 1 Code of Judicial Procedure, a court may not entertain a dispute that shall be entertained by an authority. The preparatory work to the Electronic Communications Act grants some guidance to this question of scope.[112]

According to this guidance, disputes that concern purely contractual issues between the parties should be entertained by a civil court even when the issue results from an obligation required by the Electronic Communications Act or from Regulations, or as imposed by another public authority. Disputes regarding obligations such as to provide interconnection or to apply a cost-oriented price would, however, be entertained by the supervisory authority. The grounds cited by a plaintiff in its action will typically decide whether a court or a public authority is the competent forum. Where an action or a complaint is primarily based on the Electronic Communications Act, the supervisory authority will typically be the forum of first instance. Decisions by a public authority can be appealed to the Administrative Court.

§3. Policy Objectives and Regulatory Principles

44. The initial sections of the Electronic Communications Act[113] set out the policy objectives and regulatory principles of the Act. These objectives and principles closely mirror the catalogue in Article 8 Framework Directive.

Chapter 1 section 1 Electronic Communications Act states that the provisions of this Act aim at ensuring that private individuals, legal entities, and public authorities shall have access to secure and efficient electronic communications, and the greatest possible benefit regarding the range of electronic communications services

111. Government Bill (Proposition) 2002/03:110, 355 et seq.
112. Government Bill (Proposition) 2002/03:110, 117 et seq.
113. Chapter 1 ss 1–3 Electronic Communications Act.

and their price and quality. This objective shall mainly be achieved through the promotion of competition and the international harmonization of the sector. However, universal services shall always be available for everybody on equivalent terms throughout Sweden at affordable prices. When applying the Act, particular regard shall be given to the importance of electronic communications for the freedom of expression and freedom of information.

Chapter 1 section 2 states that measures that are implemented in accordance with the Act may not be more extensive than appears to be reasonable, and should be proportional having regard to the objectives of the Act and the other interests referred to in section 1.

Chapter 1 section 3 states that the public authority appointed by the Government shall receive reports, consider applications, decide on obligations and otherwise consider issues and deal with matters, and also exercise supervision under this Act or under regulations issued in accordance with the Act. In accordance with section 2 Ordinance on Electronic Communications, the Swedish PTS is the public authority appointed as the supervisory authority for the Electronic Communications Act, the National Regulatory Authority.

§4. The National Regulatory Authorities

I. The Legal Framework for Regulatory Authorities

45. Under Chapter 8 sections 1 and 3 Instrument of Government,[114] provisions concerning the relations between private subjects and the public institutions which relate to obligations incumbent upon private subjects, or which otherwise encroach on the personal or economic circumstances of private subjects, must be laid down in law.

While the Parliament enacts the laws,[115] the Government 'governs the Realm'.[116] Where so authorized by law, the Government may adopt provisions relating to certain matters in areas enumerated in the Instrument of Government, transport and communications being one of these.[117] Where the Parliament authorizes the Government to adopt provisions in a particular matter, it may authorize the Government in such context to delegate the power to adopt regulations in the matter to an administrative authority. The Electronic Communications Act contains a large number of such authorizations, many of which the Government has made use of through the Ordinance on Electronic Communications.

46. The Swedish administrative tradition is for the Government to maintain comparatively small central ministries while the day-to-day administrative work is carried out by a wealth of large and small independent public authorities. It is

114. The Instrument of Government (*Regeringsform*) is one of the constitutional laws in Sweden. See Introduction Ch. 1 s. 4 *supra*.
115. Chapter 1 s. 4 Instrument of Government.
116. Chapter 1 s. 6 Instrument of Government.
117. Chapter 8 s. 7 Instrument of Government.

enshrined in the Instrument of Government that no authority – such as the Government, the Parliament, and the decision-making bodies of local assemblies – may determine how an administrative authority shall decide in a particular case relating to the exercise of public authority vis-à-vis a private subject or a local authority, or relating to the application of law.[118] This said, administrative authorities such as PTS receive formal instructions from the relevant Government department, the Ministry for Enterprise, Energy and Communications on goals, priorities, tasks such as investigations, etc. Once a matter has been lodged before an authority such as PTS, for example, a dispute between telecom operators on interconnection requirements, the Government is constitutionally prohibited from directing the outcome of the matter.

The Ministry for Enterprise, Energy and Communications, as do the other sector Ministries, focuses on its roles as policymaker and supervisor of the public authorities under its responsibility. While more or less elaborated suggestions for new legislation may originate from the Parliament, public authorities, and other public or private bodies, the Ministry commissions committees to draft legislative proposals and then after a public consultation, drafts the legislative bills that are tabled in the Parliament. The Ministry negotiates the budget for PTS's, approves fee structure for telecommunications operators and actively supervises PTS's execution of its regulatory obligations. While the Ministry formally represents Sweden in international fora, most importantly the institutions of the EU and intergovernmental organizations such as International Telecommunication Union (ITU), Internet Corporation for Assigned Names and Numbers (ICANN), World Summit on the Information Society (WSIS), its functionaries are often accompanied and advised by experts from PTS or other relevant authorities.

47. The Swedish PTS is the National Regulatory Authority. It was created as *Telestyrelsen* in 1992 as part of the reorganization of the Telecom Administration (*Televerket*) from a government authority to an incorporated limited liability company.[119] *Telestyrelsen* took over the activities of the Government Telecom Council (*Statens telenämnd*) and the Radiospectrum Administration (*Frekvensförvaltningen*).[120] The *Telestyrelsen* became *Post- och telestyrelsen* in 1994 when the regulatory functions of the Swedish Post were added to its mandate.

The PTS Director-General is appointed by the Government for a term of six years (renewable). While decisions are taken by the Director-General and are issued under her or his name, more important decisions are reviewed by the PTS Board. The Board shall according to the Ordinance Instructing the PTS consist of between five and ten persons. For the term of 1 July 2013 to 30 June 2014, the Board consists of ten persons, one of whom is the Director-General.

---

118. Chapter 11 s. 7 Instrument of Government.
119. Government Bill (Proposition) 1992/93:200, 48 et seq.
120. The Government Telecom Council was formed in 1989 and was charged with the task of issuing regulation for equipment that was to be connected to Telecom Administration facilities, to follow developments in technical standardization bodies and to advise the Government on telecommunications, technical and market developments. The Radiospectrum Administration, originally a department of the Telecom Administration, was responsible for the allocation of radio frequencies.

48. The functions of PTS are set out in some detail in the Ordinance Instructing the Post and Telecom Agency (*Förordning (2007:951) med instruktion för Post- och telestyrelsen*) (hereinafter 'Instruction Ordinance'). The Ordinance designates PTS as the public authority with the overarching responsibility for the area of electronic communication. The authority is directed to promote the information society goals and the objectives set out in the Electronic Communications Act. The authority is tasked with describing and analysing developments and results in its area of responsibility, and to report on these to the Government. It is PTS's duty to note and analyse problems occurring in this area, acting on these and suggesting solutions to the Government as necessary. PTS is instructed to ensure that its regulations and routines are cost efficient and easy to apply for industry and consumers.[121] PTS is charged with promoting the efficient functioning of the electronic communications market from a consumer, regional development, and competition point of view.[122]

The main duties of PTS are to establish and supervise the specific obligations of the operators, to promote competition in the audio-visual services market, and to resolve conflicts between operators. The most important tasks of PTS under the Electronic Communications Act are those related to competition in the market and in relation to allocation and supervision of the radio spectrum. PTS is the national regulatory authority in charge of defining the relevant markets, carrying out analysis with the purpose of determining whether a relevant market is effectively competitive, declaring that an operator has a Significant Market Power (SMP), and imposing sector specific obligations on that operator.

The Instruction Ordinance contains a catalogue of PTS's obligations. It shall:

- promote access to safe and efficient electronic communications and the availability of universal service, and the supply of a broad selection of electronic communication services;
- ensure the opportunity for efficient use of radio communication and other radio usage;
- ensure the efficient use of numbers in the national numbering plan; promote effective competition;
- follow the development of prices and services;
- provide consumer information;
- follow developments regarding health and safety and environmental aspects of electronic communications;
- promote establishment of secure high capacity physical infrastructure in all parts of the country;
- take decisions on permits and obligations;
- define the relevant markets and perform the analysis with the purpose of determining whether a relevant market is effectively competitive, declaring that an operator has an SMP, and imposing sector specific obligations on that operator;
- provide information as requested by the European Commission;
- plan and allocate radio spectrum;

121. Sections 1 and 2 Instruction Ordinance.
122. *Ibid.*, s. 11.

- carry out supervision in accordance with the Radio- and Telecommunications Terminal Equipment Act and the Top Level Domains Act;
- promote network and information security with regard to electronic communications, and advise public authorities and private parties on network security;
- promote increased crisis management capabilities and robustness in electronic communication including by procuring endurance-enhancing resources.[123]

49. PTS's enforcement of its supervisory duties is facilitated by far-reaching inspection rights and rights to demand information from operators and other market actors. It also has the authority to impose sanctions on operators, mainly with regard to the infringement of its instructions and resolutions as well as in matters related to notifications, numbering and operators' information duties. PTS's officials sometimes describe their methods and tools of supervision as an escalating set of stairs. Beginning with description and analysis, it progresses to publishing information and guidelines. PTS may address some concerns, for example, of general network security by public procurement of equipment and facilities. Further up the stairs, PTS may perform supervision, for example, by using its powers of inspection in requiring disclosure of information. More forceful is PTS's power to impose obligations and to settle disputes between operators. At the top of the stairs lies PTS's power to issue regulations and its regularly used opportunity to report concerns to the Government, suggesting remedying legislation.

PTS is mainly funded through fees on telecommunication operators and through the general government budget.

§5. Provisions of Electronic Communications: Requirements and Conditions

I. General Authorization of Electronic Communications Networks and Services

50. The provision of electronic communication networks and services in Sweden is subject to a general authorization only, following Article 3 Authorization Directive. Chapter 2 of the Electronic Communications Act sets out the requirement to notify the supervisory authority PTS of an intention to provide public communications networks of such a kind as are normally provided for payment or public electronic communications services.

There are no restrictions on who may provide networks or services, such as requiring certain nationality or legal form. There is no obligation to notify the establishment of a self-provision of networks and services.

PTS has published guidance as to which types of networks and services require notification.[124] The notification form recognizes wired or wireless access networks;

123. *Ibid.*, s. 4.

124. Swedish Post and Telecom Agency (PTS), 'Guidance for notification of operations', present Swedish edition dated 3 Nov. 2010. The English version is available at http://www.pts.se/upload/Ovrigt/Tele/Anmalningsplikt/guidelines-for-notification-of-operators.pdf.

other communication networks, fixed or mobile telephony, 'Internet services', 'other' data communication service and 'other public electronic communication services'. Anecdotal evidence suggests that potential operators sometimes find these classifications confusing. The notification form is otherwise very short, focussing on collecting the contact details of the operator and restricting descriptions of the service provided to a maximum of five lines. The notifying operator is required to also submit a Certificate of Incorporation.

51. There have been a few cases where the question of notification has been contentious. PTS on 5 November 2008 required Telemar Scandinavia AB to notify PTS of its provision of mobile satellite-based services using the satellite networks Inmarsat, Iridium, Globalstar, and Thuraya.[125]

In another case, PTS on 2 July 2009 required Skype Communications to submit a notification of its provision of it services branded as SkypeIn, SkypeOut, and Skype To Go.[126]

The Skype case is illuminating as an example of PTS's approach where an operator for whatever reason has been providing a network or service without submitting a notification. The decision requiring Skype to notify the provision of these services was the culmination of a dialogue between the parties that had been going of for almost three years.[127] PTS's approach in supervision is typically characterized by an initial soft-handed approach even though PTS has the power to order the cessation of operations or to demand compliance with its interpretation of the Electronic Communications Act under sanction of an administrative fine. Where seen as necessary, PTS regularly issues decisions under sanction of administrative fines. In accordance with general Swedish administrative law, PTS has to ask the Court to order payment of an administrative fine where the recipient of the PTS decision fails to comply. It is very rare for PTS to proceed to asking for such a court order.[128]

II. Rights and Obligations Attached to the General Authorization

A. *Establishment of Rights and Obligations*

52. In the structure of the Electronic Communications Act, the Act is short on explicit rights for operators and long on obligations. Rights to access to capacity from the national numbering plans (most importantly the E.164 plan) and to radio spectrum require special, separate permissions.[129]

---

125. Decision by Swedish Post and Telecom Agency (PTS) of 5 Nov. 2008, no. 08-9691.
126. Decision by Swedish Post and Telecom Agency (PTS) of 2 Jul. 2009, no. 06-14224.
127. *Ibid.* See also PTS Report PTS-ER-2009:12 on provision of services and networks that require notification.
128. The only example known to the author is *PTS v. Teracom AB*, where the Stockholm Administrative Court denied PTS's request, see Decision by Stockholm Administrative Court from 26 Aug. 2009, no. 11868-09.
129. See Ch. 3 ss 1 (radio spectrum) and 19 (numbering capacity) Electronic Communications Act.

53. The main obligations attached to the general authorization are the following:

(a) to be subject to a notification procedure as well as to a decision issued by the competent national or regional authority for the use of numbers, radio frequencies and rights of way;
(b) to negotiate interconnection when requested by other operators of publicly available networks in order to ensure the provision and interoperability of services;
(c) to comply with universal service obligations;
(d) when allocated a number or a range of numbers, not to discriminate against other providers of electronic communications services with regard to the number sequences used to give access to their services;
(e) to use numbering resources effectively and efficiently, and to comply with number portability requirements;
(f) when supplying public telephone networks or publicly available telephone services, to route calls to the national, European and international numbering ranges, in the terms specified in the applicable plans;
(g) to comply with the applicable technical specifications and requirements;
(h) to guarantee the confidentiality of communications (although enabling the legal interception of the communications by national competent authorities), personal data and privacy protection rules as well as the rights of the users of the service;
(i) to comply with environmental and town and country planning requirements as well as with the requirements and conditions linked with the granting of, access to, or use of public or private land, or linked with the co-location and facility sharing;
(j) to comply with the regulation established for the use of frequencies especially when related to its effective and efficient use or to the establishment of measures regarding the limitation of exposure of the general public to electromagnetic fields caused by electronic communications networks;
(k) to pay the applicable fees;
(l) to allow and facilitate the carrying out of inspections by the competent national regulatory authorities.

Finally, operators shall provide all the information required by the competent national regulatory authority which in these cases means PTS. PTS is entitled, for the purpose of supervision, to gain access to areas, premises and other space, though not personal residences, where operations that are subject to the Electronic Communications Act are conducted.[130]

130. Chapter 7 ss 3 and 2 Electronic Communications Act.

54. The supervisory authority is entitled to seek enforcement with the assistance of the Enforcement Authority of decisions that relate to measures under the Electronic Communications Act.[131]

55. Information disclosed to PTS in the course of an investigation or other supervisory activity is protected by secrecy legislation. The statute regulating secrecy for information at PTS is somewhat obscure. The Public Access to Information and Secrecy Act (*Offentlighets- och sekretesslag (2009:400)*) stipulates secrecy for information held by a supervisory authority which regulates production, trade, transport, and other industrial or commercial activities, if it may be presumed that a private subject would be negatively affected if the information is disclosed, if the Government has adopted regulations to this effect.[132] Such specific regulation regarding secrecy for information held by PTS has been issued.[133]

B. *Modification of the Obligations Attached to the General Authorization*

56. The Electronic Communications Act does not explicitly address modifications to the obligations attached to the General Authorization.

C. *Provision of Services by Entities with Special or Exclusive Rights, or by Public Administrations*

57. Especially following the introduction of the 2002 EU Regulatory Framework, special or exclusive rights are in present times generally rare in the EU. The Swedish telecom market has been exposed to competition since the early 1990s. In consequence, there are no regulations in the Electronic Communications Act regarding entities with special or exclusive rights.

58. The European Commission opened a case against Sweden in 2007 for failing to implement correctly Article 2 Directive 2002/77/EC of 16 September 2002 on competition in the markets for electronic communications networks and services.[134] Government requirements related to grants of TV broadcasting licenses in effect ensured a monopoly for access control services to the state-owned company Boxer Access AB. Following changes to the digital terrestrial television broadcasting licenses affected by the Government, the Commission withdrew its case.

59. The Government holds a 37.3% ownership share of the telecom incumbent TeliaSonera,[135] but does not control TeliaSonera's operations. There are also some

131. Chapter 7 s. 2 Electronic Communications Act.
132. Chapter 30 s. 23 Public Access to Information and Secrecy Act.
133. Section 9 Ordinance on Public Information and Secrecy and s. 99 Appendix to the Ordinance.
134. Case C-419/07, *Commission of the European Communities v. Kingdom of Sweden.*
135. As of 30 Sep. 2013.

150 municipally owned or controlled broadband networks.[136] These municipal networks typically (but not completely) restrict their operations to providing a network infrastructure, with commercial market entities providing communication services to users utilizing the public networks. From the point of view of the Electronic Communications Act, these municipal networks are treated the same as networks and operations owned and operated by private companies. Following changes to the Competition Act (*Konkurrenslag (2008:579)*), the Swedish Competition Authority (*Konkurrensverket*)[137] has been allowed to intercede against commercial sales activities by publicly owned entities when these distort or restrict competition on the market, or are likely to do so.[138] Reportedly, the Competition Authority has received a number of complaints against the municipal networks but to date no decisions have been taken regarding these.

§6. Access and Interconnection

60. Chapter 4 of the Electronic Communications Act is titled 'Interconnection and Other Forms of Access'. Interconnection is defined as the physical and logical connection of public communications networks to make it possible for users to communicate with each other or to gain access to services that are provided in the networks.[139] The Electronic Communications Act does not provide a definition of 'access', as the concept is not exhaustively defined in the Access Directive,[140] and the legislator wanted to leave the demarcation open.[141] The definition of the Access Directive serves as a useful starting point in applying the Electronic Communications Act: the making available of facilities and/or services, to another undertaking, under defined conditions, on either an exclusive or non-exclusive basis, for the purpose of providing electronic communications services. It covers *inter alia*: access to network elements and associated facilities, which may involve the connection of equipment, by fixed or non-fixed means (in particular this includes access to the local loop and to facilities and services necessary to provide services over the local loop); access to physical infrastructure including buildings, ducts, and masts; access to relevant software systems including operational support systems; access to number translation or systems offering equivalent functionality; access to fixed and mobile networks, in particular for roaming; access to conditional access systems for digital television services; access to virtual network services.

61. There are few general rules in the Electronic Communications Act regarding interconnection. An operator of a public communications network is under a duty to negotiate on interconnection with a party that provides or intends to provide public

136. Swedish Post and Telecom Agency (PTS), 'Good Functionality and Technical Security in Municipally Owned Networks', PTS-ER-2010:2.
137. <www.konkurrensverket.se/>.
138. Chapter 3 ss 27–32 Competition Act.
139. Chapter 1 s. 7 Electronic Communications Act.
140. Article 2(2) a.
141. Government Bill (Proposition) 2002/03:110, 166.

electronic communications services.[142] There is a corresponding general secrecy obligation that forbids negotiating parties to improperly forward or utilize information they have become cognizant of or gained access to concerning another undertaking's business or operating circumstances.[143]

The obligation to negotiate on interconnection is not the same as an obligation to actually reach an agreement. In the event that lack of an agreement has the effect of or threatens to prevent communication between end users, PTS has the power to impose an interconnection. A party that controls access to end users may be ordered to, in return for fair market reward, conduct interconnection or implement other measures that are required to ensure that end users can reach each other.[144] 'Fair' market reward implies the existence of limits to what an interconnecting operator may charge, which is less then 'all the market will bear'.[145]

Operators may not be ordered to apply different conditions for equivalent services, as this would breach the requirement in Article 3 paragraph 2 Access Directive that operators must afford other operators equal treatment. An obligation that relates to access has to be linked to the services that are actually provided, unless otherwise prescribed by conditions determined in accordance with a decision to grant a radio license.[146]

More detailed or far-reaching obligations than those listed above may only be imposed on operators who have been found to hold SMP in a particular market in the course of the regulatory market analysis.[147]

62. In practice, the absence of a general obligation of interconnection and access becomes near academic. As is set out in the SMP decisions, PTS holds the view that all operators that control access to their subscribers in the form of call termination have SMP on the respective markets for fixed and mobile termination. PTS has thus on 10 June and 24 October 2013 issued decisions directed at twenty-eight operators, large and small, obliging them to accept every reasonable request for interconnection from present or intended providers of electronic communication services. These decisions are nominally subject to continuing review, but can be expected to be in force for approximately five years.[148]

63. An operator which PTS has found to have SMP ('SMP-operators') may be ordered to satisfy reasonable requirements on access to and the use of the network and associated facilities with the aim of providing electronic communications services. Such an obligation may relate to the operator providing another with access to specified parts of the network and associated facilities, extending access already granted to associated facilities, offering other operators specified services for resale, granting access to technical interfaces, protocol and other key technology that is

142. Chapter 4 s. 1 Electronic Communications Act.
143. Chapter 4 s. 2 Electronic Communications Act.
144. Chapter 4 s. 3 Electronic Communications Act.
145. Government Bill (Proposition) 2002/03:110, 195 et seq.
146. Chapter 4 s. 13 Electronic Communications Act.
147. See Ch. 2 *infra*.
148. PTS publishes an excellent overview of its SMP decisions, though only in Swedish, < http://www.pts.se/sv/Bransch/Telefoni/Konkurrensreglering-SMP/SMP-beslut-2012-2013/>.

necessary for interoperability between the services, offering co-location or other opportunities for joint use of associated facilities, offering specified services that are required to ensure interoperability between services, right up to the end user, offering access to operational support systems or similar programme systems that are required to guarantee sound competition as regards the provision of services, or conducting interconnection or otherwise implementing measures so that networks or associated facilities can be connected.[149]

In imposing the access obligations set out above, PTS is required to take account of:

- technical and financial strength for the use and installation of alternative network parts or associated facilities, having regard to market developments and the nature and kind of interconnection and other forms or access;
- the available capacity;
- the risks that a new investment involves for the owner of the network or associated facilities, the need to protect competition in the long term;
- the intellectual property rights involved;
- the interest in the cross-border services within the EEA.[150]

64. SMP-operators may be ordered to, in a reference offer or in another way, publicize specified details concerning accounting, technical specifications, network characteristics, conditions for provision and use, pricing, or other circumstances that are needed for openness on matters relating to interconnection and other forms of access. A decision on obligations as above shall include a notice concerning what information is to be provided, how detailed this should be and in which way it should be publicized. The operator may be ordered to change an item of information.[151]

65. An SMP-operator may be ordered to apply non-discriminatory conditions in its operations. Such an obligation shall in particular ensure that the operator in similar circumstances applies equivalent terms in relation to others who provide equivalent services, and the services and the information that the operator offers to others are provided on the same conditions and are of the same quality as apply for the operator's own services or for the services of a subsidiary or collaborating partner.[152]

66. An SMP-operator may be ordered to account separately and report specified operations with links to interconnection and other forms of access. Such an obligation may refer to an operator applying open pricing for other operators and for internal transfer or to provide an authority with its accounts, including details of revenues from others.[153]

149. Chapter 4 s. 8 Electronic Communications Act.
150. Chapter 4 s. 10 Electronic Communications Act.
151. Chapter 4 s. 5 Electronic Communications Act.
152. Chapter 4 s. 6 Electronic Communications Act.
153. Chapter 4 s. 7 Electronic Communications Act.

I. Local Loop

67. Where an access obligation is imposed on an SMP-operator that consists of access to the network between a main distribution frame or a similar interconnection point and a subscriber's fixed network termination point, and if the network there comprises a 'twin cable of metal', then the operator shall also be obliged to publish a reference offer for this specific access, often referred to as the local loop. Only TeliaSonera has had a local loop obligation imposed on it.[154]

A decision may be combined with a sanction in the form of a set administrative fine, which PTS can ask a court to execute if the decision is respected.

II. Functional Separation

68. Inspired by the Open Reach solution in the United Kingdom, in 2008 provisions for imposing a 'functional separation' of the metal based access network from the operator's other business were added to the Electronic Communications Act. By forcing the operator to transfer network assets and facilities to a separate corporate organization independent from its services operations, the operator is meant to become incentivized to treat all service providers utilizing its network without discrimination and with transparency. The network assets may be required to be placed under independent management or even transferred to a separate corporate entity. The criteria for imposing functional separation are demanding. Only operators who have been obliged to provide local loop and bitstream access can be an addressee of this obligation, and only under 'exceptional circumstances'.[155] The only possible recipient of a separation order is the incumbent, TeliaSonera.

The operator which may qualify for an order of functional separation may decide to carry out such a separation on its own accord in order to guarantee non-discrimination and transparency. The regulator, under the same exceptional circumstances, may accept this self-imposed transfer. While this voluntary separation lasts, an order imposing a functional separation may not be issued.

§7. Numbering

69. As Recital 20 Framework Directive explains, 'access to numbering resources on the basis of transparent, objective, and non-discriminatory criteria is essential for undertakings to compete in the electronic communications sector'.

PTS determines the national numbering plans for electronic communications and issues regulations concerning the plans and their use. The plans shall be designed so that electronic communications networks and electronic communications services can be reached in an equivalent way.[156]

---

154. Decision by Swedish Post and Telecom Agency (PTS) of 24 Nov. 2004, no. 04-6948/23.
155. Chapter 4 s. 12 a–c Electronic Communications Act.
156. Sections 10, 16, and 17 Ordinance on Electronic Communications.

70. A party that conducts operations that are subject to a notification obligation in accordance with Chapter 2 section 1 Electronic Communications Act, or provides electronic communications services in interconnection with the party that conducts such operations, is liable to comply with the approved numbering plans.[157]

A party that provides a public telephony service shall be capable of dealing with all calls to the European Telephony Numbering Space 3883.[158] PTS is required to keep the national numbering plans publicly available, insofar as there are no secrecy concerns. The numbering plans are available at PTS website.[159]

I. License to Use Numbers

71. The allocations of numbers from a national numbering plan require a license. A license refers to a series of numbers or individual numbers such as for example, numbers from the 118 series which are allocated for directory services. The Government and PTS are authorized to issue regulations concerning the principles for allocation of numbers.[160]

72. A party that has been allocated a number series may not discriminate against others who provide electronic communications services as regards which numbers allow access to services in the networks.[161]

73. A license to use numbers may be combined with conditions concerning:

(1) the kind of service for which the number shall be used;
(2) the actual and efficient use of the number;
(3) a reasonable term of validity with reservations for possible changes in the national numbering plan;
(4) undertakings that have been made in conjunction with licenses being granted for numbers of substantial economic value; and
(5) obligations in accordance with applicable international agreements regarding the use of numbers.

Examples of conditions regarding the services are the requirement to provide free calls for calls to the 020 series, the requirement to provide directory services at numbers in the 118 series and the requirement to provide public health information at numbers in the 1177 series.

---

157. Chapter 3 s. 16 Electronic Communications Act.
158. Chapter 3 s. 17. This implements Art. 27(2) Universal Services Directive.
159. The numbering plan is available in English at <www.pts.se/en-gb/Industry/Telephony/Numbering/National-numbering-and-addressing-plans/>.
160. PTS has issued regulations on numbering PTSFS 2003:3 and 2003:4.
161. Chapter 3 s. 20 Electronic Communications Act.

Requirements on actual and efficient use are used to prevent operators from unnecessary stockpiling of numbers. PTS has had issues with mobile operators locking in large amounts of numbers in Subscriber Identity Module (SIM) cards for prepaid accounts distributed to retail outlets for eventual sale.

II. Numbers of Substantial Economic Value

74. Licenses to use numbers of substantial economic value may be granted by PTS following an open invitation to apply. Such a license may be granted the following:

(1) a comparative selection procedure;
(2) a tender procedure where the price that the applicant is willing to pay for the license shall be decisive;
(3) a procedure with random allocation; or
(4) a combination of the procedures under items (1) to (3).

The Government and PTS are authorized to issue regulations concerning the content of an open invitation and concerning related procedures.[162]

75. Numbers that are perceived by PTS as more attractive are deemed to potentially have substantial economic value. Directory service providers complained in the early 1990s that PTS had allocated the number 118118 to what was then Telia's directory service without first offering the number for sale on the market.

A. Number Portability

76. A provider of public telephony services is required to ensure that its network allows subscribers to retain their telephone numbers when changing service provider. If the subscriber so requests, the telephone number that is used for such a service shall be transferred to another to enable it to provide the service. Numbers whose figure structure has geographical significance, as is the case for most fixed-line residential subscriptions in Sweden, need only be transferred for the provision of telephony services within the same geographical area (area code district). Providers are not required to permit transfer of telephone numbers between fixed and mobile network respectively, though some chose to offer this service anyway.[163]

The Government or, if authorized by the Government, the supervisory authority may issue regulations concerning the way in which the obligations shall be satisfied and concerning exemptions from the obligations and also may, in individual cases, grant exemptions from the obligations, if there are special reasons.[164]

162. Chapter 3 s. 22 Electronic Communications Act and ss 19 and 20 Ordinance on Electronic Communications.
163. Chapter 5 s. 9 Electronic Communications Act.
164. *Ibid.*

77. Charges for number portability must be based on the operational cost for the transfer. A provider that has transferred a telephone number is only entitled to payment for the operational costs that comprise increased traffic costs for a message to the telephone number. The charge is invoiced to the operator taking over the number; the transferring provider may not charge the subscriber for the service.[165]

78. The transferring provider is required to immediately provide such information as is necessary for routing messages to the telephone number to the Swedish Number Portability Administrative Center (SNPAC), the independent non-profit industry organization set up to administer number portability routing.[166] SNPAC operates the Reference database for number portability. Other information than the telephone number and the service provider that may be directly or indirectly referable to a natural person may not be released without the consent of such person.

B. Domain Names

79. Unlike the numbering plan, the provision of domain names for Internet communication falls outside of the operational scope of PTS. Domain names under the top-level domain associated with Sweden.se are allocated by the independent non-profit foundation Internet Infrastructure Foundation (*Stiftelsen för Internetinfrastruktur*). PTS, however, supervises the administration of all 'national top-level domains for Sweden' in accordance with the National Top-Level Domains for Sweden on the Internet Act (*Lag (2006:24) om nationella toppdomäner för Sverige på Internet*).[167]

§8. Radio Spectrum

I. Introduction

80. Radio frequencies are considered a scarce resource in the public domain. The Electronic Communications Act defines radio waves as electromagnetic waves with frequencies from 9 kilohertz to 3,000 gigahertz propagated without artificial guide. The definition is derived from Article 2 of Decision No. 676/2002/EC of the European Parliament and of the Council of 7 March 2002 on a regulatory framework for radio spectrum policy in the European Community.

165. Chapter 5 s. 10 Electronic Communications Act.
166. More information at <www.snpac.se>.
167. See Part II Ch. 6 *infra*, paras 207 et seq.

II. Management of the Radio-Electric Public Domain

81. PTS is the designated supervisory authority for issues relating to the right to use radio spectrum and radio transmitters in Sweden.[168] PTS decides on permits and licenses for such use, and is authorized to issue regulations on exemptions from the license obligation. Licenses to use radio transmitters are awarded for a limited period of time. As a separate or a distinct part of this decision, PTS decides on conditions for the use of the license. Questions such as commercial usage, geographic areas, specific technology, and frequency band are decided in the Conditions decision.

82. A license shall be granted for a fixed term. The term for license conditions may be shorter than the term of the license. When the term of validity for the license and the license conditions is decided, particular regard shall be taken to:

(1) future changes in radio use;
(2) the period that the transmitter is intended to be used;
(3) the technical development that may be expected;
(4) the period that is required to achieve reasonable financial return on the equipment; and
(5) whether a license under a separate Act constitutes a precondition for a license to use a radio transmitter.[169]

III. Rights of Use for the Radio-Electric Public Domain

A. *General Statement*

83. A license is required in order to use a radio transmitter in Sweden or on a Swedish vessel or aircraft abroad.[170] If the use of frequencies and the conditions and procedure for the grant of a license to use a radio transmitter have been harmonized in accordance with international agreements to which Sweden has acceded or provisions adopted in accordance with the Treaty establishing the European Community, the party that has been granted such a license shall be deemed to have a license. This means that when a completely harmonized selection procedure in accordance with Article 8 Authorization Directive has been used in granting a license in one EU Member State, the license will also be valid in other Member States that have implemented this regulation.[171]

84. Allocation of radio spectrum and licenses for transmitters to certain public bodies relating to security and law enforcement such as the Police (*Polisen*), the

168. Sections 10 and 11 of the Ordinance on Electronic Communication.
169. Chapter 3 s. 12 Electronic Communications Act.
170. Chapter 3 s. 1 Electronic Communications Act.
171. Chapter 3 s. 2 Electronic Communications Act.

Swedish Armed Forces (*Försvarsmakten*), the National Defence Radio Establishment (FRA/*Försvarets radioanstalt*), and the Defence Materiel Administration (FMV/*Försvarets materielverk*) are decided in accordance with separate procedures.[172] PTS may also issue regulations on exemptions from the license obligation. In this connection, conditions may be prescribed that the radio installation where the transmitter is included should meet specific technical requirements and other conditions on usage.

B. The Rights of Use for the Radio-Electric Public Domain

85. The general rule of the Electronic Communications Act on issuing permits is that a license to use a radio transmitter shall be granted, if:

(1) it may be assumed that the radio transmitter will be used in such a way that the risk for prohibited harmful interference does not arise;
(2) the radio use constitutes an efficient use of radio frequencies;
(3) it may be assumed that the radio use will not impede such radio communications as are particularly important having regard to the free moulding of opinion;
(4) the radio use does not utilize radio frequencies that are required to maintain a reasonable preparedness for the development of existing and new radio uses or frequencies for which the radio use has been harmonized in accordance with international agreements to which Sweden has acceded or provisions adopted in accordance with the Treaty on the Functioning of the European Union;
(5) it may be assumed that the radio use will not infringe on radio frequencies that are required for public security and law enforcement operations; and
(6) having regard to the fact that the applicant has previously had a license revoked or some other similar circumstance, there is no reasonable cause to assume that the radio transmitter will be used in violation of the license conditions. A license to use a radio transmitter for broadcasts that require licenses according to another Act or according to provisions issued under another Act, may only be issued if such a license exists.[173]

C. Procedure for Limiting the Number of Rights of Use

86. The number of licenses that are granted within one part of the radio spectrum may be restricted when this is deemed necessary by PTS to safeguard the efficient use of radio frequencies. A decision to limit the number of licenses shall be reconsidered as soon as there is cause to do so.[174]

---

172. Chapter 3 s. 3 Electronic Communications Act. See <www.polisen.se>, <www.forsvarsmakten.se>, <www.fra.se> and <www.fmv.se> respectivly.
173. Chapter 3 s. 6 Electronic Communications Act.
174. Chapter 3 s. 7 Electronic Communications Act.

87. When the question arises of granting a license to use a radio transmitter for new or fundamentally altered radio uses, and it may be assumed that the frequencies that can be assigned to the operation will not be sufficient to grant a license to everyone who wishes and who would be able to conduct such operations, allocation shall take place following an open invitation to apply, provided that there are not special reasons to do otherwise. This also applies when the radio spectrum that is assigned to a certain radio use is increased or in some other way allows further licenses to be granted.

The requirement to issue an open invitation does not apply to such radio use that:

(1) primarily relates to the broadcasting of sound radio programmes to the public or other activities such as television programmes and certain other transmissions of sound, pictures or text made using electromagnetic waves, or the content of certain public playbacks from databases;
(2) is intended for private use; or
(3) exclusively relates to operations that are conducted with the purpose of ensuring public order and security.[175]

When allocation under an open invitation is decided in accordance with a comparative selection procedure, or following a tender procedure where the price that the applicant is willing to pay for the license shall be decisive or following a combination of these proceedings. PTS may issue regulations concerning the content of an open invitation and on the comparative selection or tender procedure.

D. Conditions Attached to the Rights of Use

88. A license to use a radio transmitter is generally not required to relate to a particular radio use, such as mobile telephony and computer communications, fixed wireless access, etc.

89. A general license to use a radio transmitter may be combined with conditions concerning:

(1) the frequencies to which the license relates;
(2) which electronic communications services or kind of electronic communications networks or techniques the license relates to;
(3) coverage and roll-out within Sweden;
(4) the geographical area to which the license applies;
(5) an obligation for the applicant to share frequency space with another;
(6) such matter as in accordance with a decision on the harmonized use of radio frequencies should be imposed as conditions when the party to be allocated a radio frequency has been nominated in accordance with international agreements or

175. Chapter 3 s. 8 Electronic Communications Act.

provisions adopted in accordance with the Treaty on the Functioning of the European Union;
(7) obligations in accordance with applicable international agreements as regards the use of frequencies;
(8) undertakings that have been made in conjunction with the grant of a license in a selective procedure; and
(9) otherwise as required to ensure the actual and efficient use of radio spectrum.[176]

89.1. Conditions requiring the license be used for a particular electronic communications services or kind of electronic communications networks or techniques may only be issued if necessary to avoid harmful interference, ensure efficient use of radio spectrum, to protect peoples life and health, serving a public interest that certain electronic communications services are available in certain parts of the country, or serving a public interest in promoting the supply of broadcast radio and TV licensed under another Act.[177]

89.2. A license to use a specific radio transmitter may, in addition to the conditions set out in (89 above) be combined with conditions relating to:

(1) the nature of the antenna and the radio transmitter generally;
(2) the geographical area in which a mobile radio transmitter may be used;
(3) where the antenna for a fixed radio transmitter shall be located;
(4) competence requirements for those who will manage the radio installation.

E. The Transfer of Rights to Use the Radio-Electrical Public Domain

90. Recital 19 Framework Directive suggests that:

> Transfer of radio frequencies can be an effective means of increasing efficient use of spectrum, as long as there are sufficient safeguards in place to protect the public interest, in particular the need to ensure transparency and regulatory supervision of such transfers.

91. The Electronic Communications Act states that a license or part of a license to use a radio transmitter may be assigned to another party with PTS's permission. Such permission shall be granted, provided:

(1) the assignee satisfies the requirements imposed on the applicant in conjunction with the license being granted;
(2) there is no cause to assume that the assignment will have an adverse impact on competition;
(3) the assignment will not result in changed use of the radio frequencies, if these are harmonized according to provisions adopted in accordance with the Treaty

176. Chapter 3 s. 11 Electronic Communications Act.
177. Chapter 3 s. 11 Electronic Communications Act.

establishing the European Community and there are no other special reasons against doing so.[178]

An inefficient use of radio spectrum is an example of a special reason not to grant permission to an assignation of part of a license.[179]

The assignee takes over the rights and obligations of the assignor under this Act for the period following the consent. In the case of an assignment of part of a license, the assigned part shall be deemed to be a new license.

Upon granting consent, the authority may issue new or amended conditions resulting from the assignment. An assignment in violation of this section is invalid.

An assignment of a license to use numbers follows the same rules as assignments of licenses to use a radio transmitter.

F. Measures against Interference

92. If harmful interference occurs, license holders are required to immediately ensure that the interference ceases or is reduced to the greatest possible extent, unless the interference is permitted. The same applies to a party using a radio receiver that interferes with the use of another radio receiver. Electrical or other electronic installations, excluding radio installations, that are intended to generate radio frequency energy for communications purposes in lines or for industrial, scientific, medical or any other similar purpose, may only be used in accordance with the regulations issued by the Government or PTS.[180] Section 14 Ordinance on Electronic Communications prohibits possessing electrical or electronic installations whose purpose is the interference with radio transmissions.

§9. Public Service Obligations and Other Public Rights and Obligations

I. General Statement

93. Chapters 5 and 6 Electronic Communications Act set out the regulations concerning public service obligations and other rights and obligations with a public character. The concept of public service obligations refers to the universal service and other public service obligations aimed at protecting the public interest. The expression ‘other public rights and obligations’ concerns the regulation of those aspects that refer to the provision of electronic communications networks and services which, to some extent, have a public character. They include the regulation on conveyance of emergency calls, directory services, services for the disabled, co-location, facility sharing, personal data processing, the protection of privacy and users’ rights.

178. Chapter 3 s. 23 Electronic Communications Act.
179. See Government Bill (Proposition) 2002/03:110, 164.
180. Chapter 3 s. 14 Electronic Communications Act.

II. Universal Service Obligations

A. Introduction

94. Universal service obligations may be imposed if required in the opinion of PTS to ensure adequate public electronic communications services. They may be imposed on a 'party that is, considered appropriate for this' which may be ordered to, at an affordable price, provide a number of services.[181]

Before proceeding to list and describe the possible universal service obligations, it should be remarked that there presently is no operator designated to provide universal service in the form of telephony or Internet access services. Access to telephony is a service that historically has been provided by TeliaSonera (formerly operated by the Swedish State as a public service corporation, known as Televerket and later Telia AB), as the only operator. Before the Telecommunications Act came into force in 1993, only Televerket could offer a telephony service. The policy when the Telecommunications Act was introduced was that the state was responsible for providing access to telephony at uniform prices to everyone in Sweden. When Televerket was incorporated in 1993, it had licensing conditions imposed requiring it to provide telephony services to anyone who requested it. In 2003, the Telecommunications Act was replaced by the Electronic Communications Act and the licensing conditions that were in force for TeliaSonera since before, remained in force transitionally until 24 April 2004. In 2005, PTS placed TeliaSonera under an obligation to meet reasonable requests for access to the public telephone network at an affordable price. TeliaSonera appealed against PTS's decision and the Stockholm Administrative Court annulled the decision on 5 February 2007.[182] No new decision requiring the provision of universal telephony service has been issued.

95. PTS has in October 2008 in a report to the Government proposed the introduction of a universal service fund to finance provision of universal service of fixed telephony and other electronic communications services.[183] PTS has also studied the question of provision of a universal 'functional access' to the Internet, that is broadband access.[184]

B. Universal Service

1. Concept and Scope

96. The Electronic Communications Act authorizes PTS to order 'appropriate parties' to:

181. Chapter 5 s. 1 Electronic Communications Act.
182. Stockholm Administrative Court, decision no. 20346-05.
183. Swedish Post and Telecom Agency (PTS), 'Samhällsomfattande tjänster. Rätt till telefoni', PTS-ER 2008:20.
184. PTS report matter of 18 Feb. 2010, no. 10-658.

(1) satisfy reasonable requirements for connection to a public communications network to a fixed network termination point at a permanent place of residence or a regular business location;
(2) satisfy reasonable requirements for access to public telephony services to a fixed network termination point at a permanent place of residence or a regular business location, for everyone who demands this service;
(3) in a subscriber directory, which shall be updated annually, make information about all telephone subscriptions available to the extent they are not subject to secrecy or a duty of confidentiality according to law;
(4) provide a complete directory inquiry service, regarding telephone subscriptions to the extent that the information, that is, provided is not subject to secrecy or a duty of confidentiality according to law;
(5) provide public payphones or other places with public access to voice telephony to the extent that, as regards quality, amount and geographical distribution, satisfies the needs of the public; or
(6) provide access for people with disability to services according to items (2)–(5) to the same extent and on equivalent terms as for other end users, and satisfy the needs of people with disability for such special services.[185]

97. Access to universal services shall be safeguarded through procurement by the State if this is found necessary with regard to the costs for the provision of the service or the network.

98. A party which becomes obliged to provide a service as listed above may have an obligation imposed on it to achieve particular performance objectives within a given time. This time may not be less than three months.[186]

An obligation to provide fixed-line access shall be designed so that the end user can conduct and receive local, national and international calls, telefax and data communication with a particular specified minimum data rate that allows functional access to the Internet.[187] While no such requirements have been imposed, section 29a Ordinance on Electronic Communications states that an access speed of 1 Mbit/s achieves functional access.

A party that becomes obliged to provide subscriber directories and directory inquiry services shall treat the information received in a non-discriminatory way.

A party that becomes obliged to provide universal service may, in appropriate cases, have an obligation imposed on it to:

(1) apply common tariffs throughout Sweden or apply a specified maximum price;
(2) make it possible for the consumer to pay in advance for connection to the public telephone network and for the use of public telephony services;
(3) allow the consumer to pay for a connection to the public telephone network through payments that are spread over time; and

185. Chapter 5 s. 1 Electronic Communications Act.
186. Chapter 5 s. 2 Electronic Communications Act.
187. *Ibid.*

(4) on subscriber request give information on alternative tariffs which incur lower costs.[188]

2. Designation of Operators

99. PTS is empowered to designate an operator as an appropriate party to shoulder a Universal Service Obligation (USO).[189]

The preparatory works to the Electronic Communications Act set out the requisite conditions. A decision to impose an obligation shall be founded on objective criteria and the receiving undertaking's ability to carry out the obligation. The selection shall take regard of the principle of proportionality. No undertaking may be excluded from the possibility of receiving an obligation beforehand. While the wording of the Electronic Communications Act is open to finding any undertaking as appropriate, only undertakings which already commercially offer relevant services, such as operators, can in reality be chosen.[190]

3. Costing and Financing of Universal Service Obligations

100. The Electronic Communications Act sets out that if the cost to the receiving operator of having a service obligation imposed proves unreasonably burdensome, the service shall instead be procured by the State. In deciding when costs to an operator are too high, PTS shall take regard to the costs, revenue and immaterial rights related to providing the service. Where the operator holds a dominant position for the service to be provided, additional costs are deemed to be low.[191]

101. PTS has in a report found that several factors serve to ameliorate the burden of a service provision requirement. The operator will be able to sell other services to the subscribers gained through a USO obligation. The operator will have its coverage increased, which may increase respect for its brand. The increase of customers may lead to better economies of scale, for example in procuring equipment. Customers gained through the service obligation may also prove more loyal to the operator than other subscribers, which would be valuable when the customer moves.[192]

Even so, PTS proposed in the report the establishment of a universal service fund to finance compensation for or procurement of service provision obligations. Funding is suggested to be collected through charges on operators who have notified service and/or network provision to PTS. Charges are to be calculated based on criteria

188. Chapter 5 ss 4 and 7 a–b Electronic Communications Act.
189. Section 29 Ordinance on Electronic Communications.
190. Government Bill (Proposition) 2003/04:110, 217 and 383, and PTS decision of 19 Aug. 2005, no. 05-1072/23.
191. Chapter 5 s. 1 Electronic Communications Act.
192. Swedish Post and Telecom Agency (PTS), 'Samhällsomfattande tjänster. Rätt till telefoni' PTS-ER-2008:20, 23 Oct. 2008.

that are transparent, objective, non-discriminatory, and proportional. No such fund has however been introduced by 2013.

C. Other Public Service Obligations

102. A number of general public service requirements are demanded of all providers of public electronic communications services and networks.

A basic but, in practice, very important obligation is the requirement that operators take appropriate technical and organizational actions to ensure that operations satisfy reasonable reliability demands.[193] PTS has issued guidelines for the operator's work in this regard.[194]

102.1. *A* provider of a public communications network or a publicly available electronic communication service is required to without unnecessary delay report service disruptions or interruptions of any significance to PTS. PTS may, if it deems it to be in the public interest, oblige such providers to inform the general public of service disruptions or interruptions that have taken place.[195]

102.2. The Government, or the authority authorized by the Government, may adopt Regulations regarding minimum service levels offered by providers of public communication networks, if it deems it necessary to prevent obstructed or slow network transmission, or the degradation of the quality of a publicly available electronic communication service. This measure implements Article 22.3 USO Directive, providing the regulator with tools in the event of an actionable breach of network neutrality.[196]

Providers of a public telephony service are further required to:

- assist in emergency calls being conveyed without interruption and free of charge for the user;
- provide those who receive emergency calls with location data free of charge;
- satisfy every reasonable request to release subscriber data that are not subject to secrecy or a duty of confidentiality according to law, to those who conduct or intend to conduct subscriber directory services, on terms that are fair, cost-orientated and non-discriminatory;
- provide without charge a subscriber with specified telephone bills relating to the use of a public telephone network to a fixed network termination point or public telephony services belonging thereto, provided the subscriber has not requested that the bills should be unspecified;
- ensure that end users can reach all numbers in use within the EEA, provided this is technically and economically feasible and the subscriber called has not chosen

193. Chapter 5 s. 6b Electronic Communications Act.
194. Guideline by PTS, PTSFS 2007:2.
195. Chapter 5 s. 6c Electronic Communications Act. PTS has issued Regulations and Guidelines regarding notification of service disruption or interruptions, PTSFS 2012:2.
196. Chapter 5 s. 6d Electronic Communications Act.

to limit access for incoming calls from certain geographical areas for commercial reasons; and
- have regard to the needs of people with disability for special services in operations.[197]

Calls that are free of charge for the caller may not be specified on her or his telephone bill. Telephony service providers are obliged to at subscriber's request block certain numbers or certain types of calls (e.g., international calls or calls to premium services), or to block calls when the accrued charges have reached a limit set by the subscriber. Subscribers must be informed of this right when entering into a contract for a publicly available telephony service, and must have the right to change any set block during the contract period free of charge. A self-imposed limitation of calls shall not prevent placing calls to emergency services or calls that can be made free of charge.[198]

Operators who provide payphones that are available to the public shall ensure that emergency calls from these payphones are forwarded free of charge and without a demand for means of payment.[199]

Operators who provide a public communications network or a publicly available electronic communication service shall keep information about applicable prices, tariffs and general terms for access to and the use of the telephony service available to the public.[200] A party that provides public electronic communications services may be ordered to provide comparable, adequate and up-to-date information about the quality of the services to end users.[201]

If a subscriber falls behind on payments for access to a public communications network or a publicly available electronic communication service, provision of the network or service may be only discontinued after the subscriber has been prompted to pay within a specified reasonable time, and was informed that the provision of the service may otherwise be discontinued. If the service is paid for within the specified time, the provision of the service may not be discontinued. If a subscriber has paid too late on repeated occasions, the provision of the service may however be discontinued immediately. The party that provides the service shall in such a case immediately notify the subscriber of the cessation of service and during a period of at least ten days from the discontinuance offer the subscriber the opportunity to make emergency calls and other free phone calls. If the unpaid or repeated late payment relates to a particular service, the discontinuance may be limited to that service, provided it is technically possible and the subscriber has not previously received a demand for payment or misled the service supplier.[202]

197. Chapter 5 ss 6e and 7 Electronic Communications Act.
198. Chapter 5 s. 7a and 7b Electronic Communications Act.
199. Chapter 5 s. 8 Electronic Communications Act.
200. Chapter 5 s. 17 Electronic Communications Act.
201. Chapter 5 s. 18 Electronic Communications Act.
202. Chapter 5 s. 19 Electronic Communications Act.

III. Other Public Rights and Obligations

A. *Rights of Way*

103. Operators require access for placing equipment and laying down cables across public and private property to serve end users. Rights of Way are regulated in the Utility Easements Act (*Ledningsrättslag (1973:1144)*) and not in the Electronic Communications Act. Under this Act, a party wishing to use a space within a property unit for a utility or other device can obtain the right to do so (a utility easement). Questions concerning utility easements are examined by cadastral procedure. A utility easement comprises, as determined in the cadastral procedure, a power to take within the property unit those measures which are needed for the installation and use of a utility or other devise. At the request of the proprietor of the utility easement, an order can be made to the effect that a utility easement shall belong to that party's property unit or registered site leasehold.

The Utility Easements Act encompasses utilities included in an electronic communications network for a public purpose and a public low-voltage line for signalling, remote control, data, etc. communication or some similar purpose, if it benefits economic activity or a communications installation of importance for the whole country or a certain locality and entails only slight encroachment compared with the benefit and does not provide for the domestic needs of one property unit only.[203] It used to be unclear if a mast carrying transmitters for a mobile network was strictly a 'utility' as in Swedish the Act speaks of 'cables'. The Act was clarified to include masts in 2004.

The cadastral authority may ordain that an operator as proprietor of the utility easement is entitled to sublet space and let another party install and use additional utilities within the space granted, if there is a need for such a right with regard to the nature of the utility.[204]

B. *Co-location and Facility Sharing*

104. Recital 23 Framework Directive considers that facility sharing can be of benefit for town planning, public health or environmental reasons.

An operator may be obligated to provide, in return for commercial reward, co-location or other opportunities for shared use of property or other resources, if this is required to protect the environment, public health or public security or in order to achieve the objectives of physical planning. An obligation may consist of strengthening or expanding a radio mast or similar actions required to provide access. The operator may not be required to replace an existing mast for a new one.[205] The right to demand co-location is restricted to other operators; a municipal or other public authority is not entitled to demand that operators co-locate, for example, for zoning or environmental reasons. An operator may not demand that

203. Section 2 Utility Easements Act.
204. Section 11a Utility Easements Act.
205. Chapter 4 s. 14 Electronic Communications Act.

another operator co-locates with it in order to share costs; only operators seeking access to another operator's facilities may exercise the right to request co-location. Compensation for providing co-location shall be calculated at market rates, as far as they can be established.[206]

An operator, or someone who owns cable or wires in a public communication network that the operator may dispose of, may on request become obliged to provide shared use of the lines in a building or up to the first exit or point of divergence. This obligation may only be imposed in the event the construction of further infrastructure is deemed unprofitable or physically impractical.[207]

104.1. Operators may also become obliged to allow reasonable requests for access to and use of networks and affiliated installations in order to provide electronic communication services. Article 12.1 and 12.3 of the Access Directive on obligations of access to, and use of, specific network facilities is implemented through detailed regulations in the Electronic Communications Act, whereby SMP-operators may be required to provide a range of forms of access. PTS has however not included any co-location or facility sharing requirements in the 2013 SMP decisions.

C. *Users' Rights*

1. Generally

105. The Electronic Communications Act makes a distinction between subscribers, users and end users. The definitions given to each category is relevant, for it determines who is a beneficiary of a specific right or not.

A subscriber is a person who has concluded a contract with a provider of public electronic communications services concerning the provision of such services; a user is a person who uses or demands the provision of a public electronic communications service; an end user is a user who does not provide public communications networks or public electronic communications services.[208]

2. Contracts

106. The Electronic Communications Act sets out a long list of specific requirements regarding contracts between network and/or service providers and subscribers.

206. See regarding calculation of compensation Government Bill (Proposition) 2005/06:191, 'Ändring i lagen om elektronisk kommunikation', 15 and 22. The PTS 2013 SMP decisions are available at http://www.pts.se/sv/Bransch/Telefoni/Konkurrensreglering-SMP/SMP-beslut-2012-2013.
207. Chapter 4 s. 13a Electronic Communications Act.
208. Chapter 1 s. 7 Electronic Communications Act.

A contract between an end user and a party that provides electronic communications services or a connection to a public telephone network shall contain information about:

(1) the provider's name and address;
(2) the services to be provided;
(3) access to calls to emergency services and availability of localization data;
(4) conditions that restrict access to or use of other services and applications then those of (3);
(5) the lowest level of quality that is offered;
(6) time until delivery;
(7) which measures have been taken to measure and direct traffic in order to prevent network congestion, and how these measures may affect the quality of service;
(8) the maintenance and customer services that are offered;
(9) any restrictions on the use of terminal equipment;
(10) subscriber options regarding entering of personal data in directory services;
(11) detailed prices and tariffs;
(12) how payments can be made, difference in cost for the payment options and how information on applicable tariffs and maintenance charges can be obtained;
(13) the term of the contract;
(14) conditions for extension and termination of the service;
(15) conditions for extension and termination of the contract;
(16) actions that will be taken in the event of a security breach;
(17) conditions for compensation if services are not provided according to the contract; and
(18) how dispute resolution proceedings for consumers out-of-court can be commenced.[209]

Electronic communications service providers must offer end users the option to enter into contracts with a maximum duration of twelve months. A contract between a service provider and a consumer may not have a binding period in excess of twenty-four months. Other subscribers than consumers may request that a contract have a maximum duration of twenty-four months.[210]

If a service provider wishes to amend the contract, the subscriber must be notified of the amendment at least one month before it enters into force. A subscriber who does not accept the new conditions may give notice terminating the contract without therefore being adversely affected by any cost, charge or other obligation. The notification to the subscriber shall advise her or him about her or his right to give notice terminating the contract.[211]

---

209. Chapter 5 s. 15 Electronic Communications Act.
210. Chapter 5 s. 15a Electronic Communications Act.
211. Chapter 5 s. 16 Electronic Communications Act.

§10. ADMINISTRATIVE CHARGES

107. The Electronic Communications Act sets out that PTS may charge a processing fee on a party that notifies operations concerning:

- the provision to the public of electronic communications networks;
- the provision to the public of electronic communications services; or applies for:
  - a license to use a radio transmitter;
  - a license to use numbers from the national numbering plan;
  - consent to assign a license or part of a license to use a radio transmitter or numbers.[212]

The processing charge shall correspond to the authority's costs for processing the matter. PTS may also charge an annual fee of the provider of a notified network or service, or of a license holder for radio transmission or use of numbers.

The annual charges shall in aggregate correspond to the costs that an authority otherwise has for its operations according to the Electronic Communications Act. The charges shall be allocated with a reasonable proportion to those who conduct notified operations or hold licenses.

Network and service providers are also liable to pay a charge for the financing of measures against serious peacetime threats and stresses that relate to electronic communications. The charges that are imposed shall be allocated in reasonable proportions among those who conduct notified operations.[213]

108. PTS annually issues a regulation on the calculation of the administrative charges. Operators are obliged to pay an annual percentage of their gross revenues to finance the costs incurred in the management, control and enforcement of the regulatory framework. Currently (2013) the applicable percentage is 0.165 of the revenue of the notified operation, for operators with revenue in excess of SEK 5 million for the preceding year. Operators with less annual revenue pay a fixed sum of SEK 1100. The fee for financing measures against serious peacetime threats and stresses that relate to electronic communications is set at 0.155 of the revenue of the notified operation, for operators with revenue in excess of SEK 30 million for the preceding year. The Government however sets an annual total cap of what fee may be collected for this purpose. The fees for use of numbers and various radio transmitter usages are listed in the PTS regulation.[214]

212. Chapter 8 s. 17 Electronic Communications Act, s. 11 Ordinance on financing the operations of the Post and Telecom Agency and s. 37 Ordinance on Electronic Communications.

213. Chapter 8 s. 18 Electronic Communications Act.

214. PTS issues an annual regulation on the calculation of the fees; the latest one is PTSFS 2012:5 covering the year 2013.

Chapter 2. Regulation of Competition in the ICT Market

§1. General Statement

109. The present EU regulatory framework aims at reducing or even withdrawing *ex ante* sector specific rules. The mechanism for doing so is based on an initial analysis of the relevant markets with a view to assessing whether competition is effective in a given market. If so, *ex ante* regulatory obligations should not be imposed. If there is not effective competition or if competition is not deemed durable, *ex ante* obligations may be imposed on undertakings having a SMP.[215]

§2. Market Definition Procedure

110. PTS is in charge of defining the relevant markets concerning the provision of electronic communications networks and services. To this end, it must take into account the EU Commission guidelines for market analysis and the assessment of SMP, as well as the Recommendation on relevant product and service markets.[216]

PTS is enjoined to continuously determine which product and service markets have such characteristic features that it may be justified to introduce obligations under the Electronic Communications Act. The territorial scope of the markets shall be defined in that connection.[217]

§3. Market Analysis Procedure

111. PTS shall continuously analyse the relevant markets that it has determined, having had regard to the Commission Recommendation. For each market, it shall be determined whether effective competition prevails. If, when making an assessment, it is concluded that effective competition does not prevail in a market determined, then the undertakings with significant power in this market shall be identified and decisions issued concerning obligations.[218]

If it is concluded that effective competition prevails in a market determined, the obligations that have been decided will be revoked. The time of revocation of an obligation shall be decided having regard to the interests of the parties affected.

As regards cross-border markets determined in accordance with a decision of the European Commission, measures shall be decided following consultation with the competent authorities in the States affected.[219]

215. See Art. 16 Framework Directive.
216. See Art. 15 Framework Directive.
217. Chapter 8 s. 5 Electronic Communications Act.
218. Chapter 8 s. 6 Electronic Communications Act.
219. Chapter 8 s. 11 Electronic Communications Act.

§4. OPERATORS WITH SIGNIFICANT MARKET POWER

I. Identification of Operators with SMP

112. An undertaking shall be deemed to have significant power in a market determined if it, either individually or together with others, has a position of such financial strength that it can to a significant extent act independently of its competitors, its customers and ultimately the consumer. PTS shall issue regulations concerning guidelines and documentation for making an assessment.[220]

The Electronic Communications Act uses a concept of SMP equivalent to the one established in the EU Framework Directive, that is, equivalent to the concept of dominance as defined in the case law of the Court of Justice and the Court of First Instance.[221] As a result, PTS will find that an operator has an SMP if – either individually or jointly with others – it enjoys a position equivalent to dominance, that is, a position of economic strength affording it the power to behave to an appreciable extent independently of competitors, customers, and consumers.

II. Special Obligations for Undertakings with Significant Power in a Market

113. If an operator has been found to have SMP in a market that PTS finds to be signified as lacking in effective competition, PTS shall decide on appropriate obligations to be imposed.[222] A catalogue of available obligations is listed in Chapter 4 of the Electronic Communications Act. Any obligations shall be chosen for the purpose of achieving effective competition.[223]

The main obligations that may be imposed on an operator with SMP in a relevant market are as follows.

An operator may be obliged to:

- publish specified information in a reference offer or otherwise regarding accounting, technical specifications, network characteristics, conditions on access and usage including conditions that restrict access to or use of certain services, pricing, or other matters necessary to afford transparency regarding interconnection or other forms of access;[224]
- apply non-discriminatory conditions in its business, aiming to ensure that the operator applies the same conditions towards other who offer equivalent services, and that the services and information offered to others are supplied on the same terms and with the same quality as are the operator's own services, including the services of group companies or affiliated companies;[225]
- maintain separate accounting of and reporting on specified enterprise relating to interconnection and other forms of access. The obligation may entail an open

220. Chapter 8 s. 7 Electronic Communications Act.
221. See Case 27/76 *United Brands v. Commission* [1978] ECR 207.
222. Chapter 8 s. 6 Electronic Communications Act.
223. Chapter 4 s. 4 Electronic Communications Act.
224. Chapter 4 s. 5 Electronic Communications Act.
225. Chapter 4 s. 6 Electronic Communications Act.

pricing towards other operators or in inter-group transfers, or opening the operator's accounting to a public authority;[226]

- accommodate reasonable requests for access to and use of networks and related installations in order to supply electronic communication services. This obligation may entail the operator granting access to specified network components and related installations, including such access necessary to enable carrier selection and carrier pre-selection as well as retail of subscriptions; extending previously granted access to related installations; offering other operators specified services they can retail; granting access to technical interfaces, protocols and other key technologies necessary for interaction of services; offering co-location and other opportunities of shared use of related installations; offering specific services necessary to ensure interaction between services through to the end user; offer access to operational support systems or similar systems necessary in order to guarantee a healthy competition with regard to the supply of services; offer access to such services that enable, support or may support the provision of services over an electronic communications network or electronic communications services; to interconnect or otherwise act in order to enable the connection of networks or related installations. Obligations such as these may be enjoined with conditions required to ensure regular network operations. Any condition to observe particular technical standards or specifications must correspond to such standards designated as obligatory by the European Commission and published in the Official Journal of the European Union;[227]
- apply cost-covering or cost-oriented pricing or other set pricing for specific types of interconnection or access; to use a specified method of accounting for costs and to make public a description of the method. The operator shows its prices to be fair and reasonable with regard to costs, and may be ordered to adjust its pricing. When imposing this obligation, regard shall be taken to the operator's investments, allowing the operator a reasonable return on capital investment.[228]

113.1. Under exceptional circumstances, a vertically integrated operator that has been obliged to provide access, may become required to detach the business units related to the access obligation into a separate organizational structure in what is known as 'functional separation'. The detached business units shall operate as if independent, ensuring non-discrimination, and transparency. If functional separation is imposed, it may be joined with conditions seeking ensure operational independence, such as being placed in a separate legal entity or under an independent management.[229]

*113.2. An o*perator who could have a functional separation imposed may have a commitment to self-detach concerned business units accepted, if there are exceptional reasons. Such acceptance shall have the legal effect of requiring the operator to observe the commitment. As long as the acceptance decision is in force, an order

226. Chapter 4 s. 7 Electronic Communications Act.
227. Chapter 4 s. 8 Electronic Communications Act.
228. Chapter 4 s. 11 Electronic Communications Act.
229. Chapter 4 s. 12 a–b Electronic Communications Act.

of a functional separation may not be imposed on the operator. The acceptance decision may be revoked, should the circumstances the decision was based on fundamentally change, the operator fails to honour the commitment or the decision was based on incomplete, false or misleading information provided by the operator.

114. An operator that has SMP in a particular end user market may if necessary be ordered to implement extra measures. Such an obligation may relate to:

(1) application of a particular maximum or minimum price;
(2) not implementing measures that impede competition; or
(3) not performing a service that can be provided independently as a result of another service also being provided.[230]

230. Chapter 5 s. 13 Electronic Communications Act.

Chapter 3. Regulation of Cryptography and Other Dual-Use Products

§1. The Regulation of Cryptography

115. In Sweden the import, use and production of cryptographic products is not restricted. It is also possible to import and produce cryptography products.

The Swedish Commission for ICT (*IT-Kommissionen*, hereinafter 'ICT Commission')[231] was an advisory board that was set up by the Swedish Government and advised the Government on issues relating to information technology. It has in various reports provided guidance to the Swedish Government on the issue of cryptography. One of the conclusions it came to was that it was impossible to separate cryptography from normal computer technology. In a report entitled 'The Importance of the Use of Encryption', the ICT Commission indicated that the discussion on cryptography involves three areas: (1) the availability of strong encryption techniques and products; (2) the use of encryption together with attempts to limit its use; and (3) the export control of encryption techniques and products. The ICT Commission furthermore made the following proposals:

- All forms of mandatory system for depositing keys should be opposed.
- Swedish users need to be able to use encryption products to the same extent as companies.
- Encryption is important for international communication.
- Government policy should encourage the use of strong encryption.
- Government should send a clear message that it is acceptable to use strong encryption.

Finally, the ICT Commission recommended that exports of cryptography should be stimulated and encouraged as well as the import and use of strong cryptography products.

116. The Swedish policy on cryptography was proposed in Government Communication 1998/1999:116 on cryptography.[232] The origin of this Government Communication is the establishment in 1996 of a Swedish Government Office Reference Group in order to formulate a national policy with regard to encryption. The Swedish Government presented this Communication to the Swedish Parliament on 6 May 1999. It outlined the Swedish Government's attitude towards cryptography and a main area of focus was the use of cryptography, both in regard to its import as well as export.

231. The ICT Commission ceased to exist on 30 May 2003, <www.itkommissionen.se>. See Introduction Ch. 5 *supra* (para. 33).

232. Skrivelse 1998/99:116 Om kryptografi. The basis of this Communication was a report from the ICT Commission entitled 'Inför en svensk policy för säker elektronisk kommunikation', IT-kommissionens rapport 6/97, SOU 1997:73.

According to the Government Communication, the following points should be considered when deciding on a policy with regard to cryptography products:[233]

- The importance of trustworthy electronic documents.
- The trustworthiness of electronic signatures as well as attaining confidentiality for electronic communication and other information.
- The fight against crime.
- Export controls to prevent cryptography ending up in the wrong hands.

In Communication 1998/1999:116, the Swedish Government also stated that there was no reason to limit the use of cryptography in Sweden. Rather, emphasis was on the fact that all should be free to choose technology themselves. Therefore, there were to be no limitations on the import of encryption products. Here the emphasis was on the advantages that could be gained from these products. For example, encryption is a means of ensuring security within e-commerce, it enhances ways of attaining privacy and it secures communications not only between individuals, but also between individuals and public authorities.

117. It can also be mentioned that authorities investigating a crime are able to use various means in order to get access to cryptographic keys, however, a person who is suspected of committing a crime cannot be forced to actively assist or participate in the investigation of the crime.

Therefore, in summarizing the status of cryptography within Sweden, there are no restrictions regarding the import, use and production of cryptographic products. However, considering that cryptography is also considered a dual-use product, its export is regulated together with other dual-use products.

§2. The Regulation of Dual-Use Goods

118. The term 'dual-use' has its origin in the fact that certain products, due to their nature, can be used for both civilian purposes as well as for military ones. Therefore, dual-use products can have consequences which jeopardize the security interests of nations. However, dual-use products can also have far-reaching benefits. For example, cryptography is important in the creation of a secure information technology environment and the technology is used in e-commerce and digital signature technologies. However, in the wrong hands it could also be used to conceal crime or acts of terrorism. Cryptography is considered a dual-use product and most of the legislation in respect of other dual-use products also applies to cryptography.

In the opinion of the ICT Commission, referred to above, it was unfortunate that cryptography fell under the same regulations as other dual-use products, due to the fact that it has many commercial advantages, and it is important that trade in cryptography products be allowed to occur, with Swedish companies being allowed to trade on equal footing with other international companies.[234]

---

233. *Ibid.*, 4.

234. IT Commission, 'The Importance of the Use of Encryption', Dnr ITK99/19, 9.

I. Legislative Framework

119. The legal framework with regard to dual-use products is comprised of international regime controls, EU legislation and national legislation. It can be said that most of the legislation on dual-use products originates from the EU in the form of EU Council Regulations and which is in turn supplemented by national legislation regarding export control.

The international framework outlining Swedish policy in regard to the export of dual-use products is determined by five multilateral regimes of which Sweden is a member. They are the following:

- The Zangger Committee.[235]
- The Nuclear Supplies Group.[236]
- The Australia Group.[237]
- The Missile Technology Control Regime.[238]
- The Wassenaar Arrangement.[239]

The main aim of these regimes is to restrict export and in so doing prevent the spread of weapons of mass destruction and dual-use products. The regime specifically dealing with cryptography products is the Wassenaar Arrangement.[240] It was established in 1995 and Sweden became a signatory that same year. The Arrangement has as its aim the prevention of the dissemination of ammunitions and dual-use products in order to create international security. Each signatory to the Wassenaar Arrangement is required to implement the arrangement by enacting national legislation.

120. Council Regulation No. 428/2009[241] (hereinafter 'the Regulation') regulates the export of dual-use products both within the EU and to countries outside of the region. Chapter I Article 3 paragraph 1 of the Regulation states that authorization is required for the export of dual-use products listed in Annex I. In addition, an authorization may also be required if the dual-use product is not specified in Annex 1, according to Article 3(2). Annex I stipulates which types of products may be exported as well as what type of license is required. This annex is updated on a regular basis. The overriding factors to be considered in determining whether a specific product is to be considered a dual-use product are the type of dual-use product as well as its proposed destination. According to the Council Regulation, dual-use products should be subject to effective control when they are exported from the

235. <www.zanggercommittee.org>.
236. <www.nuclearsuppliersgroup.org>.
237. <www.australiagroup.net>.
238. <www.mtcr.info>.
239. <www.wassenaar.org>.
240. Wassenaar Arrangement on Export Controls for Conventional Arms and Dual-Use Goods and Technologies.
241. Council Regulation (EC) No. 428/2009 of 5 May 2009 setting up a Community regime for the control of exports, transfers, brokering and transit of dual-use items.

European Community. Adherence to this principle in turn allows for the free movement of dual-use products within the EU.

National legislation in Sweden is comprised of the Act on Control Over Dual-use Products and Over Technical Assistance (*Lag (2000:1064) om kontroll av produkter med dubbla användningsområden och av tekniskt bistånd*), and the corresponding Ordinance (*Förordning (2000:1217) om kontroll av produkter med dubbla användningsområden och av tekniskt bistånd*). The Department for Disarmament and Non-Proliferation at the Swedish Ministry for Foreign Affairs determines policy, initiates legislation and regulates international negotiations in this area.[242] The local public authority responsible for export controls of dual-use products is The Swedish Agency for Non-Proliferation and Export Controls, ISP being the Swedish acronym (*Inspektion för strategiska produkter*).[243] It has also enacted a Regulation relating to the export of strategic products (TFS 2000:24).[244]

121. The term 'export' is defined in the above Council Regulation.[245] It refers to goods leaving the Community, the re-export of non-Community goods and the transmission of software or technology by electronic media, including by fax, telephone, email or any other electronic means to a destination outside of the European Community. The export of cryptography products without the required license can lead to someone being convicted of the crime of smuggling.[246]

II. Supervision of Cryptography and Dual-Use Exports

122. The main function of the Swedish Agency for Non-Proliferation and Export Controls (ISP) is to control not only the export of military equipment, but also the export of equipment that could have both civilian and military uses, in other words dual-use products. The role of ISP is to see to it that dual-use products are not exported to certain governments and other actors, thereby contributing to the production of weapons of mass destruction. It therefore can be said to play a role in Swedish foreign and security policy. It is also responsible for ensuring compliance with the regulations that must be observed in connection with dual-use products as well as the handling of targeted sanctions aimed at specific countries.

ISP also consults with the Export Control Council (ECC), which is an advisory body consisting of twelve members. All export matters are referred to the ECC, along with cases where ISP needs advice where developments have occurred or when assessing new recipient countries.[247] The members are appointed by Government, and represent the various Swedish political parties.

---

242. <www.regeringen.se/sb/d/11557>, 5 Apr. 2014.
243. <www.isp.se/sa/node.asp?node=410>, 5 Apr. 2014.
244. Föreskrifter om ändring i Inspektionens för strategiska produkter föreskrifter (TFS 2000:24) om generellt exporttillstånd. There is an additional Regulation that sets out the application document to be used when applying for an export license (TFS 2000:25).
245. The definition can be found in Ch. I, Art. 2, point 2. (i) through (iii).
246. Agne Lindberg & Daniel Westman, *Praktisk IT-rätt*, 3rd edn (Stockholm: Norstedts Juridik AB, 2002).
247. <www.isp.se/sa/node.asp?node=1212>, 5 Apr. 2014.

123. In determining matters of export control, there is a general presumption in favour of allowing the export of dual-use products. In other words, the export of dual-use products is allowed unless there are specific reasons for not allowing this. According to ISP, matters concerning the export of dual-use products are dealt with either by focusing on the dual-use product itself or by focusing on the end use of the dual-use product.

As mentioned above, cryptography products are treated as dual-use products and are subject to export control if they have a key length that exceeds 56 bits for symmetric keys and 512 bits alternatively 112 bits for asymmetric keys (dependent upon the mathematical function used).[248] Authorization is not required for the transfer of cryptography that is intended for personal use, for example, for individuals to secure personal files.[249]

124. When focusing on the dual-use product itself, the general rule is that a license is required for the export of dual-use products if they appear in Annex I of the Regulation. However, exports within the EU do not require a license, except in those circumstances involving dual-use products that are very specialized and appear in Annex IV of the Council Regulation.[250]

If a company is unsure of whether a dual-use product can be exported, it is able to ask ISP for advice on the matter. This consideration of the dual-use product can result in either a positive or negative presumption. A positive presumption means that an export license is required whereas a negative presumption entails a denial, in other words export is not allowed.

125. The end use approach to dual-use products is relevant in circumstances where a product is not found on the product list, but which may still be subject to export controls. For example, the ISP may suspect that a dual-use product is to be exported to a country which intends to use it for undesirable ends. In such cases, ISP has the authority to classify dual-use products with reference to a specific end user as controlled even if it does not appear on the above-mentioned Annex I.[251] This is known as a catch-all clause, and is referred to in Chapter II Article 4 of the Regulation. Any denial by ISP for an export license is reported to the EU or to the relevant regime, for example, the Wassenaar Arrangement, if it concerns cryptography products.

In circumstances where a license is required, ISP can also require an end user certificate, which verifies what the dual-use product is, the purposes that the dual-use product will be used for, contract numbers and finally also what it can be used for.

---

248. <www.isp.se/sa/node.asp?node=998>, 5 Apr. 2014.

249. This is dealt with in Annex I, Category 5 part 2 of Regulation (EU), No 388/2012 of the European Parliament and of the Council of 19 Apr. 2012 amending Council Regulation (EC) No 428/2009 setting up a Community regime for the control of exports, transfer, brokering and transit of dual-use items.

250. <www.isp.se/sa/node.asp?node=1139>, 5 Apr. 2014.

251. ISP Annual Report 2008, 13, <www.isp.se/documents/_English/Publications/AR/ISP_AR2008_web.pdf>, 5 Apr. 2014, available on the publications page of ISP at <www.isp.se/sa/node.asp?node=528>.

Also, Chapter II Article 7 states that the Regulation does not apply to the supply of services or the transmission of technology if it involves the cross-border movement of persons. Therefore, a person travelling with a laptop computer which contains a cryptography product is not subject to the Regulation.

126. There are various types of export licenses applicable to the export of dual-use products. Chapter III Article 9 of the Regulation refers to a Community General Export Authorization for exports. It specifies certain non-European Union countries to which the export of dual-use products is treated the same as exports to countries within the EU.[252] Furthermore, the above article states that all other exports require authorization from the relevant authority in Member States. In addition, all authorizations are valid throughout the Community.

In addition to this, ISP can issue three other types of national export licenses, namely an individual license, a global license, and a general license. These licenses are valid throughout the EU.[253] They become relevant in cases where the export of a dual-use product is not covered by the Community General Export Authorization. An individual license is applicable to a certain dual-use product from a specified exporter and to a specific destination. A global license can be granted to a specified exporter. This allows for unlimited export to multiple countries while the license is valid. The general license is an open authorization and does not require an application. ISP has promulgated an Ordinance in respect of this license (TFS 2000:24). It is valid for the export of cryptography of a temporary nature, for repair, for replacement or for demonstrations. Furthermore, this applies only for cryptography that is to be used for civilian purposes and does not apply to especially sensitive cryptography products, according to section 3. The Ordinance also specifies the countries to which cryptography may be exported in accordance with the general license.

---

252. The United States of America, Australia, Japan, Canada, New Zealand, Norway and Switzerland are the countries stipulated in this export exception according to export authorization EU001 in Annex II of the Regulation.

253. <www.isp.se/sa/node.asp?node=1065>, 5 Apr. 2014.

Chapter 4. Legal Status of Standardization

127. In Sweden, developments with respect to standardization in the area of ICT are reflected in both the private sector as well as within the public administration. Sweden is a country with a long tradition of developing a sound and well-functioning public administration and standardization has been identified as necessary in order to stimulate progress within this sector.

Since 1 January 2012, the main organization involved in standardization in Sweden is the Swedish Standards Association.[254] The Association is a collaborative body for the three Swedish standardization organizations: ITS (*Informationstekniska Standardisering*),[255] SEK (*Svensk Elstandard*),[256] and the Swedish Standards Institute (SIS).[257] These organizations in turn are members of international standardization organizations. For example, SIS is a member of the International Organization for Standardization (ISO)[258] and the European Committee for Standardization (CEN).[259]

The purpose of the Association is to promote standardization in Sweden, promote the use of standards, streamline standardization through collaboration and apply for state funding.[260] The Association does not maintain an official register of adopted standards, but rather refers to the respective standardization organization's website, where a full catalogue is kept.[261]

A new national IT Standards Council was established in March 2014 under the authority of the E-Government Delegation. Management of the Council is to be handled by the Swedish Standards Institute (SIS).[262] The Council's role is to be the Government's platform for addressing standardization issues with the area of ICT.[263] More specifically, the Council is to:

- assist the Government in preparing Swedish positions on matters relating to standards and standardization within the area of ICT;
- lead and coordinate matters of IT standardization with representatives of major stakeholders within the state, local government, and interested organizations and corporations;
- follow developments with the field and participate in discussions and the exchange of information on issues affecting international efforts on standardization issues with the area of ICT; and

---

254. Sveriges Standardiseringsförbund, <www.standardiseringsforbundet.se>. The Swedish Standards Association replaced Swedish Standards Council (*Sveriges Standardiseringsråd, SSR*), the public authority that previously was responsible for the oversight and control of standards in Sweden.
255. <www.its.se>.
256. <www.elstandard.se>.
257. <www.sis.se>.
258. <www.iso.org>.
259. <www.cen.eu>.
260. < www.standardiseringsforbundet.se/om-standardiseringsforbundet>, 6 Apr. 2014.
261. SSR previously maintained an official register of adopted standards in Sweden. However, this is no longer available since October 2012, see <www.standardiseringsforbundet.se/register-over-svensk-standard>.
262. <www.sis.se/itstand>, 6 Apr. 2014.
263. <www.edelegationen.se/Stod-och-verktyg/It-standardisering/>, 6 Apr. 2014.

– manage cases that may involve different sectors of society which do not purely relate to e-Government.

The initiative for the inception of a standard can come from individuals, private organizations or public government authorities. When a standard is proposed, the matter is investigated by experts who then form committees and working groups. This process ends with an open consultation before the standard is approved. In addition, all standards that are adopted on the European level are almost always accepted on the national level.[264]

§1. Private Sector

128. The legal framework in Sweden within the area of standardization in the private sector is regulated by a number of Acts and Ordinances that implement Directives from the EU.

The rationale behind the EU legislation is that the EU merely specifies the technical demands that need to be met by products, and then it is for manufacturers to determine how these demands can technically be achieved. For example, it is the responsibility of the manufacturers of radio and telecommunications terminal equipment to see to it that products adhere to the standards set on the European level. The CE certification[265] in turn functions as a guarantee that products put on the market adhere to the Directives' specifications. This is referred to as 'the new method' whereby the EU merely specifies what demands are to be met, and it is then up to the individual manufacturers to determine how they wish to technically meet these demands. An effect of this is that States may not prohibit or hinder the placing of products on the market that bear the CE mark.[266] It is then the function of the responsible authority to determine whether these standards have been adhered to. This differs from the previous situation, where manufacturers of radio and telecommunications terminal equipment were required to obtain clearance prior to putting a product on the market. A positive effect of this legislative process is that manufacturers no longer need to wait for a decision by the local authorities before putting products on the market, which previously had the effect that there was a delay before products would reach the market.

129. The Act on Radio and Telecommunications Terminal Equipment (*Lag (2000:121) om radio- och teleterminalutrustning*) as well as a corresponding Ordinance (*Förordning (2000:124) om radio- och teleterminalutrustning*) is one such example of the above-mentioned legislative technique. The above legislation puts into effect Directive 1999/5/EC of the European Parliament and of the Council of 9 March 1999 on radio equipment and telecommunications terminal equipment and

---

264. <www.its.se/om-standardisering/hur-standard-blir-till/>, 6 Apr. 2014.

265. CE stands for Conformité Européenne.

266. Article 8, Directive 1999/5/EC of the European Parliament and of the Council of 9 Mar. 1999 on radio equipment and telecommunications terminal equipment and the mutual recognition of their conformity.

the mutual recognition of their conformity (hereinafter 'Directive 1999/5/EC'). According to section 3 Ordinance on Radio and Telecommunications Terminal Equipment, PTS[267] is the local authority specializing and having jurisdiction within the operation area of the corresponding Act. Section 4 gives it the authority to introduce Regulations within the above-mentioned area.

130. The aim of Directive 1999/5/EC is to open up the telecommunications market and to allow for the free movement of products as long as they fulfil the Directive's 'essential requirements'. Another aim is to stimulate technical advances within the area of ICT. Directive 1999/5/EC specifies 'essential requirements' that need to be met in order to provide a high level of protection to users of this equipment. Article 3 specifies two general essential requirements. They are: (1) the protection of the health and safety of the user and any other person as well as the objectives contained in Directive 73/23/EEC[268] and (2) the protection requirements regarding electromagnetic compatibility found in Directive 89/336/EEC.[269] The article also contains other essential requirements that are specific to radio equipment. However, it does not specify how these essential requirements are to be fulfilled and it is up to each manufacturer to devise the best methods of achieving this end. Compliance is mandatory and products are not allowed to be placed on the market until they have satisfied the necessary requirements.[270]

Directive 1999/5/EC also prescribes other security arrangements. These are reflected in section 7 Act on Radio and Telecommunications Terminal Equipment. Accordingly, an operator can, with the permission of the responsible local authority (PTS in Sweden), refuse to connect equipment to a network, disconnect it or take it out of use. In certain emergency circumstances, the operator can take these steps without the prior consent of the responsible authority. However, the responsible authority must later be notified of this. Article 9 paragraph 1 of the Directive states that where a product does not meet the specifications laid out in the Directive, then the responsible authority will ensure that the product is removed from the market. This control function of the local authority is reflected in sections 9 and 10 Act on Radio and Telecommunications Terminal Equipment.

131. Another Directive, also having a bearing on the private sector is Directive 2001/95/EC of the European Parliament and of the Council of 3 December 2001 on General Product Safety (hereinafter 'Directive 2001/95/EC'). The aim of this Directive is to decrease trade barriers within the EU by standardizing all products as far as health, the environment and safety issues are concerned. Directive 2001/95/EC has been incorporated into national legislation in the form of the Product Safety Act (*Produktsäkerhetslag (2004:451)*) with a corresponding Ordinance (*Produktsäkerhetsförordning (2004:469)*). The aim of the Product Safety Act is to ensure that

267. <www.pts.se>.
268. Council Directive 73/23/EEC of 19 Feb. 1973 on the harmonization of the laws of Member States relating to electrical equipment designed for use within certain voltage limits.
269. Council Directive 89/336/EEC of 3 May 1989 on the approximation of the laws of the Member States relating to electromagnetic compatibility.
270. Guide to the R&TTE Directive 1999/5/EC, Version of 20 Apr. 2009, 33, 42, <www.ec.europa.eu/enterprise/sectors/rtte/documents/guides/#h2-guide-to-the-rtte-directive-1995/9/ec>, 6 Apr. 2014.

goods and services do not cause any personal injury. Section 8 of the above Act defines a 'safe' good or product as a good or product that upon normal or foreseeable use will not entail any risks to personal health or safety or only a low risk. Low risk is a risk that is acceptable considering how the goods or services are used. Section 9 sets out the factors that must be taken into account when determining the above risk. These factors include the characteristics of the good, information that is provided, the good's effect on other goods and the risk that the good may have for certain categories of people, for example, children. Section 11 contains a presumption in favour of goods being safe if they adhere to a Swedish standard that transforms a European standard. Finally, according to section 3 Product Safety Ordinance, it is the Swedish Consumer Agency (*Konsumentverket*)[271] that is the supervisory authority for matters relating to the Product Safety Act.

§2. Public Authorities

132. Sweden has a large public administration and the issue of standardization in this sector has been examined in the form of a Government consultation. In 2006, the Swedish Government ordered an inquiry, one of the aims of which was to examine the status of standardization as well as the coordination of standardization within this public administration. The results of the IT Standards Inquiry (hereinafter 'the Inquiry') were published in 2007.[272] One aspect that was highlighted was the role of open software. Also, the conclusions that the Inquiry came to must be seen in the light of Directive 98/34/EC, which has the aim of preventing national IT standards from creating trade barriers within the EU.[273] The point of departure was the definition of the term 'standard', which was seen both as a commonly accepted example against which something is measured as well as the outcome of a standardization process.[274] The Inquiry had the view that the issue of IT standards must be seen in relation to the following factors:

- Swedish coordination in response to EU decisions;
- e-government;
- industrial policy;
- gaining an overall view of IT standardization as an organizational system.

In addition, the Inquiry referred to a Bill put forward by the Government concerning general IT policy.[275] One of the points advocated in the Bill was that the use of open standards should be promoted where possible. These are standards that have

271. <www.konsumentverket.se>.
272. Government Official Report SOU 2007:47, 'Den osynliga infrastrukturen – om förbättrad samordning av offentlig IT-standardisering'.
273. Directive 98/34/EC of the European Parliament and of the Council of 22 Jun. 1998 laying down a procedure for the provision of information in the field of technical standards and regulation.
274. Government Official Report SOU 2007:47, 30.
275. Government Bill (Proposition) 2004/5:175, 'Från IT-politik för samhället till IT-politik för IT-samhället'.

been established by recognized European institutions and include the CEN,[276] the European Telecommunications Standards Institute (ETSI)[277] and the European Committee for Electrotechnical Standardization (CENELEC).[278] The Inquiry alluded to the fact that there were other standards that indeed had a large degree of openness. In addition, the Inquiry proposed that Sweden should promote direct reference to informal standards such as those developed by bodies like the Internet Engineering Task Force (IETF),[279] the Organization for the Advancement of Structured Information Standards (OASIS),[280] the World Wide Web Consortium (W3C),[281] and the United Nations Centre for Trade Facilitation and Electronic Business (UN/CEFACT).[282] Of particular interest is the fact that it was the Inquiry's view that all Swedish public authorities should be able to receive all types of documents that are widely used in the market by the general public and based on formal standards. However, according to the Inquiry, it is up to each public authority to decide if it wants to use the open document formats in other contexts, for example, when communicating with the general public.

The Inquiry also emphasized that there was no single body that assumed control or took a leading role when it came to IT standardization. It therefore suggested the creation of a body that would oversee the entire organizational system when it came to IT standardization. It proposed that the Swedish Standards Institute[283] was the organization that was in the best position to take on this leading function.

133. A consequence of the move towards an increased reliance on and use of e-government in Sweden has also resulted in the fact that there is an increased exchange of information between the various Swedish public administrations. In addition, there are an increased number of ways in which the general public is able to communicate with these various public administrations. The result of this is that information security has an increased significance. In the Inquiry, reference is made to information security accreditations under ISO/IEC Standard 27001, as well as the Swedish version. Reference is also made to BITS[284] which is a document with recommendations issued by the Swedish Civil Contingencies Agency that can be used in order to increase the levels of security within an organization.

134. Reference must also be made to a Swedish Government Official Report 'Strategy for the Government Agencies' Work on e-government' published on 19 October 2009.[285] The e-Government Delegation was given the task of providing

276. <www.cen.eu>.
277. <www.etsi.org>.
278. <www.cenelec.eu>.
279. <www.ietf.org>.
280. <www.oasis-open.org>.
281. <www.w3.org>.
282. <www.unece.org/cefact/>, 6 Apr. 2014.
283. <www.sis.se>.
284. BITS stands for Basic Level for Information Secutiry (*Basnivå för informationssäkerhet*), see Swedish Civil Contingencies Agency (MSB) <www.msb.se/en/>.
285. Government Official Report SOU 2009:86, 'Strategi för myndigheternas arbete med e-förvaltning'.

proposals as to how public authorities and government agencies could become more productive and efficient.

One recommendation was in respect to the National Guidelines for public sector websites. The original guidelines were developed by the Swedish Administrative Development Agency (VERVA) and published in 2006.[286] The Inquiry proposed that the above Guidelines be developed so that they meet the WCAG 2.0 standards, which are a set of non-technology specific guidelines for making web content more accessible, not only to the general public but also to people with disabilities.[287] The e-Government Delegation published a new version of the Guidelines in 2012, with updated versions being published on a monthly basis on a dedicated website.[288] The new guidelines have incorporated the recommended WCAG 2.0 standards proposed in the original guidelines.[289]

§3. Conclusion

135. As can be seen, standards themselves have no inherent legal status. However, they are incorporated into various forms of legislation and thereby have an influence from within legislation. As for the Swedish Government's view on standardization, it has been highlighted that the relationship between the state and standardization would remain the same, that there is neither a law on standardization at present nor would there be one in the future.[290]

286. VERVA was closed at the end of 2008. An archive of VERVA's webpages is still kept on the e-Government Delegation's website, and as such the Guidelines, *Vägledningen 24-timmarswebben*, can be found at <arkiv.edelegationen.se/verva/upload/publikationer/2006/vagledningen-24-timmarswebben-2006-05.pdf>, 6 Apr. 2014.

287. Web Content Accessibility Guidelines, <www.w3.org/TR/WCAG20>, 6 Apr. 2014.

288. <www.webbriktlinjer.se/riktlinjer/alla-riktlinjer-som-pdf/>, 6 Apr. 2014.

289. <www.edelegationen.se/Stod-och-verktyg/Webbutveckling/>, 6 Apr. 2014.

290. Speech by Ewa Björling, Minister of Trade, 23 Apr. 2008, <www.regeringen.se/sb/d/11390/a/103692>, 6 Apr. 2014.

Chapter 5. Legal Status of Out-of-Court Dispute Settlement in the ICT Sector

§1. General Statement

136. Disputes between contracting parties in the ICT Sector are, as a starting point, regarded as civil matters in the sense that they are amenable to out-of-court settlement. They normally concern disagreements/interpretations regarding once voluntary agreed contractual relationships and the parties may therefore also amicably resolve their disagreements/interpretations within these relationships. A settlement may be reached either before a dispute is brought before the court, or during the courts' handling of it. In the latter situation, the settlement will result in the plaintiffs' withdrawal of its action and the court writing it off, or a joint request from the parties that the court enters into a judgment confirming the settlement.[291] Also non-contractual liability claims for damages brought within the ICT sector, for example, by an operator or an end user under Chapter 7 section 13a Electronic Communications Act (*Lag (2003:389) om elektronisk kommunikation*); claims under the Copyright Act (*Lag (1960:729) om upphovsrätt till litterära och konstnärliga verk*); claims under section 48 Personal Data Act (*Personuppgiftslag (1998:204)*); claims under section 1 Product Liability Act (*Produktansvarslag (1992:18)*); as well as claims under the general Tort Liability Act (*Skadeståndslag (1972:207)*), because of alleged violation of the Electronic Commerce Act (*Lag (2002:562) om elektronisk handel och andra informationssamhällets tjänster*) and/or the Electronic Bulletin Boards Act (*Lag (1998:112) om ansvar för elektroniska anslagstavlor*) are considered as disputes which in principle are amenable to out-of-court settlement.[292] This also includes that disputes within the ICT Sector involving mandatory rules which parties to a contract may not set aside in advance,[293] in principle are amenable to out-of-court settlement.

137. A court handling a civil dispute amenable to out-of-court settlement shall to the extent appropriate, and considering the nature of the case and other circumstances, work for the parties to reach a settlement. If the court considers that the case is suitable for mediation, it may *direct* the parties to appear at a mediation session before a mediator appointed by the court.[294] In practice, it rarely occurs that parties against their joint consent are compelled to enter into mediation. One reason for this is that mediation as opposed to the court action is more costly since the parties not only will have to assume their respective counsel's fees, but also a fee to the mediator.

291. Chapter 17 s. 6 Code of Judicial Procedure (*Rättegångsbalk (1942:740)*).
292. See, e.g., Government Official Report SOU 2006:88, 'Effektivare LEK. Slutbetänkande av Utredningen om översyn av lagen om elektronisk kommunikation', 239; and Government Bill (Proposition) 2006/07:119, 'En effektivare lag om elektronisk kommunikation', 37.
293. See, e.g., s. 5 Product Liability Act.
294. Chapter 42 s. 17 Code of Judicial Procedure.

§2. Out-of-Court Dispute Settlement with Regard to Access and/or Interconnection

138. The Swedish Electronic Communications Act (*Lag (2003:389) om elektronisk kommunikation*) confers upon the national regulatory authority, PTS, to adjudicate conflicts arising between those who provide electronic communication networks or electronic communication services; or associated services as regards obligations ensuing from the Electronic Communications Act; or from regulations, license conditions or decisions concerning obligations that have been issued under the Electronic Communications Act.[295] PTS's mandate includes ruling upon conflicts regarding *inter alia* rights/duties to interconnect and/or rights to access another operator's facilities, as well as to decide terms in the operator's relationships, for example termination charges and/or any other term which derives from obligations that may have been imposed *ex ante* on one or both operators. A prerequisite for PTS's jurisdiction is that the invoked obligations and requested remedies ensue from the Electronic Communications Act, its regulations, licensed conditions or decisions which follow from the Act or formally have been issued by PTS, or otherwise are *related* to obligations which stem from the Electronic Communications Act.[296] It is notable that PTS's mandate to adjudicate conflicts between operators according to Chapter 7 section 10 Electronic Communications Act only comes into play if one, or both, operator(s) so request. The decision issued by PTS in a dispute between operators is binding and, which also is important to note, replaces any former agreement made between them on the substantive matter.[297] This means that even if the parties already have an earlier agreement covering the disputed issues, for example a certain level of access charge, a party may initiate a dispute resolution procedure against the other, and request PTS to decide a new term (charge) to apply and replace the term on which the parties earlier have agreed. PTS's decision may be appealed to administrative courts – the County Administrative Courts (*Förvaltningsrätten*) in first instance and, provided that the appellate court grants leave to appeal, further to the second instance, the Administrative Courts of Appeal (*Kammarrätten*).

139. When an operator requests PTS to resolve a dispute, PTS may instead of adjudicating upon it under Chapter 7 section 10 Electronic Communications Act refer the dispute for *mediation*. The parties shall in such a case be afforded an opportunity to submit proposals to the authority concerning an appropriate party to act as mediator.[298]

If mediation has proceeded for four months or has been discontinued before that without the parties reaching agreement, the authority shall, upon a new application by any of the parties, consider the dispute in accordance with Chapter 7 section 10

295. Chapter 7 s. 10 Electronic Communications Act.

296. See Government Bill (Proposition) 2008/09:159, 'Vissa ändringar i lagen om elektronisk kommunikation'; and C-426/05 *Tele2 Telecommunication GmbH v. Telekom-Control-Kommission*, s. 39, REG 2008 I-685.

297. Article 20 Framework Directive; and Government Bill (Proposition) 2002/03:110, 'Lag om elektronisk kommunikation, m.m.', 303–304.

298. Chapter 7 s. 11 Electronic Communications Act.

Electronic Communications Act. The parties shall be jointly liable to pay reasonable compensation to a mediator for work and disbursements.[299] If a dispute referred to PTS has also been referred to an authority in another state within the EEA, PTS shall, when processing the matter, consult the foreign authority.[300]

PTS has so far referred very few disputes for mediation and the reason for it is probably (at least) two-fold. One is the cost aspect. The other and more significant reason is that PTS often chooses a third alternative when an operator requests dispute resolution. Instead of resolving the dispute in accordance with Chapter 7 section 10 or refer it to mediation according to section 11, it can choose to act in its capacity of supervisory body under the Electronic Communications Act. In this capacity PTS may, for example, compel an involved operator to adhere to *ex ante* obligations imposed on it by virtue of earlier rendered decisions on SMP. PTS also has a mandate to decide interim measures during the supervisory process.[301] Supervision instead of dispute resolution and/or mediation sometimes also serves as an attractive and cost saving alternative for a party who wishes to interconnect with a reluctant operator demanding unreasonable conditions[302] for it or simply refuses to interconnect. If a dispute concerns past time termination charges, supervision procedures will however not be an alternative since supervision is solely a *forward-looking procedure* and cannot be used to remedy historical overcharges. For this latter purpose, dispute resolution[303] is the sole alternative. It is then important to note that in such pecuniary disputes, for example when an operator wishes to recover historical overcharges from another operator, there are certain time-limits which must be observed, and that PTS may only issue binding decisions which *establishes* the correct charge level. If an operator, despite PTS's decision refuses to pay, the entitled operator must turn to an ordinary civil court in order to obtain an enforceable award.

140. The above-described means for resolving disputes between operators regarding issues falling within the scope of the Electronic Communications Act do not prevent parties to voluntarily solicit Alternative Dispute Resolution (ADR), for example, mediation, on their own initiative instead of employing the rules in Chapter 7 Electronic Communications Act. It should however be observed that certain issues are not susceptible to other courts or adjudicating bodies except PTS. Thus PTS has an exclusive competence to rule and issue decisions which replace former agreements made between the parties on issues which could be characterized as 'core' issues of the Electronic Communications Act, for example, assessments of access charges and the right to interconnection and/or access. Such matters are considered to fall exclusively within PTS's competence.[304]

---

299. Chapter 7 s. 12 Electronic Communications Act.
300. Chapter 7 s. 13 Electronic Communications Act.
301. Chapter 7 ss 1–9 Electronic Communications Act.
302. Compare Decision by PTS from 2 Oct. 2007, no. 07-10669/23.
303. Chapter 7 s. 10 Electronic Communications Act.
304. See Stockholm City Court Decision of 26 Apr. 2005 in case T 4715-02 *TeliaSonera Mobile Networks AB v. Telenor AB. See also* Government Bill (Proposition) 2002/03:110, 117 and 303; and Government Bill (Proposition) 2004/05:175, 'Från IT-politik för samhället till politik för IT-samhället', 282 and 304.

In 2012 The Supreme Court rendered an important decision and opened up for ordinary civil courts to rule upon disputes regarding interpretation of interconnection agreements. In addition, the Supreme Court stressed that civil courts have competence, *inter alia*, to comply a party to pay debts under the interconnection agreement in order to enable the party to bring its claim to the enforcement authority, which, PTS does not have the competence to do.[305] Civil courts also have jurisdiction in disputes between operators regarding issues in interconnection/access agreement which are only remotely connected to the Electronic Communications Act, for example, offset clauses, confidentiality undertakings, trademark issues, etc.

141. When operators solicit ADR (e.g., mediation) to reconcile their disagreements, it often results in a revised or a new agreement. If the new terms involve SMP-obligations or other mandatory rules which stem from the Electronic Communications Act, a party who is discontent with the result of the reconciliation could still submit the disputed issues to PTS in accordance with Chapter 7 sections 10–13 Electronic Communications Act. This is possible because of the public interest and objectives vested in the EU Directives[306] which in turn are implemented into Swedish law through the Electronic Communications Act. The Directives and the Act aim at ensuring that private individuals, legal entities, and public authorities shall have access to secure and efficient electronic communications and the greatest possible benefit regarding the range of electronic communications services and the price and quality. Further, when applying the Act, particular regard shall be given to the importance of electronic communications for the freedom of expression and freedom of information.[307]

§3. Out-of-Court Dispute Settlement Involving Consumers and Other End Users

142. Disputes between operators and consumers and other end users are solved through the dispute resolution clauses in the subscriber (service-) agreements. An example of a dispute resolution clause in a consumer agreement is the following:

> Disputes
> Disputes in relation to the interpretation or application of the Agreement shall be conclusively determined by a Swedish court pursuant to Swedish Law. Disputes may also be adjudicated by the National Board for Consumer Complaints, whose decision is a recommendation to the Parties as to the manner in

305. Decision by Supreme Court from 11 juli 2012, NJA 2012 p. 498.
306. Directive 2002/21/EC (Framework Directive), Directive 2002/20/EC (Authorization Directive), Directive 2002/19/EC (Access Directive), Directive 2002/22/EC (Universal Service Directive) and Directive 2002/58/EC (Directive on Privacy and Electronic Communications), Directive 2009/136/EC and Directive 2009/140/EC.
307. Chapter 1 s. 1 Electronic Communications Act.

> which the dispute may be resolved. The National Board for Consumer Complaints does not adjudicate disputes which concern only the basis for invoicing the Services.[308]

The National Board for Consumer Complaints (ARN)[309] is a public body authorized to impartially try disputes between consumers and business operators in a variety of consumer's product and service fields. Petitions are filed by the consumer and ARN recommends how the dispute should be resolved. ARN's recommendations are not binding, but a majority of business operators follow them.

143. More importantly, as it especially focuses on providing free information, guidance and assistance for telecom, TV and Internet consumers, is the Swedish Telecom Advisors.[310] The Swedish Telecom Advisors is an organization that provides free information, guidance, and assistance for telecom, TV and Internet consumers. It was set up in 2006 by the Swedish IT and Telecom Industry Association after an initiative from PTS and is financed by the telecom, TV and Internet operators. All telecom, TV and Internet operators who enter into an agreement with consumers are invited and offered the opportunity to co-finance the bureau. The Swedish Telecom Advisors can act as a mediator in disputes between individual consumers and telecom, TV and Internet operators. The creation of The Swedish Telecom Advisors in 2006 was an important step for the Swedish telecom, TV, and Internet industry efforts to promote a generally accepted industry practice towards consumers and other end users. The organization's board comprises representatives of telecom, TV, and Internet operators and the government. The government is represented by PTS and the Swedish Consumer Agency (*Konsumentverket*), a public body. The authorities and industry representatives have an equal number of votes on the board, and one of the state authorities has the casting vote if this is necessary to facilitate a decision on the bureau's operations.

144. Swedish consumer protection legislation, such as the Consumers Sales Act (*Konsumentköplag (1990:932)*) and the Consumer Services Act (*konsumenttjänstlag (1985:716)*), is not directly applicable on telecom, TV, and Internet services but many of its principles (mandatory in favour of the consumer) are often said expected to apply analogous if and when such disputes appear before civil courts. Chapter 5 section 15 Electronic Communications Act enumerates certain information about, for example, quality of services, price conditions, duration, etc. which must be contained in contracts between end users and operators providing electronic communications services or a connection to a public telephone network. The information is mandatory and PTS may employ its supervisory powers and compel operators who fail to live up to these minimum standards to adhere to them.

---

308. *TeliaSoneras* General Terms and Conditions for Services to Consumers, applicable from and including 1 Jan. 2012.
309. Allmänna reklamationsnämnden, <www.arn.se>.
310. Telekområdgivarna, <www.telekomradgivarna.se>.

Part II. Protection of Intellectual Property in the ICT Sector

Chapter 1. Application of Copyright in the Area of ICT

§1. General Statement

145. Sweden has been a member of the Paris Convention for the Protection of Industrial Property (Paris Convention) since 1885, and joined the Berne Convention for the Protection of Literary and Artistic Works (Berne Convention) in 1904, as well as ratified the latest amendments. Both Conventions are administered by the World Intellectual Property Organization (WIPO), a specialized agency of the United Nations. The Berne Convention was complemented in 1996 by the WIPO Copyright Treaty (WCT), which entered into force in 2002.

Regarding neighbouring rights, Sweden entered the Rome Convention for the Protection of Performers, Producers of Phonograms, and Broadcasting Organizations (Rome Convention) in 1962, and signed and ratified its successor, the WIPO Performances and Phonograms Treaty (WPPT), in 1996.

As a contracting party of the World Trade Organization (WTO), Sweden signed and ratified the Agreement on Trade-Related Aspects of Intellectual Property Rights (TRIPS).

146. On a European level, though neither the Treaty on European Union (TEU) nor the Treaty on the Functioning of the European Union (TFEU) explicitly state any legal competence within the field of intellectual property rights, Article 36 TFEU[311] stipulates that prohibitions or restrictions on imports and exports are allowed if they are justified on grounds of the protection of industrial and commercial property to the extent they do not 'constitute a means of arbitrary discrimination or a disguised restriction on trade between Member States'. According to Article 345 TFEU,[312] the Treaty 'shall in no way prejudice the rules in Member

311. Ex Art. 30 Treaty establishing the European Community.
312. Ex Art. 295 Treaty establishing the European Community.

States governing the system of property ownership'. Despite these rules, intellectual property rights have been an important issue for the internal market which has led to a number of Directives within this area.[313]

Examples include:

- Council Directive 87/54/EEC of 16 December 1986 on the legal protection of topographies of semiconductor products.
- Council Directive 93/83/EEC of 27 September 1993 on the coordination of certain rules concerning copyright and rights related to copyright applicable to satellite broadcasting and cable retransmission.
- Directive 96/9/EC of the European Parliament and of the Council of 11 March 1996 on the legal protection of databases (hereinafter 'Database Directive').
- Directive 2001/29/EC of the European Parliament and of the Council of 22 May 2001 on the harmonization of certain aspects of copyright and related rights in the information society (hereinafter 'InfoSoc Directive').
- Directive 2004/48/EC of the European Parliament and of the Council of 29 April 2004 on the enforcement of intellectual property rights (hereinafter 'Enforcement Directive').
- Directive 2006/116/EC of the European Parliament and of the Council of 12 December 2006 on the term of protection of copyright and certain related rights.
- Directive 2009/24/EC of the European Parliament and of the Council of 23 April 2009 on the legal protection of computer programs. (hereinafter 'Computer Program Directive').

Some of them will be discussed more in detail below.

§2. Legislative Framework in Sweden

147. Sweden protects intellectual property, especially copyright, in its Constitution. Chapter 2 of the Instrument of Government (*Regeringsform (1974:152)*) states fundamental rights and freedoms, and Article 16 stipulates: 'Authors, artists and photographers shall own the rights to their works in accordance with rules laid down in law.'

The first Swedish legislation on intellectual property rights was the King's Decree (*reglemente*) for book publishers in the year 1752. Today's statute was enacted in 1960: Act on Copyright in Literary and Artistic Work (*Lag (1960:729) om upphovsrätt till litterära och konstnärliga verk*; hereinafter 'Copyright Act'). Its wording was written and designed to allow its application and validity over a long period of time.[314]

313. See, e.g., Recital 4 Computer Program Directive: 'Certain differences in the legal protection of computer programs offered by the laws of the Member States have direct and negative effects on the functioning of the internal market as regards computer programs.'

314. Governmental Bill to the original Copyright Act, Proposition 1960:17, 'Upphovsrätt till litterära och konstnärliga verk. Rätt till fotografisk bild', published in NJA II 1961 s. 1, 48.

148. The Copyright Act grants the authors of literary and artistic works economic[315] and moral rights.[316] With a few exceptions, most of the rules are not mandatory, which allows for the economic rights to be transferred by contractual agreements.

The copyright protection starts at the moment of creation, in accordance with Article 5(2) Berne Convention stipulating that '[t]he enjoyment and the exercise of these rights shall not be subject to any formality'. The copyright sign © has therefore no legal validity in Sweden.

In accordance with Council Directive 93/98/EEC of 29 October 1993, harmonizing the term of protection of copyright and certain related rights the time of protection is seventy years after the year of death of the author (*post mortem auctoris*).[317] Neighbouring rights are protected for fifty years in accordance with EC Directive 93/98, and databases enjoy fifteen years of protection.[318]

§3. Object of Protection

149. According to Chapter 1 Article 1 Swedish Copyright Act, literary and artistic works include:

(1) fictional or descriptive representations in writing or speech;
(2) computer programs;
(3) musical or dramatic works;
(4) cinematographic works;
(5) photographic works or other works of fine arts;
(6) works of architecture or applied art;
(7) works expressed in some other manner.

Maps and other works of a descriptive nature executed as drawings, engravings or in a three-dimensional form shall be considered literary works.

The expression 'literary or artistic work' (*litterärt eller konstnärligt verk*) in other words includes all types of cultural products and media content. For example, the term literary works includes not only books but also scientific writings, presentations, seminar papers, meeting notes, encyclopaedias, newspaper articles, technical descriptions, texts in instruction manuals and forms, advertising texts, computer programs, and database collections. Artistic works mainly include musical compositions, film art (including video art), theatrical performances and art works (paintings, drawings, graphics, photography, sculpture, collage, textile art, and art as computer created pictures), as well as architectural designs.[319]

315. Chapter 1 Art. 2 Copyright Act.
316. Chapter 1 Art. 3 Copyright Act.
317. Chapter 4 Art. 43 Copyright Act. Compare Art. 7 Berne Convention that requires a minimum of fifty years.
318. See also Art. 10 Database Directive.
319. Mogens Koktvedgaards & Marianne Levin, *Lärobok i immaterialrätt* (Stockholm: Norstedts Juridik, 2007), 69 et seq.

The Copyright Act does not make any distinction between literary, musical, and artistic works. Some exemptions, however, are reserved for a specific type, such as literary works.

150. Swedish copyright law explicitly exempts certain works from protection. According to Article 9, copyright does not subsist in laws and other regulations; decisions by public authorities; reports by Swedish public authorities; or official translations of these texts. In other words, there is no Crown Copyright in Sweden.

Important to mention here is also the Swedish constitutional right of access to information and public records, which supersedes copyright to some extent. For example, patent applications are considered public records unless otherwise stated in the Swedish Public Access to Information and Secrecy Act (*Offentlighets- och sekretesslag (2009:400)*).[320]

151. In order for a work to be protected, it has to be created by a human being and be the result of a personal creative effort. There is no qualitative or quantitative requirement in order for the work to be worthy of protection.

152. Pictures can be protected as photographic works[321] or as photographic pictures.[322] The former requires a higher level of originality; the latter protects all types of photographs, also the ones taken by amateurs, or within medicine or science. The protection requires some sort of photographic technique being used, which includes digital cameras as well as holograms created by laser technique.[323] The difference between the two types of work is the term of protection, which amounts to seventy years after the death of the author of a photographic work as opposed to fifty years from the year in which the photographic picture was taken.

153. Photographs always consist of still images, not sequences of pictures that amount to moving pictures which would be covered as cinematographic works[324] if they are original. Film that does not amount to a cinematographic work is protected for fifty years, pursuant to Article 46.

The Swedish Supreme Court (*Högsta Domstolen*) decided in the Nintendo case[325] that videogames are not regarded as cinematographic works as they include an interactive moment. Instead, they are protected as computer programs. Video art, however, is regarded as a cinematographic work.

---

320. See s. 22 Swedish Patents Act (*Patentlag (1967:837)*) and Ch. 31 s. 20 Public Access to Information and Secrecy Act.
321. Article 1 point 5 Copyright Act.
322. Chapter 5 Art. 49a Copyright Act.
323. Koktvedgaards & Levin, 101 et seq.
324. Article 1 point 4 Copyright Act.
325. Decision by Supreme Court from 22 Nov. 2000, NJA 2000 s. 580.

§4. Subject of Protection

154. As mentioned above, a work has to be created by a human being and be the result of a personal creative effort.

It can be discussed in this context to what extent works completely created by computer programs can be protected under the Copyright Act. Literary or artistic works, created with the help of a software program or a machine, are protected by copyright law, as the user of the computer would be the author of the work.[326] This also applies to music created on a computer.

155. The Swedish Copyright Act does not contain any general provisions with regard to works created in an employment relationship.[327] Therefore, an employee creating literary or artistic works as part of the employment is also considered to be the author of the created works. Sweden does not, in other words, follow the works made for hire principle as the UK or US.

The employer can, however, obtain exclusive rights through contractual agreements with the employee. These licensing agreements can also be included in the employment contract. In accordance with Chapter 3 Article 27 Copyright Act, the economic rights may be transferred to the employer in whole or in part, with no additional form requirements. The moral rights, however, stay with the author, that is the employee. Sweden has recognized a general principle that an employer commonly has the right, unless otherwise agreed, to exploit the copyright of an employee's work, which is created within the work tasks or due to direct instructions.[328]

§5. Exclusive Rights

156. The Swedish Copyright Act grants two types of exclusive rights for works in Chapter 1 Article 2: the right to make copies and the right of making it available to the public. Making of copies (*framställning*) is defined as 'any direct or indirect, temporary or permanent preparation of copies of the work, regardless of the form or through which method this is carried out and regardless of whether it concerns the work in whole or in part'. This also includes temporary copies on the computer or any other system, such as caches, etc.

157. The term 'making available to the public' (*tillgängliggörande för allmänheten*) includes communication to the public (*överföring till allmänheten*), public performance (*offentligt framförande*), public exhibition (*offentligt visning*), and distribution (*spridning*) such as sale, lease or rent.

---

326. Henry Olsson, *Upphovsrättslagstiftningen – En kommentar*, 2nd edn (Stockholm: Norstedts, 2009), s. 1.
327. With the exception of computer programs created as part of an employment.
328. Sanna Wolk (ed.), *Ownership of the Copyright in Works and the Patent Right in Inventions Created by Employees in Finland, Sweden, Germany, Austria, the United Kingdom, Estonia and Argentina*, Gröna Serien, No. 120 (Stockholm: Institute of Intellectual Property Law and Marketing Law – Institutet för Immaterialrätt och Marknadsrätt (IFIM), 2002), 8–11.

The term 'communication to the public' was introduced when transposing the InfoSoc Directive into Swedish law in 2005. Before that, on-demand services were interpreted as either public performance or, in a few cases, public exhibition. Today's term includes 'any making available of the work to the public by wire or by wireless means that occurs from a place other than that where the public may enjoy the work. Communication to the public includes also acts of communication that occur in such a way that members of the public may access the work from a place and at a time individually chosen by them'. This includes traditional radio and TV-broadcasts, webcasting, publication on a website, as well as any peer-to-peer file sharing.[329]

A decision by the Swedish Supreme Court in 2000 discussed if deep linking was to be considered a public performance.[330] The Court held that deep linking from a website to infringing music files on the Internet constitutes either public performance itself or abetting public performance and thereby infringes copyright. Deep linking was to be understood as linking from one web page to the other without the visitor being aware of the change of address. The Supreme Court did not deal with the question of reference links, where the visitor clearly is made aware of the change of website. The Governmental Bill transposing the InfoSoc Directive stated that this decision could still be relevant in relation to the limits of exclusive rights, even though the linking would now fall under the rights of communication to the public and not public performance.[331]

158. Another term that has been discussed is 'to the public'. The governmental bill transposing the InfoSoc Directive defines public in the context of public performance as the possibility for anyone to join the communication. Even a requirement of membership can be considered public if anybody can become a member. In order for a communication to be private, it has to be aimed at one or a few people or in case it is aimed at a more general public, the requirements must be too strict for everybody to fulfil them. Even password protection or other protection measures do not exclude a communication from being public.[332]

When transposing the InfoSoc Directive, the meaning of 'public performance' was somewhat changed in Swedish law. Before the Directive, public performance included radio, TV, and other distance broadcasting. Now the term comprises 'only such cases where the work is being made available to the public, with or without the use of a technical device, at the same place as the one where the public may enjoy the work'. This definition covers the live performance of a musician or a theatrical play, the showing of video or playing of music on a CD player publicly, or last but not least, the showing of a radio programme or a TV broadcast publicly in a restaurant. The last situation involves both public performance and communication to the public. The term public has the same meaning as regarding communication to the public.

329. Henry Olsson, *Upphovsrättslagstiftningen,* s. 2; and Government Bill (Proposition) 2004/05:110, 'Upphovsrätten i informationssamhället – genomförande av direktiv 2001/29/EG, m.m.'.
330. Decision by Supreme Court of 15 Jun. 2000, NJA 2000 s. 292.
331. Government Bill (Proposition) 2004/05:110, 70.
332. Olsson, *Upphovsrättslagstiftningen,* s. 2; and Government Bill (Proposition) 2004/05:110, 57.

The InfoSoc Directive also led to a change in the meaning of the term public exhibition. Today it includes 'such cases where a copy of a work is being made available to the public, without the use of a technical device, at the same place as the one where the public can enjoy the copy'. If a technical device is being used, the Copyright Act considers it as a public performance. Before the amendment it was unclear if the display of a work on a TV or computer screen was to be considered as a performance or an exhibition; now the legal situation is clear as this situation is covered by performance and not exhibition, as it is not the work itself that is being displayed but the content of a file.

159. According to Chapter 5 Article 48 Copyright Act, sound radio or television organizations have exclusive rights to exploit a sound radio or television broadcast, which include recording the broadcast in material format so it can be reproduced, making copies and distributing these copies, and permitting a recording to be communicated to the public.

§6. Exemptions to the Exclusive Rights

160. Chapter 2 Swedish Copyright Act contains provisions on the limitations of copyright. Some of these exceptions are voluntary and can be changed in a contract, whereas some are mandatory and surpass even contrary contractual obligations, for example Article 26g and 26h Swedish Copyright Act.

In general, the limitations can be divided into three categories:

(1) provisions that allow free use;
(2) provisions that allow limited use for remuneration (*tvångslicenser*);
(3) provisions that allow collective licenses, that is agreements between right holders' organizations and users, which are also applicable for authors not represented in these organizations (*avtalslicenser*).[333]

161. Chapter 2 Swedish Copyright Act was drafted in accordance with the Berne Convention, especially the three-step-test of Article 9.2,[334] as well as Article 13 TRIPS[335] and Article 5(5) InfoSoc Directive.[336]

333. Recital 18 InfoSoc Directive explicitly allows for collective licenses: 'This Directive is without prejudice to the arrangements in the Member States concerning the management of rights such as extended collective licences.'
334. 'It shall be a matter for legislation in the countries of the Union to permit the reproduction of such works in certain special cases, provided that such reproduction does not conflict with a normal exploitation of the work and does not unreasonably prejudice the legitimate interests of the author.'
335. 'Members shall confine limitations or exceptions to exclusive rights to certain special cases which do not conflict with a normal exploitation of the work and do not unreasonably prejudice the legitimate interests of the right holder.'
336. 'The exceptions and limitations provided for in paras 1, 2, 3 and 4 shall only be applied in certain special cases which do not conflict with a normal exploitation of the work or other subject-matter and do not unreasonably prejudice the legitimate interests of the right holder.'

The limitations mainly concern published works, that is, works that have been lawfully made available to the public.[337] The idea behind this is that only the author should be able to decide on the publication of a work.

In the following sections, two exemptions are explained in detail, as they are particularly relevant in an Information and Communications Technology (ICT) context: temporary and private copies.

I. Temporary Copies

162. As mentioned above, temporary copies are covered by the exclusive right of reproduction. In accordance with Article 5(1) InfoSoc Directive, Chapter 2 Article 11a Swedish Copyright Act states:

> Temporary forms of copies of works may be made, if the making of the copies is an integral and essential part of a technological process and if the copies are transient or have only a secondary importance in that process. The copies must not have any independent economic importance.
>
> The making of copies under the first Paragraph is permissible only if the sole purpose of that making is to enable
>
> 1. a transmission in a network between third parties by an intermediary, or
> 2. a lawful use, that is, a use that occurs with the consent of the author or her or his successor in title or another use that is, not un-permissible under this Act.
>
> The provisions under the first and second Paragraphs do not confer a right to make copies of literary works in the form of computer programs or compilations.

Article 11a has to be seen in relation to the Swedish Electronic Commerce Act (*Lag (2002:562) om elektronisk handel och andra informationssamhällets tjänster*), as well as the Directive on electronic commerce,[338] which exempt service providers from liability for mere conduit, caching and hosting.[339] The legislation on electronic commerce does, however, only cover service providers and not the temporary copying for individuals, making Article 11a Copyright Act necessary to cover this exemption.

163. The main purpose of Article 11a is to allow users to browse and surf the web without meeting the risk of infringing copyright. As the exclusive right of reproduction includes direct or indirect, temporary or permanent copies of a work,[340] temporary copies in caches, both on different routers, host and access providers, as well as on individuals' computers, fall within this exclusive right. With

337. Chapter 1 Art. 8 Copyright Act.
338. Directive 2000/31/EC of the European Parliament and of the Council of 8 Jun. 2000 on certain legal aspects of information society services, in particular e-commerce, in the Internal Market (hereinafter 'Directive on electronic commerce').
339. See Part V Ch. 3 *infra* (paras 344 et seq.).
340. Chapter 1 Art. 2 Copyright Act.

caching being an integral part of web browsing, the exemption of Article 11a is therefore necessary.

Besides the requirement that temporary copies are only permitted if the copying is an integral and essential part of the process and the copies are not the most important part of the process, paragraph 2 in Article 11a Copyright Act states that the making must try to enable either a transmission in a network or a lawful use. The typical example for the first case would be Internet Service Providers (ISPs) storing copies of websites and emails in the cache of their servers. Important to remember here is Recital 33 InfoSoc Directive, which although not explicitly transposed into Swedish law, states:

> To the extent that they meet these conditions, this exception should include acts which enable browsing as well as acts of caching to take place, including those which enable transmission systems to function efficiently, provided that the intermediary does not modify the information and does not interfere with the lawful use of technology, widely recognized and used by industry, to obtain data on the use of the information.

In other words, an intermediary should not tamper with the information, otherwise the right does not apply and it could be liable for copyright infringement. An example of the second possibility for making temporary copies, that is, the lawful use, would be private copying according to Chapter 2 Article 12 Copyright Act. This also corresponds to Recital 33 InfoSoc Directive: 'A use should be considered lawful where it is authorized by the right holder or not restricted by law.'

Article 11a paragraph 3 Copyright Act further states that this right does not include making copies of computer programs or compilations.

II. Private Copying

164. Chapter 2 Article 12 Swedish Copyright Act deals with private copies and in which situations they constitute legal exceptions to the exclusive rights granted by copyright law. The provision in the Swedish Act was amended due to the implementation of the InfoSoc Directive. It now contains four paragraphs that stipulate the following:

> On the Making of Copies for Private Purposes
>
> Article 12. Anybody is entitled to make, for private purposes, one or a few copies of works that have been made public. As regards literary works in written form the making of copies may, however, concern only limited parts of works, or such works of limited scope. The copies must not be used for purposes other than private use.
>
> The provisions in the first Paragraph do not confer a right to 1. construct works of architecture 2. make copies of computer programs, or 3. make copies in digital form of compilations in digital form.
>
> Furthermore, the provisions in the first Paragraph do not confer a right to engage, for private purposes, another person to 1. make copies of musical

> works or cinematographic works 2. make utilitarian articles or sculptures, or 3. copy another person's work of fine art by means of artistic reproduction.
> This Article does not confer a right to make copies of a work when the copy that constitutes the real master copy has been prepared or has been made available to the public in violation of Article 2.

Paragraph 1 of Article 12 stipulates the general rule for private copies being exempted from the exclusive right of reproduction. According to the provision, anybody can reproduce a literary or artistic work for private purposes. The amount of copies have to be kept to a minimum, and with regard to literary works, reproducing more than half a book, either in digital or analogue format, is not covered by Article 12.[341]

165. In general, all types of works can be copied for private purposes – regular literary works, music, film (e.g., movies on DVD or on TV), and other artistic works. Paragraph 2, however, exempts, among others, computer programs from the right to private copying. Acts of reproduction can include photocopying, recording of musical and film works, as well as downloading of creative works on a personal computer.

Furthermore, Article 12 only allows reproduction of works that have been made public. In other words, the author or right holder must have agreed to the publication the work.[342]

Private purposes cover copying for one's own use or for use within family or close circle of friends.[343] Not only the reproduction as such but also the following use has to be for private purposes. Recordings of music for private purposes can therefore not be sold to the public afterwards.

166. In transposing the InfoSoc Directive, a new paragraph 4 was introduced limiting the right to private copying to real master copies. In other words, private copying is only allowed for works that either have been reproduced with the consent of the author or in exercising one of the exemptions in Chapter 2 of the Copyright Act. With regard to the Internet, this means that the original copy that was made available online has to be authorized or otherwise be legal according to Chapter 2.

This new provision also led to an amendment regarding liability for infringement. According to Chapter 7 Article 54 paragraph 4 Swedish Copyright Act infringement of Article 12 paragraph 4 can only lead to civil liability in case of intent or gross negligence. In addition, an infringement can only lead to criminal liability if the individual carried out the violation intentionally or with gross negligence.[344]

---

341. Government Bill (Proposition) 2004/05:110, 383.
342. See Chapter 1 Art. 8 Copyright Act: 'A work is deemed to have been made public when it has lawfully been made available to the public.'
343. Before transposition of the InfoSoc Directive, the scope of private purposes even included copies for colleagues at one's workplace. See Olsson, *Upphovsrättslagstiftningen,* s.12.
344. Chapter 7 Art. 53. See more relating to sanctions in paras 170 et seq.

167. As Article 12 is voluntary, the right holders can limit its application in a contract with the user. Standard terms and conditions for video rental, for example, often include such provisions. Not abiding to these contractual rules then constitutes breach of contract, and not copyright infringement.

§7. TRANSFER OF RIGHTS

168. An author can transfer the exclusive economic rights entirely or partially to somebody else.[345] The Swedish terms are *överlåtelse* for a complete transfer and *upplåtelse* for a partial transfer or rights. The moral rights, however, can never be transferred:

> Article 27: Subject to the limitation that follows from Article 3, copyright may be transferred entirely or partially.
>
> The transfer of a copy does not include a transfer of the copyright.

169. The licensing agreements have to be specified with regard to which rights are being transferred wholly or in part. Otherwise, in line with general copyright law principles, the contract terms will be interpreted restrictively and might not cover specific rights originally thought of.[346]

The transfer of rights can also concern future works, even including all future works of the author. Under specific circumstances, contracts concerning future creative results can, however, be invalid according to Swedish contract law. In a decision from 24 April 1989, the Svea Appellate Court (*Svea hovrätt*) came to the conclusion that a contract transferring the rights of all future works of an artist combined with the right for the other party to solely decide which of the works are published infringes Article 36 Swedish Contracts Act and therefore was considered invalid.[347]

§8. ENFORCEMENT/SANCTIONS

170. Infringement of copyright provisions can lead to both civil and criminal liability, as prescribed by Chapter 7 Copyright Act. According to Chapter 7 Article 53 Copyright Act, infringing acts that are committed wilfully or with gross negligence are punishable by fines or imprisonment for a maximum of two years. Chapter 7 Article 54 further stipulates that anyone who exploits a work in violation of copyright rules shall pay 'a reasonable compensation for the exploitation' to the author. In case of intent or negligence, the liability also covers 'the further damage that the infringement' has caused.

345. Chapter 3 Art. 27 Swedish Copyright Act.
346. See more in Part III Ch. 2 *infra* (paras 221 et seq.).
347. The decision is published in Nordiskt Immateriellt Rättsskydd (Nordic Intellectual Property Law Review) NIR 1989 s. 394.

According to Article 54 the compensation should consider lost profit, any profit that has been made by the infringer, damage caused to the reputation of the work, moral damage, as well as the interest of the author or the right holder in that infringements are not committed.

The one who claims a copyright infringement has to prove it in court. The Swedish Supreme Court stated in a case in 1994 that a striking resemblance with a work can represent a strong argument for a reproduction of that work. In this case, the suspected infringer would have to show it was more likely that the second work was created independently in order to avoid conviction for infringement.[348]

171. In 2004, the EU enacted Directive 2004/48/EC of the European Parliament and of the Council of 29 April 2004 on the enforcement of intellectual property rights (hereinafter 'Enforcement Directive') in order to 'approximate legislative systems so as to ensure a high, equivalent and homogeneous level of protection in the internal market'.[349] Though it did not aim to harmonize rules for judicial cooperation, jurisdiction, or the recognition and enforcement of decisions in civil and commercial matters, it established several 'procedures and remedies necessary to ensure the enforcement of intellectual property rights'.[350] The Directive was transposed into Swedish national law by introducing some amendments in the Copyright Act, including the right of information.

A new Article 53c that implements Article 8 Enforcement Directive ('right of information'), introduces into Chapter 7 Copyright Act the possibility for right holders to apply for an 'order to provide information' (*informationsföreläggande*) before the Court, which obliges a party 'to provide information to the applicant concerning the origin and distribution networks for the goods or services in respect of which the infringement or the violation has been committed'. Such orders can only be issued 'if it can be assumed that the information would facilitate an inquiry into the infringement' and can only relate to parties that have committed or contributed to such an infringement.

The order to provide information covers Internet access providers submitting information about the subscribers to certain IP-numbers that have been used in the course of copyright infringement.[351] Some cases were initiated before the District Court of Stockholm, mainly requiring host providers and access providers to release information about their customers. The Swedish Supreme Court recently issued a judgment on the matter,[352] after a preliminary ruling from the ECJ.[353] The Supreme Court, taking into account privacy and data retention issues, confirmed that such orders to provide information may be issued, provided that rights holders have demonstrated probable cause of copyright infringement, as required under Article 53c

348. Decision by Supreme Court from 23 Feb. 1994, NJA 1994 s. 74.
349. Recital 10 Enforcement Directive.
350. Article 1 Enforcement Directive.
351. Government Bill (Proposition) 2008/09:67, 'Civilrättsliga sanktioner på immaterialrättens område – genomförande av direktiv 2004/48/EG', 263.
352. Decision by Supreme Court from 21 Dec. 2012, NJA 2012 s. 975.
353. C-461/10 *Bonnier Audio AB and Others v. Perfect Communication Sweden AB.*

Copyright Act. The interests of rights holders to investigate and potentially prosecute alleged copyright infringement was therefore deemed to outweigh interests of individual privacy.[354]

172. In the context of enforcement, the Swedish Copyright Act also contains a chapter on the protection of technological measures, which was introduced in the transposition of the InfoSoc Directive. The chapter covers provisions on the protection of technological measures as well as of electronic information on the management of rights. In accordance with the Act,[355] 'technological measure' means 'any effective technology, device or component designed to prevent or restrict, in the normal course of its operation, the reproduction or the making available to the public of a copyright-protected work without the consent of the author'.

'Information on the management of rights' is defined as:

> any information, also in the form of numbers or codes, that is linked to a copy of a copyright-protected work or appears in connection with the communication to the public of such a work and which aims at identifying the work or the author or her or his successor in title or at informing about the conditions of use of the work. The information must have been provided by the author or her or his successor in title.[356]

Chapter 6 a Article 52d prohibits any circumvention of technological protection measures. It is furthermore prohibited, according to Chapter 6 a Article 52e, to manufacture, import, transfer, distribute or possess for commercial purposes any devices, products or components, or to make available services, which:

(1) are promoted, advertised or marketed for the purpose of circumvention of a technological measure;
(2) other than to circumvent a technological measure, have only a limited interest from a commercial point of view, or a limited scope of commercial use; or
(3) are primarily designed, constructed, adapted or produced for the purpose of enabling or facilitating a circumvention of a technological measure. (Article 52e).

In addition, it is prohibited to remove or alter any electronic rights-management information relating to a work protected by copyright.[357]

354. See Part VI Ch. 2 3 s. III B *infra* (para. 421).
355. Chapter 6 a Art. 52b Copyright Act, as well as Art. 6(3) and Art. 7(2) InfoSoc Directive.
356. Chapter 6 a Art. 52b Copyright Act.
357. Chapter 6 a Art. 52g Copyright Act.

Chapter 2. Legal Protection of Software

§1. General Statement

173. Chapter 1 Article 1 point 2 Swedish Copyright Act explicitly grants copyright protection to computer programs. Sweden introduced this protection in 1989 before the Computer Program Directive entered into force. The Directive led, however, to smaller amendments in the Act, among others the introduction of Chapter 2 Article 26g and 26h Copyright Act.

§2. Object of Protection

174. In accordance with Article 10 TRIPS[358] and Article 4 WCT,[359] as well as Article 1(1) Computer Program Directive,[360] computer programs are protected as literary works, as stipulated in Chapter 1 Article 1 point 2 Swedish Copyright Act.

Neither the Act nor the Directive defines the term 'computer program'. A Swedish governmental report,[361] however, suggested a similar definition as the WIPO Model provisions on the protection of computer software from 1978:[362] 'A computer program is [a] set of instructions capable, when incorporated in a machine-readable medium, of causing a machine having information processing capabilities to indicate, perform or achieve a particular function, task or result.'

175. The copyright in software covers all expressions of a program, including any immediately readable form or any machine-readable format, such as source or object code, whether it is stored on a disk, CD, in the computer's read only memory (ROM) or on paper.[363] In accordance with the Computer Program Directive, the protection also covers the preparatory design material,[364] such as design drafts, and all other preparatory material.

Documentation for a program, however, is not protected as a computer program but as literary work in general.

358. 'Computer programs, whether in source or object code, shall be protected as literary works under the Berne Convention (1971).'
359. 'Computer programs are protected as literary works within the meaning of Art. 2 of the Berne Convention. Such protection applies to computer programs, whatever may be the mode or form of their expression.'
360. 'Member States shall protect computer programs, by copyright, as literary works within the meaning of the Berne Convention for the Protection of Literary and Artistic Works.'
361. Government Official Report SOU 1985:51, 'Upphovsrätt och datorteknik. Delbetänkande 3 av upphovsrättsutredningen', 87.
362. International Bureau of the World Intellectual Property Organization, 'Model provisions on the protection of computer software' (Geneva: WIPO, 1978).
363. Koktvedgaards & Levin, 96.
364. Chapter 1 Art. 1 Copyright Act.

The protection neither extends to the underlying ideas and principles, such as algorithms and the like, nor the interface of the program.[365] Programming languages are also not protectable by copyright.[366] This is one of the weaknesses and strengths related to software, as the algorithm can be the most valuable part of the whole software, while preventing distribution and use of good programming ideas is not in the best interest of the society as a whole. This is also an important principle in relation to interoperability and interaction between software.[367]

The program as such has to be 'the author's own intellectual creation', no additional qualitative criteria is required for it to be eligible for protection.[368]

§3. Subject of Protection

176. The general principle that the author receives all the exclusive rights to the work at the moment of creation also applies here.

177. With regard to computer programs created in employment relations, the Swedish Copyright Act, in accordance with Article 2 Computer Program Directive, regulates in Chapter 3 Article 40a:

> The copyright in a computer program created by an employee as a part of her or his tasks or following instructions by the employer is transferred to the employer unless otherwise agreed in contract.

The automatic transfer of rights according to Article 40a not only includes the economic rights but, contrary to the Computer Program Directive,[369] also the moral rights.[370]

As clear from its wording ('unless otherwise agreed in contract'), Article 40a Swedish Copyright Act is non-mandatory and can be changed in the contract of employment.

§4. Exclusive Rights

178. The Swedish Copyright Act does not stipulate any specific exclusive rights for computer programs, but the general rule of Chapter 1 Article 2 applies, which states that copyright includes making copies of a work or making it available to the public. The term 'making available to the public' in turn covers communication to

365. See Recital 11 and Art. 1(2) Computer Program Directive.
366. Recital 11 Computer Program Directive.
367. Koktvedgaards & Levin, 98.
368. Article 1(3) Computer Program Directive.
369. Article 2(1) Computer Program Directive: 'The author of a computer program shall be the natural person or group of natural persons who has created the program.'
370. Wolk, *Ownership of the Copyright in Works*, 11; and Government Bill (Proposition) 1992/93:48, 'Regeringens proposition om ändringar i de immaterialrättsliga lagarna med anledning av EES-avtalet m.m.', 117.

the public, public performance, public exhibition, and distribution such as sale, lease or rent.

As mentioned above[371] the definition of reproduction[372] is rather broad and includes, for example, temporary copies in the internal memory of a personal computer as well as cache copies on servers, which might not have a value in themselves.

This choice of legislative technique was already taken in the Computer Program Directive. In order to balance the interests of society as a whole, an exemption was introduced covering temporary copies.[373]

§5. Exemptions

179. Some of the general exemptions for literary and artistic works mentioned above[374] do not apply for computer programs.

The right of the user to make temporary copies, for example, only exists 'if the making of the copies is an integral and essential part of a technological process and if the copies are transient or have only a secondary importance in that process'. This provision does, however, 'not confer a right to make copies of literary works in the form of computer programs or compilations'.[375]

In addition, the right to make private copies is limited when it comes to computer programs. According to Chapter 2 Article 12 paragraph 2 Swedish Copyright Act, the private copying exemption does not apply to computer programs.

180. Users with a right to use a computer program are, however, allowed to:

(a) 'make such copies of the program and to make such adaptations of the program which are necessary' in order to enable use of the program for its intended purpose. This also applies to the correction of errors;[376]
(b) 'to make back-up copies of the program, if this is necessary for the intended use of the program'.[377] Contracts in contrast to this provision are void;[378]
(c) 'observe, study or test the function of the program in order to ascertain the ideas and principles which lie behind the various details of the program'. The right to reverse engineer applies 'provided that the act is performed in connection with

371. See Ch. 1 s. 5 *supra* (para. 156).
372. Chapter 1 Art. 2 Copyright Act: 'any direct or indirect, temporary or permanent preparation of copies of the work, regardless of the form or through which method this is carried out and regardless of whether it concerns the work in whole or in part'.
373. See Ch. 1 s. 6 I *supra* (paras 162 et seq.).
374. See Ch. 1 s. 6 *supra* (paras 160 et seq.).
375. Chapter 2 Art. 11a Copyright Act.
376. Chapter 2 Art. 26g para. 1 Copyright Act.
377. Chapter 2 Art. 26g para. 2 Copyright Act.
378. Chapter 2 Art. 26g para. 6 Copyright Act.

such loading, display on a screen, processing, transmission or storing of the program that the user is entitled to make'.[379] Contractual stipulations which limit these rights are void.[380]

Interesting to note here is that the rights to make backup copies (point b) and to reverse engineer (point c) are mandatory, and cannot be changed in contractual agreements.

181. Another provision based on the Computer Program Directive is Chapter 2 Article 26h Swedish Copyright Act concerning decompilation to ensure interoperability. According to the provision, codes of computer programs can be copied or translated if this is necessary to obtain interoperability between the program and another program. In order to fall under Article 26h reverse engineering has to meet the following requirements:

- the acts are performed by a person who has the right to use the program or by a person who is authorized to perform those acts;
- the information necessary to achieve interoperability has not previously been readily available to the persons referred to in the point above;
- the acts are confined to those parts of the original program which are necessary to achieve interoperability.

The information obtained through reverse engineering may not be used for the development, preparation or marketing of a computer program substantially similar in its expression to the protected program.[381] As above, contractual stipulations limiting these rights are void.[382]

§6. Enforcement/Sanctions

182. As for all other copyright infringements, not adhering to any of the exclusive rights concerning computer programs can lead to both criminal and civil liability.[383]

Under certain conditions, however, copying of a computer program that was lawfully published is exempted from criminal liability if the master copy is not used in commercial or public activities, and the individual only uses the copies for private purposes.[384]

379. Chapter 2 Art. 26g para. 4 Copyright Act.
380. Chapter 2 Art. 26g para. 6 Copyright Act.
381. Chapter 2 Art. 26h para. 2 Copyright Act.
382. Chapter 2 Art. 26h para. 3 Copyright Act.
383. See in general Ch. 1 s. 8 *supra* (paras 170 et seq.).
384. Chapter 7 Art. 53 para. 2 Copyright Act.

Chapter 3. Legal Protection of Databases

§1. General Statement

183. Sweden introduced protection for databases in 1960 by enacting Article 49 Copyright Act protecting catalogues, tables and other similar works where a large amount of data was collected and gathered. In 1997, the rule was somewhat amended due to the implementation of the Database Directive which stipulates a sui generis right for the content of databases in addition to protection for the structure.[385]

§2. Object of Protection

184. Chapter 5 Article 49 Swedish Copyright Act protects catalogues, tables or similar products:

- in which a large number of information items have been compiled (catalogue protection); or
- which are the result of a significant investment (sui generis right).

As a kind of neighbouring right, the compilation does not have to reach a certain quality or originality, it is rather the efforts of creating the database that are being protected. If a compilation reaches a certain level of originality it can, however, be protected as a literary work according to Chapter 1 Article 2 Swedish Copyright Act.

The first possibility for a database to receive protection is if a large amount of information has been collected. This is the case for sales and exhibition catalogues, timetables, compilations of currency and stock exchange prices.[386] It does not matter in which format the information is compiled, both analogue and digital versions fall within the scope of Article 49.

The second possibility for protection is databases that are the result of a significant investment. This provision transposes Article 7 Database Directive into Swedish law, which can serve as a guideline for interpreting the meaning of significant investment. Article 7 of the Directive speaks about 'qualitatively and/or quantitatively of the substantial investment in either the obtaining, verification or presentation of the contents'. In other words, the investment can be quantitatively substantial considering the time or money invested in the collecting or organizing of the material. A qualitative aspect can be, on the other hand, if the choice of material or its collection were challenging.[387]

The Swedish Supreme Court decided in a case in 2005,[388] following the preliminary ruling of the Court of Justice of the European Communities,[389] that investment

385. Koktvedgaards & Levin, 109.
386. Governmental Bill (Proposition) 1960:17, 322.
387. Henry Olsson, *Upphovsrättslagstiftningen,* s. 49.
388. Decision by Supreme Court from 28 Dec. 2005, NJA 2005 s. 924.
389. C-338/02 *Fixtures Marketing Ltd. v. Svenska Spel AB* [2004] ECR I-10497.

refers 'to the resources used to seek out existing independent materials and collect them in the database, and not to the resources used for the creation as such of independent materials'. The Court of Justice further stated that: 'the purpose of the protection by the sui generis right provided for by the Directive is to promote the establishment of storage and processing systems for existing information and not the creation of materials capable of being collected subsequently in a database'.[390]

185. Important to notice is that the protection covers the compilation and database as such and not the information stored in it. Chapter 5 Article 49 does, however, not exclude any potential rights for the works collected in the catalogue or compilation. In other words, the compiled data may – with a sufficient level or originality – be protected as literary or artistic works.[391] The database as a whole, however, will be protected according to Article 49.

186. The time of protection for databases is fifteen years 'from the year in which the product was completed',[392] which reflects Article 10 Database Directive.

To summarize, Swedish law provides three possibilities to protect databases:

(1) protection as a work pursuant to Chapter 1 Article 2 (and according time for protection);
(2) catalogue protection pursuant to Chapter 5 Article 49 (compilation of a large number of data);
(3) sui generis right pursuant to Chapter 5 Article 49 (database as the result of a significant investment).

§3. Subject of Protection

187. As Chapter 5 Article 49 Copyright Act states, anyone who produced a catalogue enjoys the copyright protection. In other words, it is the producer of the database who is granted exclusive rights. Contrary to general copyright law rules, the producer can be a legal person, not only a natural person.

This does not, however, affect any potential rights of individuals in works collected in the database.

§4. Exclusive Rights

188. Chapter 5 Article 49 Swedish Copyright Act grants 'the exclusive right to make copies of the product and to make it available to the public'. Article 7(1) of the Database Directive, which stipulates the right to prevent 'extraction and/or re-utilization of the whole or of a substantial part, evaluated qualitatively and/or quantitatively, of the contents of that database', was, in other words, not transposed

390. Point 24 in the Judgment.
391. Chapter 1 Art. 2 Copyright Act.
392. Chapter 5 Art. 49 para. 2 Copyright Act.

literally into Swedish law. Chapter 5 Article 49 protects the structure of a database, not the information compiled in it.[393]

189. The third paragraph of Chapter 5 Article 49 was added when implementing the InfoSoc Directive and refers to the general exclusive rights granted by the Copyright Act.

The right to make copies covers all types of reproduction, including temporary copies. With regards to Article 7(1) of the Database Directive, a copy emerges if it concerns the whole or substantial parts of the database. Copying single bits of information or a smaller amount of data contained in the compilation does not constitute copyright infringement, unless these parts are considered literary or artistic works according to Chapter 1 Article 2 Copyright Act, in which case the individual copying the works infringes Chapter 1 Article 2, but not Chapter 5 Article 49.[394]

In addition, the producer of the database has the exclusive right of making it available to the public, which includes communication to the public, public performance, public exhibition, and distribution.[395] Publishing a database online would therefore fall under 'communication to the public'.[396]

190. According to paragraph 4 of Chapter 5 Article 49 Copyright Act, contractual agreements that extend the exclusive rights are not valid.[397] However, within the framework of the exclusive rights, the producer can agree on specific terms and conditions regarding the licenses.[398]

§5. Exemptions

191. As for computer programs, users are not allowed to 'make copies in digital form of compilations in digital form'.[399] Digital copying of digital databases is therefore an infringement of copyright, even for private purposes.[400] However, analogue paper copies of digital material as well as digital copies of analogue material for private purposes are allowed.[401]

An authorized user has the right to make use of a database in any way that is necessary to fulfil 'its intended purpose'.[402] Typical use of a database is, therefore, allowed. This provision reflects Article 6(1) Database Directive.[403]

---

393. Government Bill (Proposition) 1996/97:111, 'Rättsligt skydd för databaser, m.m.', 59.
394. Government Bill (Proposition) 1996/97:111, 59.
395. Chapter 1 Art. 2 paras 3 and 4 Copyright Act.
396. Government Bill (Proposition) 1996/97:111, 59.
397. In this sense the provision protects the users of a database.
398. Koktvedgaards & Levin, 170–171.
399. Chapter 2 Art. 12 para. 2 point 3 Copyright Act.
400. Digital in this context means electronic information in binary code, i.e., zeros and ones.
401. Government Bill (Proposition) 1996/97:111, 53–54.
402. Chapter 2 Art. 26g para. 5 Copyright Act.
403. Article 6(1) Database Directive: 'The performance by the lawful user of a database or of a copy thereof of any of the acts listed in Art. 5 which is necessary for the purposes of access to the contents of the databases and normal use of the contents by the lawful user shall not require the authorization of the author of the database.'

192. As mentioned above, only the structure of the database is protected by Chapter 5 Article 49 Copyright Act, not the content. Therefore, copying a part of the compilation is allowed as long as it does not constitute a substantial part of the whole database. Other people can use the data for a new compilation, provided it is built upon another structure.[404]

§6. Enforcement/Sanctions

193. The general sanctions for copyright infringement, including criminal and civil liability, apply also to violations of Chapter 5 Article 49 Copyright Act.

The second paragraph of Chapter 7 Article 53 Copyright Act states an exemption from criminal liability, if a digital copy of a publicly available digital database is made for private purposes, the master copy is not used in commercial or public activities and the individual only uses the copy for private purposes.

404. Government Bill (Proposition) 1996/97:111, 59; Koktvedgaards & Levin, 199.

Chapter 4. Legal Protection of Computer Chips

§1. General Statement

194. In 1986, Sweden introduced a law on the protection of topographies for semiconductor products which led to a specific protection for computer chips. This new legislation had been influenced by American legislation on 'mask works' in 1984. The American Act required reciprocity for the protection of foreign semiconductor products; as Sweden had its own production of computer chips it was important for Swedish companies to have legal protection in America as well.[405]

195. In transposing the Council Directive 87/54/EEC of 16 December 1986 on the legal protection of topographies of semiconductor products, Sweden passed the Act on the Protection of Topographies for Semiconductor Products (*Lag (1992:1685) om skydd för kretsmönster för halvledarprodukter*), which is the applicable legislation today.

Accordingly, Chapter 1 Article 10 Swedish Copyright Act now explicitly exempts semiconductor products from copyright protection: 'Copyright does not subsist in layout designs in semiconductor products. Special provisions apply to the rights in such designs.'

§2. Object of Protection

196. The Swedish Act on the Protection of Topographies for Semiconductor Products does not define semiconductor products. However, guidance can be found in the Directive, which states in Article 1(1):

(a) a 'semiconductor product' shall mean the final or an intermediate form of any product:
   (i) consisting of a body of material which includes a layer of semiconducting material;
   (ii) having one or more other layers composed of conducting, insulating or semiconducting material, the layers being arranged in accordance with a predetermined three-dimensional pattern;
   (iii) intended to perform, exclusively or together with other functions, an electronic function;

(b) the 'topography' of a semiconductor product shall mean a series of related images, however fixed or encoded:
   (i) representing the three-dimensional pattern of the layers of which a semiconductor product is composed; and
   (ii) in which series, each image has the pattern or part of the pattern of a surface of the semiconductor product at any stage of its manufacture.

---

405. Government Bill (Proposition) 1992/93:48, 'Regeringens proposition om ändringar i de immaterialrättsliga lagarna med anledning av EES-avtalet m.m.', 44.

In accordance with the Directive, the Swedish Act requires the topography to be the 'creator's own intellectual effort' and 'not commonplace in the semiconductor industry'.[406] No further requirements are necessary. The protection for computer chips concerns their design.

197. Article 4 of the Directive allows for the requirement of registration with a public authority. Contrary to many other EU Member States, Sweden does, however, not require any registration of the topography. The protection starts at the moment of creation and lasts ten years after the topography was used commercially for the first time in some part of the world.[407]

'Commercial exploitation' is defined in Article 1(1)(c) Directive as 'the sale, rental, leasing or any other method of commercial distribution, or an offer for these purposes'.

§3. Subject of Protection

198. Section 3 Swedish Act on the Protection of Topographies for Semiconductor Products stipulates that the exclusive right applies to the physical person who is the creator of the topographies of semiconductor products. The creator has to be a citizen of or have their habitual residence in a Member State of the EEA.[408]

199. If the topography was created as part of the creator's employment, the right to protection shall apply in favour of the creator's employer unless terms of employment are to the contrary. The employer has to be a natural person who is a citizen or has habitual residence in a Member State of the EEA, or a legal person with the place of commercial establishment in the territory of a Member State.[409]

§4. Exclusive Rights

200. According to section 2 Swedish Act on the Protection of Topographies for Semiconductor Products, the protection includes the exclusive rights to authorize or prohibit any of the following acts:

(1) reproduction of the topography;
(2) importation of the topography for commercial exploitation/purposes; and
(3) making the topography available to the public through sale, rental or other ways of distribution to the public.

406. Section 1 Act on the Protection of Topographies for Semiconductor Products.
407. Section 4 Act on the Protection of Topographies for Semiconductor Products.
408. See also Art. 3(1) Directive on the legal protection of topographies of semiconductor products.
409. Section 3 para. 2 Act on the Protection of Topographies for Semiconductor Products. See also Art. 3(2) Directive on the legal protection of topographies of semiconductor products.

These exclusive rights also include computer chips that have been produced by using the topography.[410]

The right holder can, in other words, control the reproduction, distribution as well as the import of topographies and any computer chips that are built on the same design.

§5. Exemptions

201. Sections 5–7 Swedish Act on the Protection of Topographies for Semiconductor Products list the exceptions to the exclusive rights. According to section 5, topographies may be copied for teaching purposes or in order to analyse the pattern (reverse engineering). Single copies may also be made for private purposes. These copies may, however, not be used for other purposes in these cases.

According to section 6, exclusive rights do not apply to topographies that have been distributed to the public within the EEA with the consent of the right holder. This principle of exhaustion reflects Article 5(5) of the Directive.

§6. Enforcement/Sanctions

202. Infringing the rights stipulated in the Swedish Act on the Protection of Topographies for Semiconductor Products can lead to civil and criminal liability. Section 9 stipulates fines or imprisonment for up to two years in cases of intent or gross negligence and also criminalizes the attempt or preparation of such infringements. Section 11 allows for compensation for damages. Compensation is given for any infringing use; in cases of intent or gross negligence the damages can also include lost profit, any profit the infringer gained, as well as damages to the reputation of the topography.

If somebody acquires a copy of a protected topography and is neither aware of nor has a reason to believe that the topography is protected, she or he has the right to continue using the computer chip even after being made aware of the protection. However, compensation for the use shall be paid by her or him.[411]

203. In accordance with the Enforcement Directive and similar to the Swedish Copyright Act, section 9c Act on the Protection of Topographies for Semiconductor Products grants right holders the possibility to apply for an 'order to provide information' (*informationsföreläggande*) which can be issued by a court.

410. Section 2 para. 2 Act on the Protection of Topographies for Semiconductor Products.

411. Section 10 Act on the Protection of Topographies for Semiconductor Products.

Chapter 5. Other Intellectual Property Rights in the ICT Sector

§1. Patents

204. Chapter 1 section 1 Swedish Patent Act (*Patentlag (1967:837)* explicitly exempts computer programs or business plans from the definition of invention.[412] According to paragraph 1 of the same section, only inventions can be eligible for patent protection, which therefore excludes computer programs. Section 1 paragraph 2 states the following:

The following shall never be regarded as an invention: that which is merely:

(1) a discovery, scientific theory or mathematical method;
(2) an aesthetic creation;
(3) a scheme, rule or method for performing mental acts, for playing games or for doing business, or a program for computers;
(4) a presentation of information.

205. Following a decision by the Supreme Administrative Court (*Regeringsrätten*) in 1974, computer programs were not protectable by patent in Sweden.[413] This situation changed, however, with a court decision from 1990.[414] In its decision,[415] the Supreme Administrative Court dealt with the patentability of an invention concerning a method of determining the pitch in human speech, for which the Swedish Patent and Registration Office (*Patent- och registreringsverket*)[416] originally denied a patent registration. The Court held that the Swedish patent legislation aims to comply with the European Patent Convention (EPC), which is why the term 'which is merely' corresponds to 'such subject-matter' in Article 52 EPC. Though Swedish law is applicable on patent registrations in Sweden, case law by the European Patent Office (EPO)[417] has been of importance.

The EPO did not have a clear standpoint on patentability of inventions using computer programs. In 1985, the Guidelines for Examination in the EPO were amended and stated then that an invention that contributes with a technical step shall not be denied patentability solely on the grounds that a computer program is involved in the inventive step.

The presently valid Guidelines stipulate that a computer program that is capable of causing, when running on a computer, a further technical effect going beyond the normal physical effects is eligible for patentability.

A further technical effect which lends technical character to a computer program may be found, for example, in the control of an industrial process or in processing data which represent physical entities or in the internal functioning of the computer itself or its interfaces under the influence of the program and could, for example,

412. Section 1 para. 2 Patent Act.
413. Decision by Supreme Administrative Court from 22 Jan. 1974, RÅ 1974 ref 11.
414. Koktvedgaards & Levin, 251–253.
415. Decision by Supreme Administrative Court from 13 Jun. 1990, RÅ 1990 ref 84.
416. <www.prv.se>.
417. <www.epo.org>.

affect the efficiency or security of a process, the management of computer resources required or the rate of data transfer in a communication link.[418]

In order to comply with the common framework of the EPC, the Swedish Supreme Administrative Court (*Regeringsrätten*) held in the case from 1990[419] that the speech signal invention was not excluded from patentability simply because of the fact that a computer program was involved to a certain extent.

At present, case law is, in general, sparse within the area of patent protection for computer programs; a more open-minded granting of patents for computer programs can, however, be noted[420] in line with the development on an European level.

§2. Trade Secrets

206. Unauthorized use of know-how is protected according to the Swedish Act on the Protection of Trade Secrets (*Lag (1990:409) om skydd för företagshemligheter*), if the information is kept secret and the use of it could lead to damage for a company.[421] The knowledge does not have to be documented; even information in somebody's mind can be protected.

According to section 3 Act on the Protection of Trade Secrets, any unauthorized intentional access to trade secrets can lead to criminal liability with imprisonment for a maximum of two years. Any intentional or grossly negligent use of trade secrets, on the other hand, only leads to civil liability for damages caused by the use.[422]

In a case in 2001, the Swedish Supreme Court held that an employee who copied electronic data from a customer database that he had access to did not fall under section 3 but section 8, which only stipulates civil liability for damages.[423]

A more recent decision by the Labour Court (*Arbetsdomstol*) dealt with the case of three former employees who had created a computer program at their new workplace, which was very similar to software the former employer was using. The Court held that the employees had had access to a computer program during their work, and that this constituted a trade secret. The next question concerned the requirement of using the trade secret in an unauthorized way. The Swedish Labour Court held that similarities alone in the two computer programs were not evidence enough to prove unauthorized use, as there were other plausible reasons for the similarities. Neither did the mere fact of a short development period for the new software provide sufficient grounds for an unauthorized use of a trade secret. The employees were therefore acquitted.[424]

As is apparent by the Labour Court's decision, a conviction according to the Act on the Protection of Trade Secrets not only requires the proof of a trade secret but

418. European Patent Office, 'Guidelines for Examination in the European Patent Office', September 2013, Part G Ch. II 3.6.
419. Decision by Supreme Administrative Court from 13 Jun. 1990, RÅ 1990 ref 84.
420. Koktvedgaards & Levin, 251–253.
421. Section 1 Act on the Protection of Trade Secrets.
422. Section 8 Act on the Protection of Trade Secrets.
423. Decision by Supreme Court from 1 Jun. 2001, NJA 2001 s. 362.
424. Decision by Labour Court from 2 Sep. 2009, AD 2009 no. 63.

also demonstration of the fact that the trade secret was actually used in an unauthorized way.

Chapter 6. Internet Domain Name Registration

§1. General Statement

207. In 2006, Sweden introduced the National Top-Level Domains for Sweden on the Internet Act (*Lag (2006:24) om nationella toppdomäner för Sverige på Internet*) (hereinafter 'Top-Level Domains Act') as part of its strategy to achieve a more secure Internet.[425] The Act aims at enabling a secure and effective administration of the Swedish top-level country domain names and to allow state control over the administration.[426]

Though the registration as such is mainly done by outsourced organizations (registrars), the general terms and condition of the main Swedish registry, Internet Infrastructure Foundation.SE (*Stiftelsen för Internetinfrastruktur*), apply and take precedence over conflicting terms and conditions in individual contracts between registrars and domain holders.[427]

§2. Administration

208. The Swedish Top-Level Domains Act applies to the technical administration and registration of domain names for Sweden.[428] Technical administration with regard to domain names traditionally includes maintaining databases such as who is, approve registrars, support name servers as well as maintain the DNS-service which translates domain names to IP addresses.[429]

Section 5 Top-Level Domains Act sets up several requirements that registries have to meet. The provision mainly concerns security aspects but also stipulates obligations such as providing correct and easily accessible information to the name servers for the top-domain, ensuring traffic between the name servers and the Internet (i.e., safeguarding the accessibility of the DNS-service), securing the information on top domains and following routines that meet certain accepted standards. Registries also have to maintain a register of issued domain names and make backup copies of the data on a regular basis.[430]

Registries have to notify the Swedish supervisory authority of their services. According to the National Top-Level Domains for Sweden on the Internet Ordinance (*Förordning (2006:25) om nationella toppdomäner för Sverige på Internet*) (hereinafter 'Top-Level Domains Ordinance'), PTS is the responsible supervisory authority.[431]

---

425. Prior to the enactment in 2006 the Swedish State was not involved in the administration of domain names.
426. Government Bill (Proposition) 2004/05:175, 'Från IT-politik för samhället till politik för IT-samhället', 1.
427. Article 1.3 Terms and conditions of registration applicable for the top-level domain.SE from 3 Jun. 2013.
428. Section 1 Top-Level Domains Act.
429. Government Bill (Proposition) 2004/05:175, 245.
430. Section 6 Top-Level Domains Act.
431. Section 2 Top-Level Domains Ordinance.

209. At the moment, the Internet Infrastructure Foundation.SE (*Stiftelsen för Internetinfrastruktur*) is the only registry for the Swedish top-level and country-level domain.se. Since September 2013, .SE also administers the top-level domain.nu.[432] Established in 1997, .SE is an independent public interest foundation and not only administers Swedish domain names, but also aims at promoting a positive development of the Internet in general in Sweden.

§3. REGISTRATION

210. The rules for registration are not stipulated in any statutory provisions, but are provided in the terms and conditions of registration applicable for the top-level domain.SE, issued by the Internet Infrastructure Foundation.SE.

As in most other countries, the principle 'first come, first served' applies.[433] This means that in principle any domain name will be registered as long as it is available,[434] and no general consideration is given to possible intellectual property rights to the name.

Both natural and legal persons can apply for registration of domain names.[435] The general terms and conditions issued by.SE set up some technical requirements for domain names as well as some exemptions as to which domain names can be registered.[436]

211. According to section 3.2.1 of the terms and conditions of registration applicable for the top-level domain.SE, a domain name may only comprise ASCII characters, which include the letters a–z, numbers 0–9 and hyphens (though the domain name cannot consist only of hyphens). Domain names have to include at least two and maximum sixty-three characters.[437]

Certain domain names are reserved and can only be registered after a special assessment (reserved) or not at all (blocked). Examples include:[438]

- country codes (blocked), such as be.se, de.se, eu.se; uk.se;
- example and test domains (blocked), such as example.se, localhost.se;
- misleading domains (blocked), such as whois.se;
- specific second level domains (blocked), such as org.se, parti.se and press.se;
- domain names related to Swedish law (blocked), such as cern.se, epo.se, euratom.se and interpol.se;
- country domains in the Swedish language (reserved), such as argentina.se, japan.se and osterrike.se.

432. This domain is seen as popular due to its meaning 'now' in Swedish, Danish and Dutch.
433. Section 3.1.2 Terms and conditions of registration applicable for the top-level domain.SE from 3 Jun. 2013.
434. *Ibid.*, s. 3.2.6.
435. *Ibid.*, s. 3.1.1.
436. For statistics on Swedish domain names see <www.iis.se/domaner/statistik/>.
437. Section 3.2.5 Terms and conditions of registration applicable for the top-level domain.SE from 3 Jun. 2013.
438. See for a complete list <www.iis.se/statistics/barred_domains_list.txt>.

In a recent report, PTS, in its capacity of supervisory authority, suggested to include the name 'bank' into the block list for domain names, in part to avoid confusion for consumers.[439] However, PTS withdrew their request after.SE refused to prohibit such domains.[440]

§4. Intellectual Property Rights

212. As mentioned above the registration process for domain names does not take into account potential intellectual property rights in the names. This is very common in other European countries and internationally.

There can, however, be rights in a word or a name, both according to the Swedish Trademarks Act (*Varumärkeslag (2010:1877)*) as well as the Swedish Trade Names Act (*Firmalag (1974:156)*). Individuals may also have a right to their personal name.

Trademarks have to be registered with the Swedish Patent and Registration Office (*Patent- och registreringsverket*),[441] according to Chapter 1 section 6 and Chapter 2 section 1 Trademarks Act, or can be protected due to incorporation pursuant to Chapter 1 section 7 Trademarks Act. In addition, trade names can be protected upon registration with the Swedish Companies Registration Office (*Bolagsverket*)[442] or incorporation, according to section 2 Trade Names Act.

Though rights on trademark or trade names are not considered during the registration of domain names, the Swedish Internet Infrastructure Foundation.SE takes account of intellectual property rights, especially trademarks, in allowing right holders to apply for a transfer or deregistration of a domain name through ADR.

§5. Disputes

213. Just as the Domain Name Dispute Resolution (UDRP) by WIPO, the Swedish organization requests individuals and companies registering a domain name under.se to agree to their General terms and conditions and thereby agree to the use of dispute resolution when settling a conflict.

214. Under certain conditions, a registered domain name can be deregistered or transferred after an ADR proceeding.[443] Point 7.2 of the General terms and conditions stipulates the following requirements which all have to be fulfilled:

(1) the domain name is identical or similar to:
   - a distinguishing product feature;

439. Swedish Post and Telecom Agency (PTS), 'Allocation of domain names under the national top-level domain.se', PTS-ER-2009:17, 26 Mar. 2009.
440. See.SE's report <www.iis.se/om/organisation/beslut-fran-ses-styrelse/>.
441. <www.prv.se>.
442. <www.bolagsverket.se>.
443. Section 6.3 Terms and conditions of registration applicable for the top-level domain.SE from 3 Jun. 2013.

- a distinguishing business feature;
- a family name;
- an artist's name (if the name is not associated with someone who deceased a long time ago);
- a title of another party's copyrighted literary or artistic work;
- a name that is protected by the Regulation concerning Certain Official Designations (*Förordning (1976:100) om vissa officiella beteckningar*);[444]
- a geographic designation or a designation of origin that is protected by the European Council's Regulation EU 510/2006;[445]
- a geographic designation that is protected by the European Council's Regulation (EU) 110/2008;[446]
- a geographic designation that is protected by the European Council's Regulation (EU) 1234/2007;[447] or
- the name of a government authority that is listed in the registry that Statistics Sweden must maintain under the Swedish Code of Statutes SFS 2007:755 (Government Agencies Register Ordinance), or its generally accepted abbreviation;

(2) the domain name has been registered or used in bad faith; and
(3) the domain holder has no rights or justified interest in the domain name.

All relevant circumstances are assessed when determining whether a domain name has been registered or used in bad faith.[448] Examples of circumstances supporting bad faith claims (a lack of which potentially implying that bad faith does not exist) are:

- the domain holder is utilising or plans to utilise the good reputation, market position or characteristic feature of the petitioner[449] to attract traffic to the own website or to increase revenue in this matter;
- the domain holder's registration of the domain name prevents or makes it difficult for the petitioner to register the brand as domain name;
- the domain name is being used or planned to be used to disrupt the petitioner's operations;
- the domain name has been registered with a view to a sale to the petitioner.

444. For example the Council of Europe (*Europarådet*) or the International Monetary Fund (*Internationella valutafonden*).
445. Council Regulation (EC) No. 510/2006 of 20 Mar. 2006 on the protection of geographical indications and designations of origin for agricultural products and foodstuffs.
446. Regulation (EC) No 110/2008 of the European Parliament and of the Council of 15 Jan. 2008. on the definition, description, presentation, labelling and the protection of geographical indications of spirit drinks.
447. Council Regulation (EC) No 1234/2007 of 22 Oct. 2007 establishing a common organization of agricultural markets and on specific provisions for certain agricultural products.
448. Instructions pertaining to ADR (paragraph 7), Instructions concerning the bad faith condition (condition 2) found at the end of Terms and conditions of registration applicable for the top-level domain.SE from 3 Jun. 2013.
449. That is, the party requesting dispute resolution proceedings.

As above, all relevant circumstances are assessed when determining whether a domain holder has no right or justified interest in the domain name.[450] Examples of circumstances supporting such claims (a lack of which potentially implying that the domain holder does not have any right or justified interest) are:

- the domain holder owns a registered brand (or other right) that is identical or similar to the domain name;
- the domain name is being used or has been registered to be used in its linguistic meaning; or
- the domain name is being used or has been registered to be used in commercial or private operations that do not infringe on the petitioner's rights;
- the domain name is older than the brand (or other right) on which the petitioner bases the application.

215. As of April 2014, 566 decisions have been taken through ADR; out of these, 384 were in favour of the plaintiff.[451] Normally, if the trademark is not registered, the plaintiff has to prove incorporation with evidence such as number of sales, costs for and extent of marketing, or use market research to show the trademark's reputation on the market.[452]

The requirement 'similar to'[453] has been confirmed for the domain name locket.se with the trademark blocket.se, the domain name vovlo.se with the trademark Volvo, iloveikea.se with the trademark IKEA, and igoogle.se as well as googlephone.se with Google. In many ADR cases, the domain name and trademark were identical and therefore did not require any further investigation in this respect, for example, vuitton.se, kawasaki.se, esso.se, dole.se as well as google.se.

If a domain name is not used for commercial purposes, the domain owner is able to keep it, even though it might infringe someone else's trademark. A non-commercial purpose of a domain name cannot, however, be claimed if the website has not been launched.[454] In accordance with trademark legislation, the term 'commercial purposes' is rather broad and can include not only websites with a purpose of profit-making, but also non-profit or educational, scientific and cultural activities if they involve an economic interest and can therefore be considered businesses.[455]

Regarding the requirement of bad faith, case law by arbitration proceedings has shown that the fact that the domain holder should have known about the trademark because of its reputation and does not reply in the proceedings, lead to the presumption of bad faith at the time of registration of the domain name. Registration

450. Instructions pertaining to ADR (paragraph 7), Instructions concerning the right or justified interest condition (condition 3) found at the end of Terms and conditions of registration applicable for the top-level domain.SE from 3 Jun. 2013.
451. See for a complete list <https://www.iis.se/domaner/tvistlosning/for-se-domaner/atf-arenden/>.
452. Henrik Bengtsson, 'Svenska domännamnstvister: Praxis enligt den s.k. II-stiftelsens systems för alternativ tvistelösning', *Nordiskt Immateriellt Rättskydd* 3(2005): 257 and 263.
453. Previously referred to as 'likely to be confused'.
454. See, e.g., Decision no. 9, from 27 Aug. 2003, Peugeot.se.
455. Bengtsson, 266–267.

of several domain names in a systematic way may also be an indication of bad faith.[456]

216. According to Point 6.4 General Terms and Conditions, a domain name shall be deregistered or transferred if the applicant presents a judgment by a court stipulating that the domain name shall be deregistered or transferred. There are no statistics to what extent this is being used, but the ADR system seems to work very well regarding cybersquatters, and as it works faster than trials before the district courts, most trademark owners will preferably use it.

456. Bengtsson, 270 and 272.

Part III. ICT Contracts

Chapter 1. Hardware Contracts

217. Swedish law does not specifically govern ICT hardware contracts. In essence, such contracts stipulate the buyer's and the seller's rights and obligations in relation to the transfer (or leasing, where applicable) of movable property. This means that all hardware transfer contracts between commercial parties are subject to the Sale of Goods Act (*Köplag (1990:931)*). Consumer sales and certain international sales are subject to specific legislation in the form of the Consumer Sales Act (*Konsumentköplag (1990:932)*) and the Convention on Contracts for the International Sale of Goods (CISG) respectively. The Sale of Goods Act is non-mandatory legislation, which means that it is normally possible and also customary in ICT contracts, to overrule this legislation through the actual agreement entered into by the parties, that is, the agreed provisions in the hardware contract will take precedence in the case of any conflict with the Sale of Goods Act.

In addition, according to section 3 Sale of Goods Act, 'commercial custom or other customs which must be regarded as binding on the parties' will take precedence over the Sale of Goods Act. Within the Swedish ICT sector, standard contracts issued by trade associations play a fairly important role, and it is not unusual for small or even medium-sized IT businesses and transactions to be conducted on the basis of, or with reference to, such standard contracts. In relation to hardware contracts, Agreement 90[457] is the most common standard contract, despite the fact that it mainly focuses on turnkey contracts and system deliveries. Since Agreement 90 is often used when interpreting ICT contracts, it has been argued that Agreement 90 should be considered as customary practice within the market.[458] In such cases, the provisions in Agreement 90 could – in connection with section 3 Sale of Goods Act – be used as a reference to define the commercial custom for ICT hardware and turnkey contracts that would prevail over the Sale of Goods Act. Regardless, the explicit terms and the content of the parties' agreement will of course have precedence over both the Sale of Goods Act and Agreement 90.

457. Agreement 90 was issued by IT & Telekomföretagen and SILF in Swedish and English. The latest version was issued in 2008.
458. Agne Lindberg & Daniel Westman, *Praktisk IT-rätt*, 3rd edn (Stockholm: Norstedts Juridik AB, 2002), 390.

218. Within the Swedish ICT sector, it has been an ongoing trend over the past decades to shift the focus from hardware specifications and descriptions to more functional aspects of the delivery, that is, hardware has become more of a commodity closely connected to different services and also more of an instrument to run software applications and hosting data. In addition, many customers today tend to prefer to lease or rent hardware rather than purchase it, especially in commercial ICT deals. Such financial arrangements allow the customer to maintain agility and flexibility as well as avoid making large investments and having to deal with old or obsolete equipment. The changed focus towards functionality, services and financing models, has caused many suppliers to bundle hardware with software and different types of services, such as maintenance services, mobile solutions, financing, and consumable supplies. Such structures are often referred to as 'functional' or 'as-a-service' deliveries, where the customer pays a fee per week/month/usage which includes the costs for hardware as well as the included software and services. Where the hardware contract includes maintenance services, it is crucial for the customer to ensure that the hardware contract includes necessary service-related provisions (e.g., maintenance frequency, availability requirements, response and resolution requirements, etc.), as well as the right to receive financial compensation in case of the supplier's non-performance or non-compliance.

In regard to such service-related provisions in a hardware contract, it should be noted that it is obviously more beneficial for the customer to include a resolution requirement rather than a response requirement in the contract. A resolution requirement means that the supplier has an undertaking to correct errors within a specified time limit, whereas a response requirement simply means that the supplier is obliged to respond to the customer's error report within a specified time. A response requirement could also be effective for the customer, as long as it is connected to an escalation model. Such an escalation model typically consists of several different levels of error correction competences through which the error is escalated until it is resolved. Irrespective of whether a resolution or a response requirement (or both) is included in the contract, the customer should ensure that such a requirement is linked to a monetary incentive (e.g., penalties) in case of the supplier's non-performance.

219. For traditional hardware contracts, a critical issue to negotiate are the warranties provided by the supplier with regard to defects in the hardware. The customer will generally strive to include more functionality-based warranties, where the supplier warrants that the hardware is fit for a specific purpose or use in a specific environment, whereas the supplier will strive to limit any warranty or representation to standard documentation and descriptions of the hardware. According to section 32 Sale of Goods Act, the supplier is, as a general rule, liable for defects occurring during a period of two years after the delivery. However, this rule is usually set aside and/or modified in the hardware contract.

220. In conclusion, traditional hardware contracts are becoming increasingly unusual in Sweden due to the bundling of hardware with services, software and financing. From a legal perspective, commercial parties to a hardware contract have a general freedom of contract and may freely dispose of the agreement. Standard contracts such as Agreement 90 could, to some extent, serve as a benchmark. It is important to note, however, that these standard contracts are generally considered to be more favourable to the supplier than the customer.

Chapter 2. Software Contracts

221. A software contract can refer to different types of ICT contracts, such as license agreements, development or distribution contracts. Since distribution agreements are covered in Chapter 4 below, this chapter will focus on software license and development agreements.

Software licensing contracts are, as far as copyright issues are concerned, subject to the Swedish Copyright Act *(Lag (1960:729) om upphovsrätt till litterära och konstnärliga verk)*, which sets out specific provisions with regard to both the transfer of copyright to software as well as licensing. Although not directly applicable, it is also widely accepted that the Sale of Goods Act, in regard to the principles of commercial transactions as such (e.g., regarding issues such as when a delivery is considered to be delayed, or within which time a complaint must be raised by the customer from the time when the customer discovered a defect), will apply analogously on software contracts to the extent that the software contract does not specifically stipulate otherwise.[459]

222. A software contract is generally different from other commercial contracts since the software license concerns the provision of a license (a right to use) rather than the *transfer* of property.[460] A software license can be either exclusive or non-exclusive, although it is obviously unusual for any commercial software to be licensed on an exclusive basis.

223. The object for a software license is typically the software code along with the accompanying documentation and manuals for the software. Except for specific source code escrow arrangements (see below), the customer will not be provided with, or have the general right to modify the source code of the software. However, it should be noted that Article 26g Swedish Copyright Act stipulates that a licensee has a mandatory right to correct errors in computer software as well as make amendments for the purpose of compatibility. Furthermore, the licensee is free to make copies of the software for backup purposes to the extent necessary for the intended use of the software. Finally, the licensee may observe, examine and test the software as long as such activities are performed within the scope of the licensed rights.

According to Article 26h Swedish Copyright Act, the licensee also has a mandatory but limited right to decompile the software. Decompilation may, however, only be performed for the purpose of achieving intended interoperability between the licensed software and the other software. The result from the decompilation must not be disclosed to third parties unless such disclosure is necessary in order to achieve the intended interoperability. It is explicitly stated in the Swedish Copyright Act that any information gained by decompilation shall not be used for the development of software that has a similar expression as the decompiled software.

459. See Lindberg & Westman, 374 et seq.

460. Note that intellectual property rights to software can theoretically be transferred as well as licensed. The question whether to transfer of license software is a commonly negotiated part of many development agreements (see *infra*).

224. The so-called specification principle (*specifikationsprincipen*) is a fundamental aspect of Swedish copyright law. This principle states that only such rights explicitly granted in the software contract will be transferred or licensed to the licensee. This principle is partly incorporated in Article 28 Copyright Act, which states that a transfer of copyrighted material will not – unless explicitly agreed to – include a right for the buyer to modify or reassign the material. To the extent that such rights are intended to pass to the buyer, the transfer agreement should include explicit provisions regarding the right to change and reassign the copyrighted material.

225. Important provisions in a software contract based on traditional licensing include liability for defects (typically limited to a standard warranty valid for a short period from delivery, e.g., thirty or ninety days), source code escrow, support and maintenance services,[461] and infringement. The latter has gained in importance in the light of open source challenges. Warranty undertakings will generally be connected to the support and maintenance agreement between the parties, if applicable.

226. Source code escrow arrangements are rather common in Sweden for software that has been developed specifically for one customer or project but where the copyright has not been transferred to the customer. Perhaps the most important clause to negotiate in an escrow agreement is to agree on which events that should trigger release of the materials placed in escrow. Examples of commonly used release events include the supplier's insolvency, the winding-up of its business, change of ownership, and/or substantial breach of (or non-performance) the maintenance agreement. In escrow agreements between Swedish parties, the Stockholm Chamber of Commerce (SCC) is widely selected as the escrow agent, often by virtue of their model contract.[462]

227. In recent years, many software suppliers have started to distribute their software through a Software-as-a Service (SaaS) structure rather than by use of a traditional licensing model. SaaS is a broad market, and services can include anything from rather simple web-based email solutions to complex Customer Relationship Management Systems. The process towards SaaS-structures has been driven not only by suppliers, who can decrease costs for distribution and maintenance, but also by customers, who prefer not to handle issues regarding licensing, maintenance, and hosting of the software. A SaaS-contract will focus less on the right to use the software, and more on functional services descriptions, service levels (e.g., availability and maintenance requirements), service level remedies (e.g., liquidated damages), data security, and exit management provisions to ensure cooperation and transfer of data upon the termination or expiration of the SaaS-contract. The extent of copyright use (and hence the need for an explicit license provision) in a SaaS-contract is dependent on the technical solution and whether the end user is duplicating the software when using it or making it available to a third party.

461. See Ch. 5 *infra* (paras 238 et seq.).
462. See <www.chamber.se/?id=6417>, 15 Apr. 2010.

228. Software development contracts deal with a number of important issues. First of all, the development project and the management and governance thereof need to be described in detail in order to ensure a successful project. One of the most important parts of a software development contract is the regulation regarding intellectual property rights and the question of whether the customer will only have a right to use the result, hence a license, or if the intellectual property rights to the result shall be transferred to and vested in the customer. In most cases, this issue can be resolved by either a grant-back license to the supplier (if rights to results are transferred to the customer) or a wide license grant for the customer (if rights to results are retained by the supplier). It should be noted that, as a main rule and in accordance with the specification principle, the intellectual property rights to results will remain with the supplier unless otherwise explicitly agreed. Furthermore, service level arrangements regarding the development and orders are generally addressed in software development contracts. During recent years, development services for software applications have become an important outsourcing object (normally referred to as Application Development Management, ADM), which often involves offshore arrangements. One of the most common offshore destinations is India, but many IT suppliers will have a so-called global delivery model whereby resources across the world can be used to supply services to a particular customer.

An increasingly common type of development methodology is so-called agile development. In particular, such agile development projects are often based on the SCRUM[463] or KANBAN[464] methodology frameworks. Somewhat simplified, agile development methodology means that the parties have a close interaction during the development project, rather than the supplier providing one final delivery at a specific date. The results in an agile development project are provided to the customer in numerous smaller parts where the customer will react on each part during the course of the project. Hence, the final result in a project based on agile development is not as clearly defined as in traditional development contracts. An agile development methodology requires a contract that can accommodate the close interaction between the parties during the development project. The statement of work, which is basically a list of the activities of each party, as well as liability issues, confidentiality undertakings and provisions on delay and incentives for the supplier need to be made as clear as possible. On a general level, a development project implementing an agile methodology will typically mean that the customer needs to be more closely involved in the actual development process and that the customer, in most cases, should be prepared to assume a higher level of project and financial risk compared to a traditional delivery model.

There are several standard contracts for software development projects. For development projects using a traditional development model, the most commonly used standard contract is IT Projects version 2008. For agile development projects,

463. For more information on SCRUM in relation to software development, see <www.scrum.org>.
464. For more information on KANBAN in relation to software development, see Anderson, David, 'Agile Management for Software Engineering: Applying the Theory of Constraints for Business Results', Prentice Hall, September 2003.

the standard contract typically used is called Agile Projects version 2012.[465] These standard contracts are, however, supplier-friendly and will often require significant negotiation in order to reach a balanced agreement.

229. To summarize, the provisions in the Swedish Copyright Act need to be considered when drafting a software contract regardless of whether it is a license or development contract. The general rules set out in the Sale of Goods Act would also need to be taken into consideration. The software contract has traditionally been based on a grant of license, development and maintenance services. Due to the rise of cloud computing, SaaS-contracts have given rise to new issues to be dealt with by the parties.

465. Both IT Projects version 2008 and Agile Projects 2012 are issued by IT & Telekomföretagen in Swedish and English.

Chapter 3. Turnkey Contracts

230. The primary purpose of a turnkey contract is to provide the customer with a complete solution or system which is (more or less) customized to meet the customer's specific requirements. This means that the turnkey contract will per se be rather extensive and include several different types of deliverables, often including a combination of hardware, software and services (e.g., adaptations of standard software or other implementation services). Maintenance services are generally not considered to be a part of the turnkey contract and will typically be subject to a separate agreement. The maintenance agreement will however often be linked to the turnkey contract, so that the maintenance undertakings will enter into effect upon the completion of the acceptance test in the turnkey contract.

The key element of a turnkey contract is that the supplier will assume responsibility for the entire system that is delivered to the customer. Hence, the different parts of the supplier's performance (hardware, software, and services) need to fulfil the agreed specification separately as well as jointly. Since the supplier assumes responsibility for the complete system delivered under a turnkey contract, it is essential for the parties to allow due consideration and time when preparing the specifications and project plans of a turnkey contract. In many cases, a large step towards ensuring the successful purchase of an entire IT system can be taken through careful preparation measures along with effective contract mechanisms.

231. The Sale of Goods Act is directly applicable to the hardware delivery component of a turnkey contract, but not to the licensing of standard software.[466] This means that, unless otherwise explicitly agreed to by the parties, the hardware part of a turnkey contract is governed by the Sale of Goods Act while the licensing part is subject to mandatory requirements set out in the Copyright Act.[467]

As already mentioned above in Chapter 1, the use of standard contracts is common within the Swedish ICT market. With regard to turnkey contracts, Agreement 90 is a well-established standard contract and the principles set out therein could to some extent be considered as commercial customs when applying the Sales of Goods Act on ICT contracts. However, it is important to point out that Agreement 90 is not mandatory in any respect, and that the parties have the freedom of contract in relation to all aspects of the turnkey contract, except for the mandatory copyright legal principles regarding, for example, compatibility changes and decompilation.[468] Agreement 90 includes all the essential aspects of a turnkey contract, such as provisions regarding installation, delivery dates, inspection/acceptance tests, delay, payment, software license, liability for defects, confidentiality obligations, infringement indemnity, limitations of liability, and dispute resolution.

232. Most turnkey contracts include delivery of third party products, and the parties will need to stipulate the level of liability that the supplier should assume for such third party products. In general, the supplier will strive to make the third party

466. Lindberg & Westman, 372 et seq.
467. See Ch. 2 *supra* (paras 221 et seq.).
468. As described in Ch. 2 *supra* (paras 221 et seq.).

supplier's terms and conditions applicable, especially in situations where the customer has made an active selection to use a specific third party product for the delivery. This is also the general rule according to Agreement 90.

Another important component of the turnkey contract is the implementation and customization of the supplier's products and solutions to the customer's IT environment and specific requirements. Such implementation is usually set up as a joint project, where the supplier assumes the role of project manager and the customer's responsibilities are limited to allowing access for the supplier's personnel to the customer's facilities and IT environment. Due to the close cooperation between the parties in the implementation project, it is essential for the turnkey contract to include adequate undertakings with regard to non-disclosure obligations and compliance with applicable security policies.

Further, the turnkey contract will typically include an acceptance test procedure. It is essential for the customer to ensure that the acceptance criteria are properly defined and customized to suit the needs and demands of the customer. The acceptance test will also constitute the difference between 'delay' and 'error', since an error cannot occur before the system is actually delivered and accepted in accordance with the acceptance test criteria.

233. A common cause for problems and disputes during the implementation of customized solutions is the supplier's delay of the implementation project. In order to provide incentives for the supplier to provide the system on time, a turnkey contract generally includes a right for the customer to receive financial compensation (e.g., liquidated damages) in the case of delay. In addition to financial remedies, the customer should also strive for the contract to minimize and clarify all actions that the customer needs to perform in order for the supplier to successfully implement the solution. Such undertakings are often listed in a separate document. In the case of a substantial delay for which the supplier is responsible, the turnkey contract should include a right for the customer to terminate the contract prematurely.

Chapter 4. Distribution Agreements

234. With regard to distribution of hardware, software and services in Sweden, the most important forms of distribution are through the appointment of distributors and agents. Under a distribution agreement, the supplier will appoint a distributor to market, resell or sub-license the supplier's products and/or services on a designated market or worldwide. A distributor will purchase and resell products and/or services in its own name and its own account/risk. A commercial or commission agent will not purchase products or services from the supplier, but rather act as an intermediary between the supplier and the customer.

To distinguish between distributors and agents is essential from a legal perspective, since agents are subject to the Commercial Agents Act (*Lag (1991:351) om handelsagentur*)[469] and the Commission Agents Act (*Kommissionslag (2009:865)*) respectively. These statutes contain several mandatory protective provisions for the agent, such as the right to minimum termination notice periods and the right to receive severance pay in case of termination. A distributor, however, is not covered by any specific protective legislation under Swedish law. It is important to note that the Commercial Agents Act is only directly applicable in relation to supply of 'goods', that is, tangible items, and not to services and/or intangible items.

235. Specifically with regard to the distribution of software, the Swedish Supreme Court made an important ruling in 2008.[470] In this case, a German commercial agent claimed severance payment according to the Commercial Agents Act from a Swedish software supplier due to the supplier's termination of an agency agreement. The Court ruled that the provisions in the Commercial Agents Act regarding severance pay can be applicable for distribution of software. However, since software is not 'goods' according to Swedish law, the otherwise mandatory provisions in the Commercial Agents Act can be set aside by the provisions in the software agency agreement. The Court also indicated that the most important aspect of a software agency agreement which also includes ancillary services (such as after sales services) is in fact the licensing of software and not providing the services.[471]

236. In addition, there is also an important difference between distributors and agents in relation to mandatory antitrust and competition law. Whereas a distribution agreement will often conflict with such laws (see below), a commercial/commission agency agreement is normally not subject to antitrust/competition legislation, provided that the agent does not take any financial risks.

For a distribution agreement, non-competition clauses and territorial/customer restrictions are especially sensitive from an antitrust point of view. Further, the distributor must always be free to set its own prices in relation to its customers. Recommended prices or fixed maximum retail prices are however generally accepted

469. The Act is based on Council Directive 86/653/EEC of 18 Dec. 1986 on the coordination of the laws of the Member States relating to self-employed commercial agents.
470. Decision by Supreme Court from 4 Jan. 2008, NJA 2008 s. 24.
471. See Johan Hübner, 'Analog tillämpning av lagen om handelsagentur på återförsäljare av datorprogram', *Lov & Data* 93 (2008): 14–15.

under the block exemptions for vertical agreements,[472] provided that the supplier has a market share below 30%. With regard to non-competition clauses, the block exemptions for vertical agreements allow for such clauses to last no more than five years except in cases where the distributor's premises are owned or leased by the supplier or it is question of a franchise agreement. If the supplier's market share is below 15%, a non-compete obligation is however permissible under the European Commission's *de minimis* notice, regardless of its duration.[473] Competition restrictions after the termination of the agreement are permitted for a period of one year, provided that the restrictions are limited to the premises of the distributor and are indispensable to protect the supplier's know-how.[474] Further, under sections 36 and 38 Swedish Contracts Act (*Lag (1915:218) om avtal och andra rättshandlingar på förmögenhetsrättens område*), a non-competition clause (and/or a penalty clause tied to the non-competition clause) can be deemed invalid and, hence, unenforceable to the extent that such a clause is considered unreasonable 'having regard to the contents of the agreement, the circumstances prevailing at the time the agreement was entered into, subsequent circumstances and circumstances in general'.[475]

237. Other important provisions in a distribution agreement include minimum purchase obligations, forecasting and reporting requirements. Such provisions often entitle the supplier to terminate the agreement (or, in case of an exclusive agreement, change the agreement into a non-exclusive agreement) if the distributor/agent fails to reach the applicable minimum purchase obligations or forecasted sales targets. Finally, many distribution agreements include a responsibility for the distributor/agent to handle customer complaints, warranty claims and all other after sales matters. The distributor/agent will generally be reimbursed by the supplier for such after sales work during the warranty period. Unless otherwise agreed by the parties, a two year warranty period for defects applies according to section 32 Sale of Goods Act.

---

472. Act on group exceptions for vertical agreements and restrictive practices (*Lag (2008:581) om gruppundantag för vertikala konkurrensbegränsande avtal*). The Act is based on Commission Regulation (EC) No. 2790/1999 of 22 Dec. 1999 on the application of Art. 81(3) of the Treaty to categories of vertical agreements and concerted practices.
473. Commission Notice on agreements of minor importance which do not appreciably restrict competition under Art. 81(1) of the Treaty establishing the European Community.
474. Article 5 Commission Regulation (EC) No. 2790/1999 of 22 Dec. 1999 on the application of Art. 81(3) of the Treaty to categories of vertical agreements and concerted practices.
475. Article 36 Contracts Act.

Chapter 5. Maintenance Contracts

238. The objective of maintenance services is basically to keep the maintenance object 'alive', up-to-date and well-functioning. A maintenance contract may complement or substitute a software warranty in a license or intellectual property rights transfer contract by including an error resolution undertaking governed by a detailed SLA. It is common for different types of maintenance contracts that the supplier's obligation will be limited to deliver specified services to the customer in relation to one or more maintenance objects. This means that neither the Sale of Goods Act nor any other Swedish statute will be directly applicable, except for serving as supplementary legal principles for the interpretation of the maintenance contract. Further, since a large part of the supplier's undertakings in a software maintenance contract consist of providing computer code to the customer, copyright issues will need to be addressed in such maintenance contracts.

As for many other ICT contracts, there is a Swedish standard contract with regard to maintenance services. This standard contract is called 'IT-Maintenance Version 2008',[476] and includes many of the provisions necessary in a maintenance contract, such as general obligations for both parties, exceptions to the supplier's maintenance obligations, liability (and limitations), security, confidentiality and termination rights. Needless to say, each maintenance contract based on the IT-Maintenance standard contract will require careful considerations and adaptations to the actual deal. Specifically, IT-Maintenance must be supplemented with a service description, specific service levels and remedies, fees and payment terms.[477]

239. A maintenance contract will normally include both pro-active and reactive error rectification, as well as support services. Even though software maintenance is a complex and common type of maintenance contract, such services could also include an undertaking for the supplier to perform error rectification of both hardware and software. The general purpose of the rectification undertaking is to eliminate interruptions in the operations of the maintained systems, which in relation to hardware often include performance of technical repair services and replacement of parts. In relation to software, the supplier is normally obligated to: (i) reactively provide rectification and corrective measures (e.g., bug fixes, patches, etc.); (ii) advise and inform on how to work around the defect; or (iii) pro-actively provide a new version of the software where known errors are rectified. If the maintenance services are provided by the software licensor, the maintenance contract may also include an undertaking to provide the customer with new versions of the software, which may include not only error rectification but also new functionality. An essential aspect for the supplier is to have the option to carry out rectification work remotely (i.e., via virtual private network or similar network connection). Such a right to perform error correction remotely should be explicitly set out in the contract. In relation to such remote access to the customer's systems on distance, security arrangements may call for specific regulations in the maintenance contract.

---

476. IT-Maintenance is issued by IT & Telekomföretagen in Swedish and English. The latest version was issued in 2008.
477. See Lindberg & Westman, 478.

Pro-active maintenance services for hardware will normally include functional control and adjustments, replacement of worn-out parts, cleaning and similar activities. In relation to software, pro-active maintenance work can include development of the software (updates, upgrades, etc.) as well as updates and maintenance of information within databases. In addition, so-called soft maintenance services are often used for software, and will generally include an undertaking to provide the customer with new versions and updates.[478]

Furthermore, it is not uncommon to include elements of support services in maintenance contracts, which means that the contract will in fact constitute a support and maintenance agreement. In this respect, 'support' refers to the supplier's provision of a helpdesk that end users of the supported object may contact in case of errors or where there is a need of assistance in relation to the supported equipment or software. In order to avoid minor issues being reported to helpdesk, many agreements will include an undertaking for the supplier to provide education and training to a limited number of 'super-users' who will deal with Frequently Asked Questions (FAQs) and the resolution of minor issues. Such 'super-users' will then provide first line support and they will be the only users authorized to contact the supplier's helpdesk (which in such circumstances will be the second line support).

240. When negotiating a maintenance contract, much effort will normally be spent on identifying and regulating suitable service levels. The most commonly used service level is 'response time', meaning the time within which the supplier shall respond to customer inquiries and handle such in accordance with a specified escalation routine. A more demanding service level from a supplier perspective is 'resolution time'. Resolution time means the time from when an incident or problem in relation to the maintenance object is reported to the supplier until the incident or problem is solved. It is essential for the supplier to exclude factors outside the supplier's control affecting the service level results. Common exceptions include errors caused by the customer and errors caused by third party factors.

241. In cases of a service level breach/default, the maintenance contract should also contain adequate remedies. Such remedies can include both financial sanctions and other incentives for the supplier to adhere to the stipulated service levels. Such incentives and sanctions can be parallel and include a right for the customer to: (i) receive liquidated damages (penalties); (ii) price reductions and/or damages; (iii) terminate the contract; and/or (iv) intervene in the service delivery itself or through a third party (step-in). In recent years, however, many outsourcing and sophisticated maintenance contracts have also tried to incorporate pro-active remedy models such as 'balanced scorecards' that connect the service performance with the parties' governance structure by measuring certain key performance indicators. The objective for such models is to identify problems before they have caused a damage or default, rather than only providing compensation in arrears.[479] Another approach

478. See Lindberg & Westman, 481.

479. See Agne Lindberg, Johan Kahn & Björn Krouthén, *IT-avtal – särskilt om outsourcing* (Stockholm: Norstedts Juridik AB, 2009), 119.

is to combine penalties for poor performance with incentives (bonus) in case the quality of the services exceeds the agreed or expected service levels.

242. In conclusion, there are many different types of maintenance contracts and the level of detail and sophistication varies. There is no Swedish legislation which specifically governs maintenance (or any other services in a commercial context), which means that business standards and standard agreements play an important role. For the customer, it is crucial to ensure that the maintenance contract contains adequate service levels and remedies.

Chapter 6. Facilities Management

243. There is no commonly accepted definition of a facilities management contract in Sweden. With regard to ICT contracts, a 'facility' will generally refer to premises, such as a data centre or part thereof (so-called co-location).

244. Transfer and leasing of premises, or space within premises, may be subject to the Swedish Land Code (*Jordabalken (1970:994)*).[480] Transfer of immovable property (real estate) is further subject to certain legal formalities under Swedish law. The purchase contract for such transfer must be in writing and contain the following information:[481]

- the names of the seller and the buyer;
- the name of the real estate as registered with the Swedish Land Registry (*Lantmäteriet*);[482]
- an explicit transfer of the real estate;
- the purchase price.

The transfer will also require registration with the Swedish Land Registry within three months of the execution of the sale.[483] In general, Swedish municipalities may invoke a pre-emption right to any transferred real estate. If such pre-emption right is applicable, it will be necessary to make a notification of pre-emption rights and acquisition permits to the relevant authorities. A transfer of a lease agreement for facilities/real estate will typically require the landlord's consent.

245. With regard to facilities management services, such services will generally be provided by the proprietor of such facility, who in turn may outsource such services to one or several subcontractors. In terms of co-location or storage facilities, perhaps the most important aspects of a facilities management agreement will be network access and capacity of the facilities in terms of cooling and power along with the level of security within the facilities. It is rather common for such agreements to contain strict provisions on the security of the facilities and, for example, explicit wordings to ensure that a supplier of storage facilities is responsible for maintaining a certain level of security within the premises. In some cases, the supplier will be liable for incidents which would normally be considered as force majeure events (such as fire, floods, etc.) to the extent that such incidents could have been avoided by implementing adequate pre-emptive security measures.

---

480. Chapters 7–12 specifically governs leasing of premises (or parts thereof).
481. Chapter 4 Art. 1 Land Code. See also Folke Grauers, *Fastighetsköp* (Lund: Juristförlaget i Lund, 2006), 45.
482. <www.lantmateriet.se/>.
483. Chapter 20 Arts 1 and 2 Land Code.

Chapter 7. Network Services

246. Network services are the foundation of a networked computing environment. Generally, network services are installed on one or more servers to provide shared resources to client computers (LAN,[484] WAN,[485] etc.). Except for the Electronic Communications Act (*Lag (2003:389) om elektronisk kommunikation*), which is the regulatory framework for electronic communications in Sweden, there is no specific legislation regarding the commercial service aspect of Network Services Contracts.

247. The main aspects for the customer in a network services agreement is to ensure a high quality of availability and service, which of course is closely linked to the network capacity of the service provider. Hence, service availability as well as specific service quality criteria will regularly be included in a Service Level Agreement which forms a part of the network services agreement. Fees are usually connected to usage of the network services, and could be based on an hourly, weekly, or monthly basis. Fixed subscription fees, which may include a certain level of usage, are also common. As in the case for other long-term service contracts, incentives in relation to the service levels are a central issue in network services contracts. Such incentives would generally consist of monetary penalties in relation to service level defaults. The main service level is of course availability (uptime) of the service. It should also be noted that network services by their nature are more likely to be affected by force majeure events and that the force majeure clause will need to be carefully designed.

248. Finally, it should be noted that the providers of Network Services mainly rely on their own standard contracts and service levels. In that respect, it can be argued that communication services are more standardized than other deliverables within the ICT industry. Many service providers are very reluctant to negotiate their standard terms.

484. Local area network.
485. Wide area network.

Chapter 8. Government Contracts

249. Depending on the nature of a government contract and its value, such a contract may be subject to EU public procurement directives[486] and the Swedish Public Procurement Act (*Lag (2007:1091) om offentlig upphandling*). If this is the case, the awarding authority may be required to:

- Advertise the contract in the *Official Journal* of the EU and follow special procedures.
- Ensure that all bidders are treated equally.

250. The Public Procurement Act is applicable to the awarding of all contracts that are not expressively excluded from their scope. This means that this legislation will also apply to the awarding of contracts where the contract value does not reach the thresholds for application of the EC public procurement directives. In such cases, however, the rules are less strict than those applicable to contracts which exceed the thresholds. For example, no advertisement in the *Official Journal* is required and advertisement in a publicly accessible database is sufficient.

To the extent that they are applicable, the EU public procurement rules are likely to have a significant impact on the:

- Timing of the pre-contract procedure.
- Award criteria adopted.
- Duration of the government contract.

251. A specific element of government contracts is the fact that the awarding authority will unilaterally, as a part of the tender request information, dictate a large number of the terms and conditions in the contract. The opportunity for suppliers to negotiate such terms in the government contract is often very limited, which means that the supplier must consider whether any legally or commercially unsatisfactory terms should have an impact on the pricing offered in the tender.

486. Directive 2004/17/EC of the European Parliament and of the Council of 31 Mar. 2004 coordinating the procurement procedures of entities operating in the water, energy, transport and postal services sectors; and Directive 2004/18/EC of the European Parliament and of the Council of 31 Mar. 2004 on the coordination of procedures for the award of public works contracts, public supply contracts and public service contracts.

Part IV. Electronic Transactions

Chapter 1. Legal Status of Electronic Transactions

§1. Contracts

252. Swedish contract law builds upon the principles of autonomy of will and freedom of contract. Once a contract is concluded, the principle of *pacta sunt servanda* applies. As common in other jurisdictions, a contract is legally established when a consensus is reached between two parties regarding the essential elements of the contract.[487]

253. Unlike other European civil law countries, such as Germany with its Bürgerliches Gesetzbuch (BGB), Sweden has not codified its civil law, and the statutory provisions dealing with sales of goods and services are spread over several different Acts.

The main statute for Swedish contract law is the Contracts Act (*Lag (1915:218) om avtal och andra rättshandlingar på förmögenhetsrättens område*). It comprises forty-one sections and mainly deals with the formation of a contract, rules on representation, and the grounds for invalidity of certain legal acts. It does not stipulate any rules regarding performance under a contract or remedies for breach of contract. These are to be found in other legislation, such as the Sales of Goods Act (*Köplag (1990:931)*), that deals with delivery of goods, balance of risk, quality of the goods, remedies in the event of delay in delivery or for defective goods (including damages) and remedies for breach of contract by either party.

In addition, the Consumer Sales Act (*Konsumentköplag (1990:932)*), the Consumer Services Act (*Konsumenttjänstlag (1985:716)*) and the Consumer Credit Act (*Konsumentkreditlag (2010:1846)*),[488] as well as the Act on Terms of Contract between Undertakings (*Lag (1984:292) om avtalsvillkor mellan näringsidkare*) and the Act on Terms of Contract in Consumer Relations (*Lag (1994:1512) om särskilda avtalsvillkor i konsumentförhållanden*), cover provisions regarding enforcement of a contract, potentially invalid contract terms and conditions, and other

487. Jan Ramberg & Christina Ramberg, *Allmän avtalsrätt*, 6th edn (Stockholm: Nordstedts Juridik AB, 2002), 101 et seq.

488. The Act transposes Directive 2008/48/EC of the European Parliament and of the Council of 23 Apr. 2008 on credit agreements for consumers and repealing Council Directive 87/102/EEC; and replaced the earlier in force Consumer Credit Act (*Konsumentkreditlag (1992:830)*).

requirements for specific contracts. Although these Acts mainly apply in consumer-business relationships, they often serve as guidelines for interpreting agreements between two businesses as well.

I. Formation of a Contract

254. In general, a contract is legally established when an offer to enter into a contract is accepted by the recipient. In other words, a consensus concerning the essential elements of a contract has to be reached by the contracting parties.

Though section 1 Swedish Contracts Act refers to other ways of concluding a contract ('from any other custom'),[489] the offer-acceptance model is still the prevailing thought on the Swedish market.[490]

255. According to the Contracts Act (section 1), the offer (as well as the acceptance) is binding for the offeror unless otherwise stated, that is the offer cannot be revoked after it has reached the offeree. This general principle (*löftesprincipen*) differs from the principle of contracts only being binding once both parties agree (*kontraktsprincipen*), as applied in the UK or the US.[491]

Offers also have to be distinguished from invitations to tender if they are addressed to a larger group of people. There are no formal requirements on what can constitute an offer; but traditionally, it must contain the object of the contract, as well as quantity and quality of the goods.[492]

The time spans stipulated by law (i.e., if nothing is specified in the offer) can differ depending on the form of the offer. If the offer is made in a letter the offer is binding for a reasonable time, which is 'such period of time as, at the time of the offer, the offeror could reasonably have estimated to be required'. When calculating this time, account should be paid to the message reaching the recipient in due time, leaving reasonable time for consideration for the offeree, and the reply not being delayed.[493] Oral offers must be accepted immediately, unless otherwise specified.[494]

The acceptance must reflect the offer. If it adds, restricts or includes reservations to the original offer, it will be considered a new offer.[495] Traditionally, the acceptance does not have to be explicit or in writing; acceptance by action (*konkludent handlande*) or by performance are considered valid expressions of intent to conclude a contract.

489. Section 1 Contracts Act: 'The provisions of the aforementioned sections shall apply unless the contrary may be inferred from the offer or the reply, from commercial practice, or from any other custom.'
490. Ramberg & Ramberg, 78.
491. In some cases, the principle of contract also applies in Swedish law, for example, for real estate purchases. See Ramberg & Ramberg, 84.
492. Carlson, 224.
493. Section 3 Contracts Act.
494. Section 3 para. 2 Contracts Act.
495. Section 6 Contracts Act.

256. Due to the freedom of contract and the absence of general form requirements (with a few exceptions mentioned below), both emails and any other forms of electronic messages, including SMS and chat messages, have been considered valid offers and acceptances.

II. Grounds for Invalidity

257. Besides typical grounds for invalidity and lack of consent, such as duress,[496] fraud[497] and usury,[498] the Swedish Contracts Act also contains provisions for mistake in section 32. The law distinguishes between mistakes concerning the content of an offer or an acceptance (paragraph 1, *förklaringsmisstag*) and mistakes in the transmission of the offer or acceptance (paragraph 2, *befordringsfel*). In both cases, the mistakes only result in invalidity if the other party realized or should have realized the mistake. In other words, even if a mistake occurred the sender is still bound by it if the receiver acted in good faith.

Both types of mistake have been discussed with regards to electronic messages. In relation to mistakes in transmissions, the law refers to the situation that, where a statement of intent which has been forwarded by telegram or transmitted orally through a messenger, has been distorted due to a telegraphic error or an inaccurate rendition by the messenger. It is questionable if electronic messages can be distorted during the transmission without the receiver noticing; for example, most mistakes will render the message completely unreadable, so it only consists of strings of symbols. In addition, distortions in the sender's or receiver's electronic device do not constitute errors in transmission. For these reasons, the application of section 32 paragraph 2 for electronic transactions is probably limited.[499]

Mistakes about the content of an expression are, however, possible when it comes to electronic messages, so the general rule of section 32 paragraph 2 Swedish Contracts Act applies, binding the sender to her or his statement unless the receiver noticed or should have noticed the mistake.

258. In this regard, one can also discuss Article 11(2) Directive on electronic commerce, which stipulates an obligation for service providers to make available 'appropriate, effective and accessible technical' measures that allow the user 'to identify and correct input errors, prior to the placing of the order'. It can be argued that this could lead to users not being bound by input errors and mistakes when ordering if the service provider did not introduce appropriate technical means to correct them.[500] This potential effect of Article 11 was, however, not taken into consideration when transposing the Directive on e-commerce; and sanctions are

496. Sections 28 and 29 Contracts Act.
497. Section 30 Contracts Act.
498. Section 31 Contracts Act.
499. See Ramberg & Ramberg, 125; and Christina Hultmark, *Elektronisk handel och avtalsrätt* (Stockholm: Norstedts Juridik, 1997), 56.
500. Ramberg & Ramberg, 122; Christina Hultmark Ramberg, 'The E-commerce Directive and Formation of Contract in a Comparative Perspective', *European Law Review* 26(5) (2001): 429–450.

restricted to orders by the Market Court (*Marknadsdomstolen*), and do not include any effects from a civil law point of view.

III. Form Requirements

259. In general, Swedish contract law does not stipulate any form requirements in order for contracts to gain legal effect. Corresponding expressions of intent are, in other words, sufficient for the conclusion of a contract. There are, however, two exceptions to this rule. First, the parties can agree on certain form requirements and second, the law may stipulate a specific form, such as for real estate agreements as well as within the field of family law. The difference between the two exceptions lies in the fact that the latter requirements are mandatory, and cannot be disregarded by the parties, whereas the former are part of the freedom of contract principle.[501]

260. The two main form requirements include a document having to be in writing and/or requiring a signature. The legal effects of a missing form requirement can range from invalidity of the contract or an obligation for one party to fulfil the requirement, to invalidity against third parties (e.g., the creditor, authorities, etc.).[502]

261. As the Directive on electronic commerce allows for exceptions regarding contracts that create or transfer rights in real estate, though not counting rental rights,[503] the Swedish legislator decided not to remove form requirements for the purchase of real property. Therefore Chapter 4 section 1 Land Code (*Jordabalken (1970:994)*) still requires the 'drawing up of a document of purchase signed by the seller and buyer'.

In addition, Sweden did not change the form requirements regarding the purchase of tenant-ownership apartments (*bostadsrätter*)[504] nor regarding time-shared real property. As the regulation on rental contracts does not explicitly stipulate that a document has to be in writing,[505] no change was made to Chapter 12 section 2 Land Code (*Jordabalken*) in this regard.

262. When transposing the Directive on electronic commerce, Sweden changed the rules for consumer credits, which required the credit agreement to be in writing and signed by the consumer.[506] It allowed for advanced electronic signatures in accordance with section 2 Act on Qualified Electronic Signatures (*Lag (2000:832) om kvalificerade elektroniska signaturer*).[507] With the latest amendments to the

501. Ramberg & Ramberg, 125 et seq.
502. Ramberg & Ramberg, 125 et seq.
503. Article 9(2) point a Directive on electronic commerce.
504. The Swedish system of ownership of apartments is mainly built upon housing cooperatives (*bostadsrättsföreningar*), and the fact that individuals own a right to inhabit an apartment for an unlimited time, as members of the cooperative.
505. A tenancy agreement shall be drawn up in writing *if* the landlord or tenant so requests.
506. Section 9 Consumer Credit Act.
507. See more on electronic signatures in Ch. 2 *infra*.

Consumer Credit Act, however, any formal requirements have been taken away[508] In other words, no signature is required anymore, consumer credit contracts only have to be documented and contain the information required by the Consumer Rights Directive. According to section 8 Consumer Credit Act, the information has to be provided in the standardized European consumer credit form.

The other statute amended with regards to its form requirements was the Financial Instruments Trading Act (*Lag (1991:980) om handel med finansiella instrument*). Its Chapter 3 section 1 was clarified to the extent that 'written' now entails a document, which is accessible to the parties in a readable and lasting format.

263. The Swedish legislator as well as legal academia distinguish between the form requirements of 'written form' and 'handwritten signature'. 'Written' can, at least in the majority of cases, include electronic documents and therefore the term would be equivalent to non-oral expression of intent, instead of the opposite of paper.[509] The reasons for the form requirements have, however, to be taken into consideration.[510] If a paper document is needed in order to secure evidence or if the form requirement stems from traditions and historical reasons, electronic means might not be possible. The term 'handwritten signature', however, will in most cases require some sort of physical signing, and therefore exclude electronic signatures. Again, this will depend on the reason behind the requirement,[511] for example the presence of witnesses for somebody's last will.

Swedish law requires handwritten signatures on very few occasions.[512] Examples include the already above stated real estate contracts,[513] transfer of the dwelling in owner-occupied housing associations,[514] and family related legal matters, such as pre-marital agreements,[515] and last wills.[516] In these examples, electronic means will not be possible, unless explicitly stated in the Act.

IV. Electronic Contracts

264. Sweden does not have any specific legislation for contracts that are concluded via electronic means. The Swedish Contracts Act applies to contracts in general, irrelevant of the means of transmission. All types of contracts are therefore

508. Government Bill (Proposition) 2009/10:242, 'Ny konsumentkreditlag', 60.
509. Ministry Publications Series (Ds) 2001:13, 'E-handelsdirektivet – genomförande av direktivet 2000/31/EG om vissa rättsliga aspekter på informationssamhällets tjänster', 104–105; Ministry Publications Series (Ds) 2003:29, 'FORMEL – Formkrav och elektronisk kommunikation', 12.
510. Agne Lindberg & Daniel Westman, *Praktisk IT-rätt*, 3rd edn (Stockholm: Norstedts Juridik AB, 2001), 76.
511. Ministry Publications Series (Ds) 2003:29, 88.
512. Government Bill (Proposition) 2001/02:150, 'Lag om elektronisk handel och andra informationssamhällets tjänster, m.m.', 78; Ministry Publications Series (Ds) 2001:13, 103; Ramberg & Ramberg, 130.
513. Chapter 4 s. 1 Land Code.
514. Chapter 6 s. 4 Act on Owner-occupied housing (*Bostadsrättslag (1991:614)*).
515. Chapter 7 s. 3 Marriage Code (*Äktenskapsbalk (1987:230)*).
516. Chapter 10 s. 1 Inheritance Code (*Ärvdabalk (1958:637)*).

binding, no matter whether they are concluded orally, in writing, on paper or via electronic messages.[517]

Also the previously mentioned Consumer Sales Act, Consumer Services Act and Consumer Credit Act, as well as the Act on Terms of Contract between Undertakings and the Act on Terms of Contract in Consumer Relations apply to all types of contracts, irrespective of how they are concluded, orally, in paper or by any electronic means, and there is no specific regulation which applies purely to electronic contracts.

265. Article 9 Directive on electronic commerce obliges all Member States to 'ensure that their legal system allows contracts to be concluded by electronic means'. In particular this means to 'ensure that the legal requirements applicable to the contractual process neither create obstacles for the use of electronic contracts nor result in such contracts being deprived of legal effectiveness and validity on account of their having been made by electronic means'.

As the Swedish legal system only stipulates form requirements in a limited number of situations, Article 9 did not lead to any major changes in Swedish contract law. In the Government Bill leading to the implementation of the Electronic Commerce Act,[518] the Government suggested that the requirement of 'in writing' mainly means 'not orally' and that the contract has to be in some sort of 'permanent and readable format'.

§2. Electronic Documents

I. General Framework

266. A report by the Swedish Ministry of Finance and the Government Offices from 2003 dealt with the question of the legal recognition of electronic documents. The report included a review of about approximately 2000 statutes in all areas of law, and investigated to what extent electronic documents were explicitly mentioned or excluded due to certain requirements.[519]

One of the conclusions of the report was that the majority of the statutes (around 1200) do not prevent electronic means, as certain terms and definitions do not per se exclude the use of electronic means. For example, the terms *application, registration, message, request* are not equivalent to paper documents and therefore allow for electronic means.

Around 190 of the statutes were considered to contain potential obstacles to electronic means, and therefore require amendments in order to allow for a technological neutral application. The remainder of the Swedish laws do not require any changes at the moment.

517. Government Bill (Proposition) 2001/02:150, 37–38.
518. Government Bill (Proposition) 2001/02:150, 37–38.
519. Ministry Publications Series (Ds) 2003:29.

267. The report also concluded that the introduction of a general rule stipulating the legal effectiveness of electronic documents or their equivalency to paper-based documents was not to be recommended, as it would lead to more confusion. By not specifically mentioning electronic means, the implication could then be that they are not admissible.[520]

267.1. Swedish public authorities are, in fact, encouraged to promote the use of secure and efficient electronic exchange of information among public administrations.[521] Larger agencies are even expected to handle orders of goods and services electronically.[522] The authority overseeing the financial activities of public authorities – the Swedish National Financial Management Authority (*Ekonomistyrningsverket*)[523] – has issued complementary guidelines on the information exchange between public agencies.[524]

II. Electronic Invoicing

268. A specific type of electronic documents, namely electronic invoices, has been used in Swedish businesses for a long time.[525] The techniques being used include EDI-invoice,[526] e-invoice, self-billing, invoice-files via email, online services (web-EDI, etc.) and scanning of paper invoices.[527] Standard contracts are mainly used in order to ensure interoperability between the computer system of the seller and that of the buyer.

The legal framework that applies to invoices, both electronic and paper-based, and accounting in general includes the Swedish Bookkeeping Act (*Bokföringslag (1999:1078)*), the Swedish Companies Act (*Aktiebolagslag (2005:551)*), the VAT Act (*Mervärdeskattelag (1994:200)*) and the Tax Procedure Act (*Skatteförfarandelag (2011:1244)*).[528]

269. Chapter 7 Swedish Bookkeeping Act deals with the archiving of accounting information, including electronic invoices. According to Chapter 7 section 1, accounting information shall be archived either:

520. Ministry Publications Series (Ds) 2003:29, 43.
521. Section 2 Ordinance on the Electronic Information Exchange by Public Authorities (*Förordning (2003:770) om statliga myndigheters elektroniska informationsutbyte*).
522. Section 3 Ordinance.
523. <www.esv.se>.
524. Ekonomistyrningsverkets föreskrifter och allmänna råd till förordningen (2003:770) om statliga myndigheters elektroniska informationsutbyte, 8 Nov. 2012.
525. In 2013 22 % of companies with more than ten employees sent e-invoices that could be automatically processed by the receiver; see Statistics Sweden (SCB), 'ICT usage in enterprises 2013', <www.scb.se/Statistik/_Publikationer/NV0116_2013A01_BR_IT02BR1401.pdf>.
526. EDI stands for Electronic Data Interchange.
527. The Swedish Alliance for Electronic Business (*Nätverket för Elektroniska Affärer*/NEA), 'Report on electronic invoices (GEAs rapport Elektroniska fakturor)', Oktober 2006, <www.nea.nu>. See also 'Good Practices in the adoption and promotion of e-invoicing in Europe: An ACCA Discussion Paper', prepared for Activity Group 2 of the European Multistakeholder Forum on e-invoicing, August 2012, www.nea.nu/wp-content/uploads/2013/09/Activity-2-Consultation-Report1.pdf>, 13.
528. The Act replaced the previously in force Tax Payment Act (*Skattebetalningslag (1997:483)*).

(1) in normal readable format (document);
(2) in micro format; or
(3) in any other form that can be read, listened to or otherwise comprehended only using technical aids.

According to Chapter 7 section 2 Bookkeeping Act, accounting information shall be stored for seven years. Computer equipment that is necessary in order to retrieve this accounting information shall be accessible in Sweden during this time.

In 2012, the VAT Act was amended to include archiving provisions for invoices in general, including electronic invoices. According to the new Chapter 11a VAT Act the authenticity of the invoice as well as the integrity of the content have to be ensured during the period it is stored (section 2). In addition, the invoice has to be readable during this time. According to Chapter 11a section 2 the term authenticity refers to ensuring the identity of the supplier, the service provider or the issuer of the invoice.

270. The Directive 2001/115/EC amending Directive 77/388/EEC with a view to simplifying, modernizing and harmonizing the conditions laid down for invoicing in respect of value added tax (hereinafter 'Directive on electronic invoices') was transposed into Swedish national law in 2003 by amending the Bookkeeping Act, the VAT Act and the previous in force Tax Payment Act. Council Directive 2006/112/EC of 28 November 2006 on the common system of value added tax was transposed into Swedish law in 2007 by amending the VAT Act and the Tax Procedure Act. The latest amendment to the Directive – Council Directive 2010/45/EU of 13 July 2010 amending Directive 2006/112/EC on the common system of value added tax as regards the rules on invoicing – has to this date not been transposed explicitly into Swedish law.

Following the 2003 amendments, a new section 17a was introduced in Chapter 1 of the VAT Act defining the term 'transmission of invoices or other documents electronically' which correlates with Article 2(2) point (e) Directive on electronic invoices. This provision was amended in 2012 and now defines electronic invoices as invoices that are 'issued and received in an electronic format'. The VAT Act also includes a provision that electronic invoices only may be issued if the receiver has approved it.[529]

The VAT Act does not state any additional requirements regarding invoices that are being sent electronically. This means that even other methods than advanced electronic signatures and EDI are accepted from a security point of view.[530]

In 2012 a provision was introduced in the VAT Act that allows public authorities in another EU Member State immediate electronic access to invoices stored by a business if the VAT has to be paid in that country (Chapter 11a section 3).[531]

529. Chapter 11 s. 6 VAT Act.
530. Report on electronic invoices, 55–56.
531. See also Government Bill (Proposition) 2011/12:94, 'Nya faktureringsregler för mervärdeskatt m.m.', 1.

270.1. The legal framework with regards to electronic invoices seems rather undisputed at this stage. The discussions rather circuit about which standards should be used for electronic invoices. The Swedish Alliance for Electronic Business (*Nätverket för Elektroniska Affärer*/NEA), the Swedish National Board of Trade (*Kommerskollegium*)[532] as well as the Swedish Banker's Association (*Svenska Bankföreningen*)[533] are all involved in different initiatives. At the moment, many standards are based on EDI, e.g., UN/EDIFACT standard messages, and XML at the moment.[534]

270.2. Swedish public authorities are expected to use electronic invoicing according to section 21f Regulation on Public Authorities' Accounting (*Förordning (2000:606) om myndigheters bokföring*). The standard that is mainly used for e-invoices by public authorities is Svefaktura, developed by Single Face To Industry (SFTI), a forum that is lead by Swedish Association of Local Authorities and Regions (SALAR) (*Sveriges Kommuner och Landsting – SKL*).

§3. Evidence

271. In Swedish law, there are no exclusionary rules regarding evidence.[535] Any evidence is therefore admissible in court.[536] The procedural law rules are laid down in the Swedish Code of Judicial Procedure (*Rättegångsbalk (1942:740)*), which covers both criminal and civil procedural law.

In accordance with this principle, proving that a contract exists can be done in any possible way, with the exception of contracts that require a certain form. The burden of proof is usually placed on the party that has the best possibility to secure the evidence.[537]

532. <www.kommers.se>.
533. www.swedishbankers.se. In Sweden many B2C services regarding electronic invoices are provided by banks; see Good Practices in the adoption and promotion of e-invoicing in Europe: An ACCA Discussion Paper, 20.
534. 'Good Practices in the adoption and promotion of e-invoicing in Europe: An ACCA Discussion Paper', 22 and 24.
535. Chapter 35 s. 1 Code of Judicial Procedure (*Rättegångsbalk (1942:740)*).
536. Carlson, 230.
537. Hultmark, 87 et seq.

Chapter 2. Regulation of Electronic Signatures and Certification Services

§1. LEGISLATIVE FRAMEWORK

I. General Statement

272. Directive 1999/93/EC of 13 December 1999 on a Community framework for electronic signatures (hereinafter 'Directive on electronic signatures') was transposed into Swedish legislation through the Act on Qualified Electronic Signatures (*Lag (2000:832) om kvalificerade elektroniska signaturer*). As the Act mainly stipulates rules regarding certificate providers established in Sweden and issuance of qualified certificates to the public, it was suggested that 'qualified' be included in its name.[538]

The Directive further led to the enactment of the Ordinance on Qualified Electronic Signatures (*Förordning (2000:833) om kvalificerade electroniska signaturer*) and the Ordinance on the financing of the National Post and Telecom's operations (*Förordning (2003:767) om finansiering av Post- och telestyrelsens verksamhet*). In addition, the rules by the supervisory authority are of importance, for example, the Post and Telecom Agency's regulations on fees (*Post- och telestyrelsens föreskrifter om avgifter; PTSFS 2011:6*).

II. Definitions

273. Swedish legislation does not reflect the Directive's definition[539] of electronic signatures word-for-word. Rather, a Swedish electronic signature includes both authentication and integrity requirements. An electronic signature is defined, in section 2 Act on Qualified Electronic Signatures, as 'data in electronic form attached to or logically associated with other electronic data, and used to verify that the content originates from the alleged issuer, and has not been altered'. The definition thus includes not only the authentication aspect, but also an integrity requirement.

In addition, it should be mentioned that the notion of an electronic signature has two implications, a technical one focused on electronic signatures as a technology to ensure information security (especially safeguarding integrity and authenticity of signed data) and a legal one, trying to ensure the equality of electronic signatures with handwritten signatures.[540]

---

538. Government Bill (Proposition) 1999/2000:117, 'Lag om kvalificerade elektroniska signaturer, m.m.', 34.
539. Article 2(1): electronic signature 'means data in electronic form which are attached to or logically associated with other electronic data and which serve as a method of authentication'.
540. Cecilia Magnusson Sjöberg & Anna Nordén, *Managing Electronic Signatures: Current Challenges*, Scandinavian Studies in Law, vol. 47 (IT Law) (Stockholm: Stockholm Institute for Scandinavian Law, 2004), 83.

274. Another slight difference is the definition of a signatory. According to Article 2(3) Directive on electronic signatures, signatory means 'a person who holds a signature creation device and acts either on her or his own behalf or on behalf of the natural or legal person or entity she or he represents'. The Swedish Act defines a signatory as 'a natural person who is authorized to control a signature creation device'. According to the preparatory works, the reason for this was that acting on behalf of another natural or a legal person is part of general private law rules and therefore does not need to be mentioned specifically.[541]

As in the Directive, 'Signature creation data' ('unique data, such as codes or secret cryptographic keys, used to create an electronic signature') means the secret/private key, while 'signature verification data' ('data, such as codes or open cryptographic keys, used to verify an electronic signature') refers to the public key.

275. The definitions for advanced and qualified electronic signatures in the Swedish Act are also based on the definitions and requirements of the Directive. An advanced electronic signature is therefore 'an electronic signature' that:

(a) is uniquely linked to a signatory;
(b) is capable of identifying the signatory;
(c) is created using means that are under the signatory's sole control; and
(d) is linked to other electronic data in such a way that any alteration to the said data can be detected.

Whereas, a qualified electronic signature is defined as 'an advanced electronic signature based on a qualified certificate and created by a secure signature creation device'.[542]

As mentioned above, some legislation might allow for electronic means or electronic signatures in general, some might stipulate the use of a specific type of electronic signature, though the latter is less common.[543]

§2. Electronic Identification

276. There is no specific legislation that describes the basic requirements for electronic identifications (eIDs) in Sweden. The Act on Qualified Electronic Signatures deals with electronic signatures in general and makes no specific reference to eIDs. Regulations by authorities concerning the provided e-services refer in many cases to the use of an eID, but without defining any eID requirements.

The reason for the lack of a definition for eIDs in Swedish laws and regulations is that traditionally, Swedish eIDs have been issued by the private sector, mainly

541. Government Bill (Proposition) 1999/2000:117, 40.
542. Section 2 Act on Qualified Electronic Signatures.
543. See Ch. 1 s. 1 III *supra* (para. 262).

banking institutions and electronic communications providers.[544] Until 2011, eIDs were selected in a public procurement process, organized by the Swedish Legal, Financial and Administrative Services Agency (*Kammarkollegiet*).[545]

In 2011 the Swedish eIdentification Board (*E-legitimationsnämnden*)[546] was established as an authority under the Swedish Ministry of Enterprise, Energy and Communications.[547] Its task is to promote and coordinate electronic identification and electronic signatures for e-services provided by the public sector. The eIdentification Board has issued a regulatory framework that describes the identify federation and technical specifications for eIDs in Sweden.[548] The goal is, *inter alia*, to develop a new infrastructure for eIDs in Sweden, and introduce a standardized identity assertion (based on the SAML standard). As the EU framework STORK[549] is also based on SAML, this development should increase cross-border interoperability.

277. Any physical person with a Swedish personal identity number can obtain an eID. Legal persons can also use an eID, but it must be linked to a user with a Swedish personal identity number. Currently a legal person as such cannot have an eID, but the plan is to offer companies the possibility to apply for eIDs for their employees – 'employment eIDs' (*e-tjänstelegitimation*).[550] 'Employment eIDs' have been used within the public sector for a while, for example, SITHS is a smart card solution with the Swedish health care sector.[551]

§3. Certificates

278. As the Directive, the Swedish Act on Qualified Electronic Signatures builds upon a Public Key Infrastructure (PKI) with the use of private and public keys and certificates issued by trusted third parties confirming the electronic signature user.

---

544. Despite or because of this over 4 million out of 9 million citizens have an e-id and made over 250 million transactions in numerous private and public e-services during 2011. One of the largest providers of eIDs in Sweden, BankID (<bankid.com/>), also offers eIDs on mobile devices.
545. The Swedish Legal, Financial and Administrative Services Agency (*Kammarkollegiet*) is the responsible authority for the public procurement, see <www.kammarkollegiet.se>.
546. <www.elegnamnden.se/>.
547. Ordinance with Instructions for the eIdentification Board (*Förordning (2010:1497) med instruktion för E-legitimationsnämnden*).
548. <www.elegnamnden.se/regelverket11.4.77dbcb041438070e039a8b6.html>, 5 Apr. 2014.
549. STORK stands for Secure idenTity acrOss boRders linKed and aims at establishing a European eID Interoperability Platform that will allow citizens to establish e-relations across borders, just by using their national eID; <www.eid-stork.eu>.
550. See Government Official Report SOU 2010:104, 'E-legitimationsnämnden och Svensk e-legitimation', 26.
551. SITHS (*Nationell identifieringstjänst*) is a national security solution for electronic identification and secure communication of information. The company Inera (<inera.se>), owned by the Swedish county councils, is responsible for the implementation. See more at <www.inera.se/TJANSTER--PROJEKT/SITHS/>, 5 Apr. 2014.

In accordance with Article 2(9) Directive on electronic signatures,[552] section 2 Act on Qualified Electronic Signatures defines a certificate as 'an attestation in electronic form that links signature verification data to a signatory and confirms the said signatory's identity'.

279. In order to be called qualified, a certificate must fulfil certain conditions.[553] The requirements from Annex I of the Directive are also stated in the Swedish Act, sections 6 and 7. According to section 6, 'a certificate shall be issued for a specific period of validity by a certificate provider that meets the requirements set forth in sections 9–12' and shall contain:

(1) an indication that the certificate has been issued as a qualified certificate;
(2) the name and address of the certificate provider, and information regarding the state in which it is established;
(3) the name of the signatory, or a pseudonym which shall be identified as such;
(4) special information regarding the signatory if that information is relevant to the purpose for which the certificate is intended;
(5) signature verification data that corresponds to the signature creation data under the control of the signatory at the time of issue;
(6) information regarding the period of validity of the certificate;
(7) the identity code of the certificate;
(8) the advanced electronic signature of the certificate provider, or an electronic signature with an equivalent level of security; and
(9) an indication of any limitations on the use of the certificate, or of any limits on the value of transactions for which the certificate can be used (transaction limit).

In addition, section 7 establishes the requirements for certificate providers that are not established in Sweden. In this case, a certificate, which meets the conditions of points (1)–(9) above, shall be deemed to be qualified if:

(1) the certificate provider is established in another state within the EEA, and is permitted to issue qualified certificates there;
(2) the certificate provider satisfies requirements equivalent to those contained in sections 9–12 and the regulations issued under section 13, and is accredited in another state belonging to the EEA; or
(3) the certificate is guaranteed as being qualified by a certificate provider referred to in point (1) or the first clause of section 6.

Section 6 paragraph 1 transposes Article 2(10) as well as Annex I of the Directive into Swedish law. Section 7 implements Article 4(1) as well as Article 7(1) Directive on electronic signatures, and stipulates that certificates issued in another EEA country are to be considered qualified, if they meet the requirements of section 6 paragraph 1.

552. Certificate 'means an electronic attestation which links signature-verification data to a person and confirms the identity of that person'.
553. Section 2 Act on Qualified Electronic Signatures.

280. As the task of a certificate provider as a trusted third party is to confirm that the signature verification data belongs to a certain signatory, the certificate provider has to meet certain requirements in order to prove its trustworthiness. The conditions of the Directive were transposed into Swedish law without further amendments and are stipulated in sections 9–12. These conditions are, *inter alia*, that the certificate provider has to conduct its operations in a reliable manner, and shall:

(1) employ personnel who possess the expert knowledge and experience required for these operations, especially with regard to management, technology and security procedures;
(2) apply such administrative and management routines that conform to recognized standards;
(3) use trustworthy systems and products that are protected against modification, and which ensure technical and cryptographic security;
(4) maintain sufficient financial resources to conduct its operations in accordance with the provisions set forth in this Act, and bear the risk of liability for damages;
(5) have secure routines to verify the identity of those signatories to whom qualified certificates are issued;
(6) maintain a prompt and secure system for the registration and immediate revocation of qualified certificates; and
(7) take measures against forgery of qualified certificates and, where applicable, guarantee full confidentiality during the process of generating signature creation data (section 9).

Section 9 implements Article 2(10) as well as Article 3(5) Directive on electronic signatures, and points a, b, d, e, f, g, h, and j in Annex II of the Directive.

Section 10, transposing point c in Annex II of the Directive as well as Article 6(1) point c and Article 6(2), states that a certificate provider that issues qualified certificates to the public shall:

(1) immediately revoke a certificate at the request of the signatory, or where there are other grounds for doing so;
(2) ensure that the date and time when the certificate is issued or revoked can be determined precisely; and
(3) ensure that the signature creation data and the signature verification data generated by the certificate provider can be used in a coordinated manner.

281. Section 11 concerns a duty for certificate providers to keep a record of certain 'relevant information concerning the certificates for a reasonable period, depending on the type of certificate and other circumstances', and thereby transposes points i, j and l of Annex II of the Directive. Certificate providers are, however, not allowed to 'store or copy signature creation data'.

Lastly, Section 12 states certain obligations regarding what information has to be provided to the signatory, at least in electronic form. It implements point k of Annex II of the Directive and mentions:

(1) limitations and other conditions for the use of the certificate;
(2) the existence of a voluntary accreditation or certification scheme pursuant to the Act on Accreditation and Technical Conformity Assessment (*Lag (2011:791) om ackreditering och teknisk kontroll*);[554] and
(3) procedures for complaints and dispute settlements.

There is no approval process, but certificate providers must notify the supervisory authority before they initiate their services or operations.[555] Additional requirements may be issued by the supervisory authority according to section 13 Act on Qualified Electronic Signatures.

282. In accordance with the Directive,[556] Sweden introduced a voluntary accreditation scheme for certification bodies. The existing Technical Conformity Assessment Act (*Lag (1992:1119) om teknisk kontroll*) already established a framework for a voluntary accreditation scheme. Accreditation is seen as a tool to create trust in the services that accredited bodies provide, which in turn creates trust in the certificates themselves, especially in an international context.[557] The 1992 Act was replaced in 2011 by the Act on Accreditation and Technical Conformity Assessment (*Lag (2011:791) om ackreditering och teknisk kontroll*).[558] Either of the Acts does, however, explicitly refer to electronic signatures.

283. SignGuard Europe AB[559] was the first Swedish company to offer qualified electronic signatures to public authorities and private companies. In accordance with section 8 Swedish Act on Qualified Electronic Signatures, SignGuard is registered with the PTS.[560] In the last years, two more organizations joined: the company Comfact AB,[561] and Myndighets CA,[562] which is a CA for Swedish government authorities.

554. And pursuant to Regulation (EC) No 765/2008 of the European Parliament and of the Council of 9 Jul. 2008 setting out the requirements for accreditation and market surveillance relating to the marketing of products and repealing Regulation (EEC) No 339/93.
555. Section 8 Act on Qualified Electronic Signatures.
556. Article 3(2): 'Without prejudice to the provisions of paragraph 1, Member States may introduce or maintain voluntary accreditation schemes aiming at enhanced levels of certification-service provision. All conditions related to such schemes must be objective, transparent, proportionate and non-discriminatory.'
557. Government Bill (Proposition) 1999/2000:117, 45.
558. According to its s. 1 the Act complements Regulation (EC) No 765/2008 of the European Parliament and of the Council of 9 Jul. 2008.
559. <www.signguard.se>.
560. See for a list <www.pts.se/sv/Bransch/Internet/Elektroniska-signaturer>, 5 Apr. 2014.
561. <comfact.com>.
562. Among others, employees from the Swedish Pensions Agency, Swedish Social Insurance, Swedish Enforcement Authority and Tax Agencies are using this CA and end users certificates which conform to ETSI TS 102 042 NCP+; <www.myndighetsca.se>.

§4. SUPERVISION

284. The preparatory works discussed the question of supervision with regards to electronic signatures and decided to implement a system of supervision under governmental power, where control is market oriented and does not entail burdensome administration for the providers of electronic signatures.[563] The supervisory authority should first of all control the issuers of qualified certificates and also intervene in cases where issuers wrongly describe their certificates as qualified, as well as control the market for secure-signature-creation devices.

According to section 18 Act on Qualified Electronic Signatures, the 'supervisory authority shall supervise the compliance with this Act and the regulations issued based on the Act. The supervisory authority shall also keep and make public a list of the certificate providers that have provided notification pursuant to section 8, and that issue qualified certificates pursuant to this Act'.

285. The PTS was chosen as the National Regulatory Authority, as stipulated in section 2 Ordinance on Qualified Electronic Signatures (*Förordning (2000:833) om kvalificerade electroniska signaturer*).

All certificate service providers who plan to issue qualified certificates have to submit an application to PTS. As mentioned above, accreditation is voluntary, so there is no approval process, however, the notification to PTS is mandatory.[564]

§5. LEGAL RECOGNITION

I. General Recognition by Law

286. As mentioned above, Swedish private law contains relatively few rules on form requirements, especially regarding rules requiring a signature. The fact that a signature can have significance as evidence to support a certain statement should of course be taken into consideration; however, in Swedish law, signatures are rarely mentioned as a form requirement in order for a statement to receive legal recognition.

Instead of being a legal requirement, signatures have become important from a practical point of view within everyday life for both individuals and businesses. Signing has become an established method for confirmation, control and proof of any statement. In this regard, Chapter 15 section 13 Swedish Penal Code (*Brottsbalk (1962:700)*) should be mentioned, stating:

> A person who denies her or his signature on a document, shall, if the act jeopardises proof, be sentenced for denial of signature to a fine or imprisonment for at most six months or, if the crime is gross, imprisonment for at most two years.

563. Government Bill (Proposition) 1999/2000:117, 60.
564. Section 8 Act on Qualified Electronic Signatures.

In other words, non-repudiation, as one of the purposes of a signature, is, in the context of evidence, punishable by criminal law.

287. In transposing Article 5(1) point a Directive on electronic signatures, stating that Member States shall ensure that qualified electronic signature 'satisfy the legal requirements of a signature in relation to data in electronic form in the same manner as a handwritten signature satisfies those requirements in relation to paper-based data', Sweden implemented section 17 Act on Qualified Electronic Signatures:

> If a requirement of a handwritten signature or its equivalent, contained in a law or regulation may be satisfied by electronic means, a qualified electronic signature shall be deemed to fulfil this requirement. However, in communication with or between government authorities, the use of electronic signatures may be subject to additional requirements.

It was, however, not considered appropriate to introduce a general rule that gives electronic signatures the same legal value as handwritten signatures.[565] Section 17 explicitly states that if a requirement of a handwritten signature may be fulfilled by electronic means, a qualified signature will always meet this requirement. This rule does, however, not prevent other types of electronic signatures with a lower level of security, such as advanced or 'normal' electronic signatures from being accepted by law or business practice.[566]

Section 17 also allows for the origin of the electronic signature to be questioned, that is, whether the right person signed a specific document. As for handwritten signatures, the origin can always be questioned if there is reason to doubt it.[567]

288. The explicit reference to communications with or between public administrations in section 17 allows for specific form requirements with regards to electronic signatures. Examples for this include the regulations of the National Tax Agency (*Skatteverket*) and the Social Insurance Agency (*Försäkringskassan*) where an explicit reference is made to eIDs and not only to electronic signatures in general, for example Regulation SKVFS 2009:8 by the Swedish National Tax Agency (*Skatteverkets föreskrifter om e-tjänsten Inkomstdeklaration*).

II. Evidence Value

289. Even in situations where a signature is not required by law, it can have significance with regards to proof. Signing a document can mean that a specific person is the signer and has approved the terms and conditions of the written contract.

565. Government Bill (Proposition) 1999/2000:117, 58.
566. *Ibid.*
567. *Ibid.*

Swedish law, as mentioned previously, has no exclusionary rules regarding evidence. This principle means on one hand that all sorts of sources can be used as evidence in a court trial, and on the other hand that the judge is not bound by any legal rules when it comes to evaluating the evidence and its weight. In other words, electronic signatures or any other electronic documents can be used as evidence in Swedish courts.[568] This also means that Article 5(1) point b Directive on electronic signatures requiring Member States to ensure that qualified electronic signatures 'are admissible as evidence in legal proceedings' did not need specific legislative measures in Sweden. The same applies for Article 5(2) stipulating that electronic signatures should not be 'denied legal effectiveness and admissibility as evidence in legal proceedings'.[569]

290. One rule that does exist, however, both in statute and case law is burden of proof. Even though there is no statutory rule regarding the situation where somebody denies having signed a contract and claiming that the signature is a forgery, the Swedish Supreme Court has established some guidelines in a case from 1976.[570] According to this decision, if a party claims not to have signed a document, the other party has to prove that the signature is not a forgery. If one party claims, however, that although the signature is genuine (i.e., not a forgery), the content was changed, it is that party who has to prove any change in the document content.

291. The Governmental report preceding the bill[571] stated that admissibility of evidence should never be restricted and there should be no special rules when it comes to electronic evidence as opposed to any other sort of evidence. Neither should there be any specific rules concerning burden of proof when it comes to electronic evidence.

§6. Damages

292. In a PKI system, there are three possibilities of liability, which are given below:

(1) the liability of the signatory, if the signature is used by an unauthorized person;
(2) the liability of the certificate provider towards the signatory;
(3) the liability of the certificate provider towards the receiver of the signature.[572]

Section 14 Swedish Act on Qualified Electronic Signatures transposes Article 6 Directive on electronic signatures and only applies to qualified certificates. According to the rule, 'a certificate provider issuing certificates declared to be qualified to

568. Government Bill (Proposition) 1999/2000:117, 17.
569. *Ibid.*
570. Decision by Supreme Court from 3 Dec. 1976, NJA 1976 s. 667.
571. Ministry Publications Series (Ds) 1998:14, 'Digitala signaturer – en teknisk och juridisk översikt'.
572. Government Bill (Proposition) 1999/2000:117, 48.

the public is liable for damages for any injury or loss caused to anyone relying on such a certificate, due to:

(1) the certificate provider not having fulfilled the requirements set forth in section 10;
(2) the certificate provider not having fulfilled the requirements set forth in the first clause of section 6; or
(3) the certificate, when issued, having contained incorrect information.

'The certificate provider, however, is not liable to pay damages if the provider can show that the injury or loss was not caused by the negligence of the certificate provider.' According to section 14, the certificate provider can limit its liability if this is clearly stated in the certificate.

Section 14 mainly focuses on the liability of the certificate provider towards the receiver of the signature, but also covers to some extent liability of the certificate provider towards the signatory. All possible other relations of liability for damages are not covered by the Swedish Act, but by general rules on damages in tort law.[573]

573. *Ibid.*, 75.

Chapter 3. Legal Aspects of Electronic Banking

§1. General Legal Framework

I. General Statement

293. The Swedish banking system is not covered by a single payment systems Act. Instead, there are a number of separate Acts forming the legal framework for the payment and settlement systems infrastructure.[574]

Chapter 9 Article 13 Instrument of Government appoints the Riksbank as the central bank of Sweden that is responsible for the monetary policy, and has the sole right to issue coinage and banknotes. The Swedish Riksbank Act (*Lag (1988:1385) om Sveriges riksbank*) stipulates in Chapter 1 section 2 that the Riksbank shall 'promote a safe and efficient payments mechanism'.

The Banking and Financing Business Act (*Lag (2004:297) om bank- och finansieringsrörelse*) contains regulations on banking and financing and lays down, *inter alia*, licensing requirements for the conduct of such operations and guidelines governing the supervision of credit institutions.

The Payment-Service Act (*Lag (2010:751) om betaltjänster*) implements large parts of the EU Payment Services Directive[575] and regulates rights and obligations of end users and payment-service providers. The Act stipulates operational requirements for payment services providers and rules concerning market access for new providers.

The Act on the Securities Market (*Lag (2007:528) om värdepappersmarknaden*)[576] transposes the EU Investment Services Directive[577] into Swedish national law, stipulates licensing requirements for securities firms and offers guidelines governing the supervision of such firms, and the types of business such firms may engage in. In addition, several other Acts regulate the financial market and are applicable to specific types of financial instruments or financial services.[578]

The previously in force Act on cross-border payments within the EU (*Lag (1999:268) om betalningsöverföringar inom Europeiska ekonomiska samarbetsområdet*) transposed the EU Directive on cross-border credit transfers[579] into Swedish

574. For detailed information on the banking sector, see European Central Bank, 'Payment and Securities Settlement Systems in the European Union', Blue Book, 4th edn, vol. 2 (Non-Euro area countries), 331 et seq.
575. Directive 2007/64/EC of the European Parliament and of the Council of 13 Nov. 2007 on payment services in the internal market amending Directives 97/7/EC, 2002/65/EC, 2005/60/EC and 2006/48/EC and repealing Directive 97/5/EC (Text with EEA relevance).
576. The Act replaced the Securities Business Act (*Lag (1991:981) om värdepappersrörelse*).
577. Directive 2004/39/EC of the European Parliament and of the Council of 21 Apr. 2004 on markets in financial instruments amending Council Directives 85/611/EEC and 93/6/EEC and Directive 2000/12/EC of the European Parliament and of the Council and repealing Council Directive 93/22/EEC.
578. More information at the website of Swedish Banker's Association (*Svenska Bankföreningen*) <www.swedishbankers.se/>.
579. Directive 97/5/EC of the European Parliament and of the Council of 27 Jan. 1997 on cross-border credit transfers.

law. In 2010, it was incorporated into the Payment-Service Act (*Lag (2010:751) om betaltjänster*) which now covers payment services provided in Sweden and performed in the European Economic Area (EEA). Sweden has, furthermore, decided to apply Regulation (EC) No 924/2009 of the European Parliament and of the Council of 16 September 2009 on cross-border payments in the Community.[580]

Sweden is also actively involved in the EU project – Single Euro Payments Area (SEPA).[581] SEPA consists of three main parts: credit transfer, direct debits and card payment and is based on. As Sweden is a non-Euro country it the transition period ends in October 2016. At the moment the majority of national Euro credit transfers are being processed as SEPA Credit Transfers. Cross-border Euro payments are also compliant with SEPA Credit Transfer. SEPA direct debit is optional for non-Euro countries, and therefore it is up to the banks to offer this possibility, which only a few banks in Sweden chose. The migration with regards to SEPA card payments is almost complete.

II. Electronic Banking

294. There is no specific legislation dealing with electronic banking as such. Most Acts stated above are technology-neutral, and apply to any form of banking.

One of the first national acts dealing to some extent specifically with electronic banking was the Swedish Act on the issuing of electronic money (*Lag (2002:149) om utgivning av elektroniska pengar*), which transposed the previous EU Directive on electronic money.[582] The Act was replaced in 2011 with the Electronic Money Act (*Lag (2011:755) om elektroniska pengar*), which is based on the 2009 E-Money Directive.[583]

The current in force Electronic Money Act states requirements for issuers of electronic money and guidelines governing the supervision of such issuers. Electronic money is defined in Chapter 1 section 2, in accordance with Article 1(2) 2009 e-Money Directive, as 'electronically stored monetary value:

(a) as represented by a claim on the issuer;
(b) which is issued on receipt of funds for the purpose of making payment transactions as defined in point 5 of Article 4 of Directive 2007/64/EC; and
(c) which is accepted by a natural or legal person other than the electronic money issuer'.

580. Sveriges Riksbank, 'The Swedish retail- payment market', Riksbank Studies, June 2013, www.riksbank.se/Documents/Rapporter/Riksbanksstudie/2013/ rap_riksbanksstudie_The_Swedish_retailpayment_market_130605_eng.pdf, 89.
581. See more at the website of the European Central Bank (ECB) <www.ecb.europa.eu/paym/sepa/html/index.en.html>, 5 Apr. 2014.
582. Directive 2000/46/EC of the European Parliament and of the Council of 18 Sep. 2000 on the taking up pursuit of and prudential supervision of the business of electronic money institutions.
583. Directive 2009/110/EC of the European Parliament and of the Council of 16 Sep. 2009 on the taking up, pursuit and prudential supervision of the business of electronic money institutions amending Directives 2005/60/EC and 2006/48/EC and repealing Directive 2000/46/EC.

Electronic money is, according to this definition, not the same as virtual currency.[584]

Issuing of electronic money in Sweden requires a permit by the Financial Inspection Board (*Finansinspektionen*/FI)[585] unless the issuer is a bank. Only Swedish limited companies (*Aktiebolag*) or Swedish economic associations (*ekonomisk förening*) can apply for a permit and have to prove, *inter alia*, a sufficient minimum start-up capital and operating capital base. The Electronic Money Act also stipulates other requirements for issuers of electronic money, for example, issuers may not receive deposits or other repayable funds from the general public.[586]

The Act is applicable to all issuers of electronic money, but only a few of its provisions are applicable to banks and credit market companies as they fall within the scope of specific legislation, according to section 1.

III. Supervision

295. In general, the Financial Inspection Board (*Finansinspektionen*/FI) is the supervisory authority for the banking sector, and also the authority granting the license to provide certain banking or financing services. Within its capacity, it also issues regulatory code (FFFS) further defining provisions stated by law.

In its capacity as the Swedish Financial Supervisory Authority, the Financial Inspection Board (FI) supervises and monitors companies and organizations operating in financial markets. In many cases, companies offering financial services in Sweden have to acquire a permit issued by FI.

According to Chapter 2 section 1 Electronic Money Act the Financial Inspection Board authorizes the issuing of electronic money.

§2. Consumer Protection

296. In general, the Swedish Consumer Credit Act regulates the granting of credit to consumers and contains, *inter alia*, provisions on marketing and information.

297. As stated above, the Payment Services Directive was transposed into Swedish national law by enactment of the Payment-Service Act (*Lag (2010:751) om betaltjänster*) in 2010. The Act, *inter alia*, stipulates the type of information that providers of payment services must present to their customers, how quickly a payment transaction is to be performed and the fees that may be charged to the user for payment services. Regarding the time frame, electronic payments in SEK or EUR must reach the payee no later than the day after the payment was initiated (Chapter 5 section 18).

---

584. Sveriges Riksbank, 'The Swedish retail-payment market', 92.
585. <www.fi.se>.
586. See more at Sveriges Riksbank, 'The Swedish retail-payment market', 92 et.sequ.

Regarding liability for unauthorized transactions with a payment instrument, the Act on Unauthorized Transactions with Payment Instruments (*Lag (2010:738) om obehöriga transaktioner med betalningsinstrument*) regulates the responsibility of the account holder. The Act defines payment instrument as a bank card or any other personalized device or personal routine that is used to electronically initiate a payment transaction. Section 4 stipulates the account holder's obligation to, *inter alia*, protect the personal code and to report to the payment-service provider as soon as possible if the payment instrument has been mislaid or been used in an unauthorized manner. Sections 5 and 6 state the liability of the account holder. If the account holder did not protect the personal code, the liability covers the amount that has been debited up to SEK 1,200. In case of gross negligence the account holder is liable for the full amount; however, if the account holder is a consumer, this amount is limited to a maximum of SEK 12,000, except in extremely reprehensible cases.

298. In addition, the Distance and Doorstep Sales Act (*Distans- och hemförsäljningslag (2005:59)*),[587] transposing, *inter alia*, the Directive on distance contracts for financial services and financial instruments,[588] covers in its Chapter 3 obligations for providers of distance contracts for financial services and financial instruments.

587. Explained more in Ch. 4 s. 3 *infra* (paras 315 et seq.).

588. Directive 2002/65/EC of the European Parliament and of the Council of 23 Sep. 2002 concerning the distance marketing of consumer financial services and amending Council Directive 90/619/EEC and Directives 97/7/EC and 98/27/EC.

Chapter 4. Protection of Users of Electronic Services

§1. General Statement

299. Though the term 'electronic services' is neither used nor defined in any of the relevant Directives or statutes mentioned below, this chapter will focus on the protection of users of information society services as well as distance contracts.

In general, the legal framework of consumer protection applies, including the Consumer Sales Act (*Konsumentköplag (1990:932)*), the Consumer Services Act (*Konsumenttjänstlag (1985:716)*), the Consumer Credit Act (*Konsumentkreditlag (1992:830)*), as well as the Act on Terms of Contract in Consumer Relations (*Lag (1994:1512) om särskilda avtalsvillkor i konsumentförhållanden*), and the Price Information Act (*Prisinformationslag (2004:347)*).

Regarding marketing practices, the Swedish Marketing Act (*Marknadsföringslag (2008:486)*) covers Business-To-Consumers (B2C) as well as Business-To-Business (B2B) relations, and is applicable in all situations where advertisement is used, not only towards consumers, but also towards competitors of the advertising company. The Competition Act (*Konkurrenslag (2008:579)*) further aims at eliminating and counteracting obstacles to effective competition in the production of, and trade in, goods and services. In this respect, it can protect both consumers and competitors from unfair trade practices.

§2. Information Society Services

I. General Statement

300. The Directive on electronic commerce[589] was transposed into Swedish national law by passing the Act on Electronic Commerce and other information society services (*Lag (2002:562) om elektronisk handel och andra informationssamhällets tjänster*; hereinafter 'Electronic Commerce Act'), as well as amending the then in force Marketing Act (*Marknadsföringslag (1995:450)*),[590] the Financial Instruments Trading Act (*Lag (1991:980) om handel med finansiella instrument*) and the Consumer Credit Act, among others.

301. The Directive[591] as well as the Electronic Commerce Act in section 1 exempts certain services from their application. The Swedish Act does not reflect the Directive word-for-word, but mentions as services that do not fall within its scope:

589. Directive 2000/31/EC of the European Parliament and of the Council of 8 Jun. 2000 on certain legal aspects of information society services, in particular e-commerce, in the Internal Market (hereinafter 'Directive on electronic commerce').
590. Now replaced by the Marketing Act (*Marknadsföringslag (2008:486)*).
591. Article 1(5) points a–d Directive on electronic commerce.

(1) taxation;
(2) processing of personal data;
(3) cooperation between companies that limits competition;
(4) activities of notaries or equivalent professions to the extent that they involve an exercise of public authority;
(5) activities that involve representation or defence of a client's interests before the courts; or
(6) gambling activities which involve wagering a stake with monetary value in games of chance.

The reason for exempting these activities is a result of the lack of competence of the EU within those fields.[592] This means, that the national legislator can enact laws within these areas, which do not necessarily have to be harmonized within the EU.[593]

Another reason for the Electronic Commerce Act not to be applicable is activities which fall under the Freedom of the Press Act (*Tryckfrihetsförordning (1949:105)*) or the Fundamental Law on Freedom of Expression (*Yttrandefrihetsgrundlag (1991:1469)*), which both have constitutional status. This is in line with Recital 9 Directive stating that the 'Directive is not intended to affect national fundamental rules and principles relating to freedom of expression.'

302. The Directive in Article 3(1), as well as Electronic Commerce Act, section 3 establish the country of origin principle (*ursprungslandsprincip*) in relation to rights and obligations of service providers. In other words, a provider of information society services has to comply with the rules of the Member State that it is established and registered in, but not with the rules of every Member State in which the service can be received (the effects doctrine – *effektlandsprincip*). The country of origin principle only concerns, however, rules regarding the taking up and pursuit of information society services ('coordinated field') and not requirements applicable to goods or their delivery.

303. The Act, in accordance with the Directive, stipulates certain rules for information society services. As will become clear from the definitions mentioned below, in particular the fact that both the Directive and the Act speak about recipients of the service and not consumers, these rules apply both in B2B as well as B2C relations.

592. Recital 12 Directive on electronic commerce: 'It is necessary to exclude certain activities from the scope of this Directive, on the grounds that the freedom to provide services in these fields cannot, at this stage, be guaranteed under the Treaty or existing secondary legislation; excluding these activities does not preclude any instruments which might prove necessary for the proper functioning of the internal market.'

593. As an example, the Swedish Lotteries Act (*Lotterilag (1994:1000)*) requires an undertaking to apply for a permit (from the Government) to organize gambling or lottery activities on the Swedish market. The law is technology-neutral and therefore applies to online gambling as well. The responsible supervisory authority is the Gaming Board for Sweden (*Lotteriinspektionen*, <www.lotteriinspektionen.se/>).

More specifically, the Swedish Electronic Commerce Act covers provisions relating to the internal market, the establishment of service providers, commercial communications, electronic contracts, the liability of intermediaries, codes of conduct, out-of-court dispute settlements as well as court actions.[594] In the following mainly the obligations of service providers will be covered, as liability of intermediaries is discussed in Part V Chapter 3 *infra*, and out-of-court dispute settlements are included in Part I Chapter 5 *supra* as well as Part II Chapter 6 *supra* with regards to domain name disputes.

II. Definitions

304. The definitions in section 2 Electronic Commerce Act reflect the definitions of Article 2 Directive on electronic commerce to a large extent.

Information society services are defined as 'services normally provided for remuneration and at a distance, by electronic means and at the individual request of a recipient of services'. All four criteria have to be fulfilled in order for a service to be covered by the Electronic Commerce Act. This reflects section 2 Swedish Ordinance on Technical Rules (*Förordning (1994:2029) om tekniska regler*) which in turn builds upon Directive on technical standards and regulations,[595] which the Directive on electronic commerce refers to in its Article 2 point a. Annex V of the Directive on technical standards and regulations mentions a list of activities that are not covered by the term 'information society services'.[596]

The term *service* is not further explained, neither in the Electronic Commerce Act nor in any other Swedish legislation, and does not have an established meaning as such. There was no discussion of this term in the Swedish preparatory works; however, the Governmental Bill[597] referred to Article 57[598] TFEU which defines services as performances that 'are normally provided for remuneration, in so far as they are not governed by the provisions relating to freedom of movement for goods, capital and persons'.

The preparatory works further mention the following examples of information society services: marketing and sale of goods and services, online newspapers, financial services and video-on-demand, under the assumption that they all are provided online. Concerning sale of goods and services, including computer programs, real estate agents, and accounting services, the Electronic Commerce Act only applies to the steps of the ordering process that are provided online. In other words, if the computer program is bought online, but delivered in physical form offline, only the ordering is covered by the Act.[599] Marketing by email is also covered as an

594. See Art. 1(2) Directive on Electronic Commerce.
595. Directive 98/34/EC of the European Parliament and of the Council of 22 Jun. 1998 laying down a procedure for the provision of information in the field of technical standards and regulations (hereinafter 'Directive on technical standards and regulations').
596. Recital 17 Directive on Electronic Commerce explicitly refers to that list.
597. Government Bill (Proposition) 2001/02:150, 'Lag om elektronisk handel och andra informationssamhällets tjänster, m.m.', 56.
598. Ex Art. 50.
599. Government Bill (Proposition) 2001/02:150, 110.

information society service. Email or other direct personal messages between individuals outside their profession do not fall within the scope, however. This also applies if the contract is concluded via exchange of emails.[600]

305. Section 2 Swedish Electronic Commerce Act further defines *service provider* as any natural or legal person providing an information society service. This can include ISPs, providers of search engines, owners of servers and companies offering goods and services online. To the extent that some economic goal exists, public authorities and universities can also fall under the definition. Typical private websites with no economic purpose are, however, not considered as service providers.[601]

The Swedish Electronic Commerce Act describes the term *country of establishment*, which in substance transposes Article 2 point c Directive on Electronic Commerce, as the Member State where the service provider has its fixed establishment. The country of origin is, in other words, the main place of business for the company, and not where the technology or website is located.[602]

The term *recipient of the service* covers any natural or legal person who uses an information society service. This includes more or less everybody who takes advantage of such a service, individuals who publish information on public networks as well as individuals who search for information on the Internet for private or professional purposes. A person or company can be both a provider and a recipient of an information society service, for example, the owner of a website is both service provider as well as recipient if a web hotel is used for the storage of the website.[603]

Section 2 describes the term *regulated profession* as a profession which according to law or ordinance requires authorization of some sort. It furthermore also defines *coordinated field* as provisions with requirements for information society services applicable to service providers regarding the taking up and pursuit of activities concerning such services.

III. Obligation to Provide Information

306. Section 8 Electronic Commerce Act, implementing Article 5 Directive on Electronic Commerce, stipulates an obligation for service providers to render certain information to the recipients of the service. This information includes, *inter alia*, data about the name, address and email address of the service provider, as well as the registration number for the company and, if applicable, the relevant supervisory authority. The information should be easily, directly and permanently accessible to the recipients and public authorities.

If the information society service concerns a regulated profession, the published information should also include the professional title and the Member State where

600. See also Recital 18 Directive on Electronic Commerce.
601. Government Bill (Proposition) 2001/02:150, 110.
602. See also Recital 19 Directive on Electronic Commerce.
603. Government Bill (Proposition) 2001/02:150, 110.

it has been granted, the professional body or similar institution with which the service provider is registered, and the applicable professional rules in the Member State of establishment and the means to access them.[604]

If the service provider refers to prices of goods or services, they should be indicated clearly and unambiguously. If tax or delivery costs are added, this should also be stated explicitly.[605]

IV. Requirements for the Online Ordering Process

307. Section 10 Swedish Electronic Commerce Act, reflecting Article 11(2) Directive on Electronic Commerce, stipulates an obligation for service providers to make available appropriate and effective technical means allowing the recipient to identify and correct input errors, prior to the placing of the order. This obligation does not include a duty for the service provider itself to correct or verify the information given by the recipient, but to provide the means for the user to notice mistakes.

308. In addition, the provider of an information society service has to render certain information in the ordering process. More specifically, according to section 11, the service provider has to inform the recipient about:

(1) the technical means according to section 10 as well as the different technical steps to follow when concluding the contract;
(2) which languages the contract is available in;
(3) whether the concluded contract will be archived by the service provider and whether it will be accessible;
(4) the relevant codes of conduct to which the service provider subscribes to and information on how these codes can be consulted electronically.

The information has to be provided clearly and unambiguously prior to the order being placed.[606]

309. After the order has been placed, the service provider has to acknowledge the receipt of the order without undue delay and by electronic means. Orders and acknowledgements of receipt are deemed received when the parties to whom they are addressed are able to access them.[607]

310. General terms and conditions of a contract must be made available in a way that allows the recipient to store and reproduce them.[608]

604. Section 8 para. 2 Electronic Commerce Act.
605. Section 9 Electronic Commerce Act.
606. Section 11 Electronic Commerce Act, transposing Art. 10(1) and (2) Directive on Electronic Commerce.
607. Section 12 Electronic Commerce Act, transposing Art. 11(1) Directive on Electronic Commerce.
608. Section 13 Electronic Commerce Act, transposing Art. 10(3) Directive on Electronic Commerce.

V. Possible Sanctions

311. If the provider of an information society service fails to adhere to the obligations to provide certain information or appropriate technical measures, it faces sanctions according to the Swedish Marketing Act (*Marknadsföringslag (2008:486)*). Section 15 Swedish Electronic Commerce Act follows the examples of other related legislation, such the Distance and Doorstep Sales Act (*Distans- och hemförsäljningslag (2005:59)*) as well as the Price Information Act (*Prisinformationslag (2004:347)*), which both refer to the Marketing Act in relation to possible sanctions.

Section 15 Electronic Commerce Act allows for sanctions under the Marketing Act for not meeting the requirements according to sections 8 and 9 (obligation to provide certain information) as well as sections 11–13 (requirements when ordering online) and section 10 (not providing technical measures). The Swedish Marketing Act stipulates in sections 24–27 and 37 the sanctions for non-compliance with the rules of the Electronic Commerce Act.

312. According to section 24 Marketing Act, a provider of an information society service, its employee or any person acting on its behalf can be ordered to provide the necessary information. This order may include providing information in advertisements or other presentations used by the company in the course of marketing, through labelling of the goods at the point of sale, or in another form to a consumer who requests such information. Similar to this provision, section 25 Marketing Act stipulates an order to provide technical aids.

In both cases, the order issued by the relevant authority can be combined with a conditional fine unless special reasons render it unnecessary.[609] If the service provider intentionally or negligently violates an order that has been issued pursuant to sections 24 or 25, it shall compensate a recipient for any damage suffered thereby.[610]

313. The proceedings for an order according to sections 24 or 25 Marketing Act shall be brought before the Market Court (*Marknadsdomstolen*).[611] They can be initiated by:[612]

(1) the Consumer Ombudsman (*Konsumentombudsmannen*);[613]
(2) the company affected by the marketing practices; or
(3) an organization of consumers, companies or employees.

609. Section 26 Marketing Act.
610. Section 37 Marketing Act.
611. <www.marknadsdomstolen.se>.
612. Section 47 Marketing Act.
613. The Swedish Consumer Ombudsman is part of the Swedish Consumer Agency (*Konsumentverket*), <www.konsumentombudsmannen.com>.

In cases of minor importance, the Consumer Ombudsman may issue orders directly, in accordance with sections 24 and 25 Marketing Act. These orders shall be combined with a conditional fine. In order to be valid, an information order must be accepted by the service provider immediately or within a specific period of time. If the order has been accepted, it shall apply as if it were a final judgment of the Market Court.[614]

314. There are no other possible sanctions for not meeting the requirements stated in the Electronic Commerce Act. For example, fines for disruptive marketing practices[615] cannot be issued in such cases.[616] It was also not deemed necessary to introduce specific rules on civil or criminal liability for not following the requirements stipulated above.[617]

§3. Distance Contracts

I. General Statement

315. Directive 97/7/EC of the European Parliament and of the Council of 20 May 1997 on the protection of consumers in respect of distance contracts (hereinafter 'Distance Contracts Directive') was transposed into Swedish law with the Distance and Doorstep Sales Act (*Distans- och hemförsäljningslag (2005:59)*).[618] According to Chapter 1 section 1, it contains 'provisions for consumer protection with regards to distance contracts for goods and non-financial services (Chapter 2), distance contracts for financial services and financial instruments (Chapter 3) and doorstep sales contracts (Chapter 4)'.

II. Definitions

316. Entering into a distance contract is not necessarily the same as providing an information society service. Chapter 1 section 2 Distance and Doorstep Sales Act defines it as a contract entered into within the undertaking's organized system for concluding contracts at a distance and where communication exclusively takes place at a distance. It is important that the undertaking has established a system for entering into contracts online, a simple advertisement to facilitate customer relations that does not include the possibility to sell goods or services at a distance, does not fulfil the criteria for a distance contract according to the definition. The threshold of 'organized' is, however, rather low; an advertisement with a telephone number that allows ordering of goods and services would constitute an organized system.

614. Section 28 Marketing Act.
615. Sections 29–36 Marketing Act.
616. Section 15 Electronic Commerce Act.
617. Government Bill (Proposition) 2001/02:150, 75.
618. This Act replaced the previous Act on Consumer protection in respect of distance contracts and doorstep sales contracts (*Lag (2000:274) om konsumentskydd vid distansavtal och hemförsäljningsavtal*).

Examples of such distance contracts include any type of offering of goods and services on the Internet that allows a consumer to order directly via the website or email or telephone. Services not included are, however, ordering of goods in a physical store, or using a telephone number in a newspaper advertisement to make an appointment with a dentist, lawyer or hairdresser. The Distance and Doorstep Sales Act is, in other words, not applicable if the undertaking and the consumer meet face-to-face.[619]

In accordance with Article 2(4) Distance Contracts Directive, the techniques used for the system or the communication are any means that can be used for a conclusion of a contract without the parties being simultaneously physically present. The preparatory works refer to the list in Annex I of the Distance Contracts Directive[620] that states, *inter alia*, the following examples of means of distance communication: addressed and unaddressed printed matters, press advertising with order form, catalogues, telephone with or without (automatic calling machine) human intervention, radio, email, television (teleshopping). An important other means of communication is, of course, the Internet,[621] and probably nowadays also SMS.

317. The definitions of consumer and undertaking in the Swedish Act reflect the Distance Contracts Directive as well as most other legislation within business law. The term *consumer* includes 'any natural person who is acting primarily for purposes which are outside her or his commercial activities', while *undertaking* covers 'any natural or legal person trading for purposes connected with her or his own commercial activities'.

As most other consumer legislation, contract terms or conditions that are 'to the disadvantage of the consumer shall be unenforceable against such consumer'.[622]

318. As is the case for information society services, some contracts are explicitly exempted from the scope of the Distance and Doorstep Sales Act. Specifically, this concerns contracts that relate to the construction of buildings, are entered into by means of an automatic vending machine or other similar automatic machines or automated commercial premises, concern public pay phones, or regard auctions that allow other means of participation.[623]

319. The Distance and Doorstep Sales Act sets up certain obligations for the service provider, to some extent similar to the Electronic Commerce Act, which will be described more in detail below.

619. Government Bill (Proposition) 2004/05:13, 'Distans- och hemförsäljningslag m.m.', 122.
620. *Ibid.*
621. *Ibid.*, 123.
622. Chapter 1 s. 3 Distance and Doorstep Sales Act.
623. Chapter 2 s. 1 Distance and Doorstep Sales Act.

III. Information

320. The duty to provide information is more detailed than the one stipulated in the Electronic Commerce Act and includes two parts. Certain information has to be provided both before[624] and after the contract has been entered into.[625]

The information that shall be provided in reasonable time prior to the conclusion of the contract includes, according to Chapter 2 section 6 Distance and Doorstep Sales Act:

(a) the name and address of the undertaking;
(b) the main characteristics of the goods or services;
(c) the price of the goods or services including taxes and charges;
(d) delivery costs;
(e) the arrangement for payment and delivery or performance in any other manner;
(f) the terms of the right of withdrawal in accordance to this Act;
(g) the cost of using means of distance communication, where it is calculated other than at the basic rate;
(h) the period for which the offer remains valid; and
(i) the minimum term of the contract, where the contract relates to the recurrent supply of goods or a service to be performed permanently.

The law does not specify what 'before the contract is entered into' means but only states 'within a reasonable time prior to entering into a distance contract'. It also stipulates that the information be 'provided in a clear and comprehensible manner and in a manner appropriate to the means of distance communication used'.

The information to be provided as soon as possible *after* the conclusion of the contract includes, according to Chapter 2 section 7, points 1–5 mentioned above in Chapter 2 section 6, as well as:

(1) the consumer's right of withdrawal as well as the name and address of the business;
(2) the address, telephone number, or email address as well as street address of the business to which the consumer may direct complaints;
(3) information on existing after sales service and guarantees; and
(4) in the event that the term of the contract is for an indefinite period or for a term exceeding one year, the terms and conditions governing termination of the contract.

The latest the information has to be provided is the time of delivery, if the contract concerns goods.

The duty to provide information according to Chapter 2 section 7 does not apply to the following types of contracts, according to Chapter 2 section 3: 'accommodation; transportation; serving, catering or any other similar services; or cultural

624. Chapter 2 s. 6 Distance and Doorstep Sales Act, transposing Art. 4 Distance Contracts Directive.
625. Chapter 2 s. 7 Distance and Doorstep Sales Act, transposing Art. 5 Distance Contracts Directive.

events, sporting events, or any other similar leisure activities', if the service shall be provided 'on a specified day or during a specified period of time'. Neither shall this obligation apply to 'distance contracts regarding sales of foodstuffs or other goods intended for everyday household consumption, where the goods are to be supplied in the consumer's residence or workplace in a distribution system with regular deliveries'. However, Chapter 2 section 3 only exempts Chapter 2 section 7, which means that certain information has to be provided prior to the conclusion of the contract, in accordance with Chapter 2 section 6 Distance and Doorstep Sales Act, but not after.

IV. Right of Withdrawal

321. A right only applicable in distance consumer contracts is the right of withdrawal, which means that the consumer can withdraw from a concluded contract by 'submitting or sending notice thereof to the undertaking within fourteen days'[626] of the delivery of goods or the day on conclusion of the contract in case of services.[627] Swedish law therefore extended the withdrawal period of seven working days granted in Article 6 Distance Contracts Directive.[628]

In case the information according to Chapter 2 section 7 Distance and Doorstep Sales Act was not provided together with delivery of the goods, or the conclusion of the contract regarding a service, the withdrawal period shall commence on the day it was provided[629] and ends the latest 'one year after the day on which the withdrawal period should have commenced'.[630]

322. A withdrawal means a cancellation of the contract, which is why the consumer has to return the goods to the supplier.[631] The goods should not be altered or destroyed, unless the changed condition was a 'consequence of any measure which was necessary to investigate the goods or due to any circumstance which cannot be attributed to the consumer'.[632] As the consumer has to return the goods, the undertaking has to refund any payments made by the consumer.[633]

With regards the notice that informs the undertaking of the consumer exercising the right of withdrawal, Chapter 5 section 3 Distance and Doorstep Sales Act shifts the risk of receipt of a correct notice to the undertaking. In other words, the consumer can claim the withdrawal even if the notice was delayed, destroyed or otherwise did not arrive. There are no formal requirements regarding the notice, but it

626. Chapter 2 s. 9 Distance and Doorstep Sales Act.
627. Chapter 2 s. 10 Distance and Doorstep Sales Act.
628. This is in accordance with the minimal clause of Art. 14 of the Directive that states that 'Member States may introduce or maintain, in the area covered by this Directive, more stringent provisions compatible with the Treaty, to ensure a higher level of consumer protection.'
629. Chapter 2 s. 10 Distance and Doorstep Sales Act.
630. Chapter 2 s. 11 Distance and Doorstep Sales Act.
631. Chapter 2 s. 13 Distance and Doorstep Sales Act.
632. Chapter 2 s. 12 Distance and Doorstep Sales Act.
633. Chapter 2 s. 14 Distance and Doorstep Sales Act.

can be expected that the consumer chooses a method in line with the situation at hand, such as regular mail, telefax, email or even a telephone call.[634]

323. As is the case for the duty to provide information, Chapter 2 section 3 exempts the right of withdrawal for the following types of contracts: accommodation; transportation; serving, catering or any other similar services; cultural events, sporting events, or any other similar leisure activities, if the service shall be provided 'on a specified day or during a specified period of time'. Neither is the right of withdrawal granted for distance contracts regarding sales of food or other goods intended for everyday household consumption, where the goods are to be supplied in the consumer's residence or workplace in a regular distribution system.

In addition, the right of withdrawal does not apply to distance contracts regarding:[635]

- a service, the performance of which has begun with the consumer's consent during the withdrawal period;
- goods which, by their nature, cannot be returned or are liable to deteriorate or expire rapidly;
- a sealed audio or video recording or sealed computer software, where the seal has been broken;
- a newspaper or periodical; or
- gaming or other lottery services.

In case the distance contract relates to goods which shall be manufactured or materially modified in accordance with the consumer's particular wishes, or which shall otherwise acquire a clear and personal character, the consumer and the supplier may agree in writing that there shall be no right of withdrawal.[636]

V. Performance of the Contract

324. In accordance with Article 7(1) and (2) Distance Contracts Directive, Chapter 2 section 17 Swedish Distance and Doorstep Sales Act stipulates a right for consumers that performance of a contract shall be carried out within thirty days after the placement of the order, unless otherwise agreed by the partners in writing.

If the undertaking cannot fulfil its obligation in time and this is not due to the consumer or any other circumstance on the consumer's side, the consumer has the right to annul the contract.

634. Government Bill (Proposition) 2004/05:13, 177.
635. Chapter 2 s. 4 Distance and Doorstep Sales Act.
636. Chapter 2 s. 5 Distance and Doorstep Sales Act.

325. If the consumer annuls the contract, the undertaking has to refund any sums already paid by the consumer, within thirty days of receipt of notice from the consumer.[637] Even if the consumer does not use this right, other legal consequences due to the Consumer Sales Act or Consumer Services Act may be applicable.[638]

326. Chapter 2 section 17 paragraph 3 Swedish Distance and Doorstep Sales Act stipulates an exemption from the right to performance, in accordance with Article 3(2) Distance Contracts Directive. According to this provision, the consumer can agree in writing to a term in the distance contract that the undertaking does not have to refund payment for distance contracts concerning cultural and sporting events, or other similar outdoor leisure events in case the activity had to be cancelled due to bad weather conditions.

As is the case for notices regarding the right of withdrawal, notices concerning the annulment of the contract can be invoked by the consumer even if they are delayed, destroyed or otherwise did not arrive.[639]

VI. Choice of Law

327. Chapter 5 section 2 Distance and Doorstep Sales Act also partly regulates the question of choice of law. It mainly protects the consumer against unfavourable terms and conditions. In general, for choice of law regarding consumer contracts, Article 6 of the Regulation (EC) No. 593/2008 of the European Parliament and of the Council of 17 June 2008 on the law applicable to contractual obligations (Rome I) would apply in these circumstances.

VII. Possible Sanctions

328. The sanctions for not meeting the information requirements in Chapter 2 sections 6 and 7 Distance and Doorstep Sales Act are stipulated in the Marketing Act.[640] As for information society services, the Marketing Act provides the possibility to issue orders to provide information,[641] which can be combined with a conditional fine unless special reasons render this unnecessary.[642] Under certain circumstances, the undertaking can be liable for damages as well.[643] Fines for disruptive marketing practices are, however, not covered by possible sanctions.[644]

637. Chapter 2 s. 17 Distance and Doorstep Sales Act.
638. Government Bill (Proposition) 2004/05:13, 144.
639. Chapter 5 s. 3 Distance and Doorstep Sales Act.
640. Chapter 2 s. 8 Distance and Doorstep Sales Act.
641. Section 24 Marketing Act.
642. Section 26 Marketing Act.
643. Section 37 Marketing Act.
644. Chapter 2 s. 8 Distance and Doorstep Sales Act.

The Consumer Ombudsman ((*Konsumentombudsmannen*) can initiate proceedings before the Market Court (*Marknadsdomstolen*),[645] or in minor cases issue orders itself.[646]

§4. Other Information Requirements

329. As is clear from above, providing consumers with reliable and relevant information has been one of the focus areas of EU legislation. In this context, section 9 Marketing Act can be mentioned, stipulating a duty to identify commercial communications as well as to clearly state the sender of the advertisement. Not following this provision intentionally or negligently can lead to fines for disruptive marketing practices according to section 29 Swedish Marketing Act.

The Price Information Act (*Prisinformationslag (2004:347)*) stipulates information obligations, concerning mainly, as the name implies, the prices of products. Failure to provide information according to this Act can lead to sanctions according to the Marketing Act.[647]

In addition, several other Swedish Acts contain provisions regarding information requirements, such as the Swedish Companies Act (*Aktiebolagslag (2005:551)*). Chapter 28 section 5 stipulates that a company's letters, invoices, order forms, and websites shall state the company's name, the place where the Board is registered as well as the company's registration number.

§5. Unsolicited Communication

330. Article 7 Directive on Electronic Commerce, dealing with unsolicited commercial communication, was not explicitly transposed into the Swedish Electronic Commerce Act in 2002, mainly because an opt-out solution did not require any specific legislative measures.

However, in transposing the Directive on Privacy and Electronic Communications, Sweden had to introduce an opt-in solution into national law, which was done in the previously in force Marketing Act (*Marknadsföringslag (1995:450)*), and was transferred into the current Marketing Act (*Marknadsföringslag (2008:486)*). The below-mentioned provision on unsolicited advertisement also implements Article 10 Distance Contracts Directive into Swedish law.

331. Section 6 point 1 Swedish Electronic Commerce Act exempts the question of direct unsolicited marketing from the country of origin principle.[648] Therefore, the effects doctrine applies and the Swedish Marketing Act is applicable on commercial communications that are aimed at the Swedish market. Factors that can help

645. Section 47 Marketing Act.
646. Section 28 Marketing Act.
647. The same rules apply as failure to meet information requirements according to ss 8 and 9 Electronic Commerce Act, see s. 2 V *supra* (paras 311 et seq.) or Ch. 2 ss 6 and 7 Distance and Doorstep Sales Act, see s. 3 VII *supra* (para. 328).
648. Sections 3–5 Swedish Electronic Commerce Act.

determine if the target market is Sweden are if the advertisement is in Swedish, if prices are in Swedish kronor, or if a Swedish address is provided.[649]

The Swedish Marketing Act defines email as an electronic text, voice, sound or image message which is addressed or otherwise individualized and sent over a public communication network, and which can be stored in the network or in the recipient's terminal equipment until the recipient collects it.[650]

As this definition is rather broad, the term email also includes SMS,[651] multimedia messages (MMS) and other types of messages that can be sent via instant message services such as Skype or ICQ. In addition, messages left on answering machines as well as communication within a network addressed directly to an IP-address can be considered email.[652]

332. Section 19 Marketing Act deals with unsolicited commercial communications and stipulates that an undertaking may only use email, telefax, automated calling systems or other similar automated systems that allow individual communication, and do not involve a natural person, in their marketing to natural persons, if prior consent has been given.

The consumer's consent is, however, not necessary if the company has acquired the contact details in the context of the sale of a product to that person and:

- the natural person has not refused that the electronic address is used for marketing purposes;
- the marketing concerns the undertaking's own products; and
- the natural person clearly and distinctly is given the opportunity to object, free of charge and in an easy manner, to use the contact details for marketing purposes when they were collected, and on the occasion of each following message.[653]

333. Last, but not least, the Swedish Personal Data Act (*Personuppgiftslag (1998:204)*) deals in section 11 with direct marketing and establishes an opt-out solution. In other words, personal data may not be processed for direct marketing purposes if the consumer has opposed in writing.

334. To conclude, besides the provision in the just mentioned Personal Data Act, Swedish law clearly applies an opt-in solution, as shown by section 19 Marketing

649. Henrik Bengtsson, 'Marknadsföring med hjälp av elektroniska meddelanden', *Ny Juridik* 3 (2009): 42–43.
650. Section 3 Marketing Act in accordance with Art. 2 Directive on Privacy and Electronic Communications.
651. As also mentioned in Recital 40 Directive on Privacy and Electronic Communications.
652. Bengtsson, *Marknadsföring,* 37. Art. 29 Data Protection Working Party, 'Opinion 5/2004 on unsolicited communications for marketing purposes under Art. 13 of Directive 2002/58/EC', MARKT/11601/03/EN - WP 90.
653. The Swedish Market Court decided on 18 Jun. 2006 in MD 2006:18 that the possibility to object can be given by clicking a button on a website and also by unselecting an already checked box. See also Bengtsson, *Marknadsföring*, 48–49.

Act, which means that undertakings and service providers have to receive the consent of their potential customers in order to be able to send out direct commercial communications to them.

The sanctions of not abiding by section 19 are, however, not very strong. In the preparatory works to the new Marketing Act,[654] it was decided that fines for disruptive marketing practices[655] cannot be issued for any unsolicited advertisements.[656] However, in the case of failure to abide by section 20 Marketing Act, which stipulates that an email used for advertisement purposes has to contain a valid contact address where the natural or legal person can object to the marketing, a fine for disruptive marketing practices can be issued by the Market Court.[657]

654. Government Bill (Proposition) 2007/08:115, 'Ny marknadsföringslag'.
655. Sections 29–36 Marketing Act.
656. Government Bill (Proposition) 2007/08:115, 121.
657. Section 29 para. 1 Marketing Act.

Part V. Non-Contractual Liability

Chapter 1. Negligence

§1. General Statement

335. The Tort Liability Act (*Skadeståndslag (1972:207)*) is the primary regulation of Swedish tort law. According to Chapter 1 section 1 of the said Act, the principles set forth in the Act apply unless another statute provides otherwise. As far as non-contractual liability is concerned, the main rule is that a person or a company is only liable for personal injury or property damage, if the damage is caused intentionally or through negligence. In general, one is only liable for damages caused by means of actions, but under certain conditions, liability can be extended to include damages caused by omission.

In a non-contractual relationship, liability for purely financial loss – that is, loss not connected to personal injury or property damage – arises in exceptional cases such as situations where the loss is caused by a criminal act, the loss is caused by a public agency in the exercise of public authority, and in some specific cases, by negligent information.[658] There are also specific statutes, such as the Personal Data Act (*Personuppgiftslag (1998:204)*) and the Copyright Act (*Lag (1960:729) om upphovsrätt till litterära och konstnärliga verk*), that include provisions that extend liability to cover purely financial loss in certain situations.

336. The purpose of compensation for damages under Swedish tort law is that of repair. As a general principle, the compensation shall put the injured in the same financial situation as before the injury or damage occurred. As far as non-pecuniary damages are concerned, such damages are only covered when stipulated in law, for example compensation for pain and suffering according to Chapter 5 section 1 Tort Liability Act. However, compensation for non-pecuniary damage rarely tends to reach any substantial amounts. It should also be noted that the system of social and collective insurance plays an important role in Swedish tort law.[659] For example, compensation can be mitigated pursuant to Chapter 3 section 6 Tort Liability Act with account to insurance. Furthermore, Chapter 6 section 2 Tort Liability Act provides for mitigation of liability in cases where the burden of liability is considered unreasonably heavy.

---

658. Chapter 2 s. 2 and Ch. 3 ss 2 and 3 Tort Liability Act.
659. See Jan Hellner & Marcus Radetzki, *Skadeståndsrätt*, 7th edn (Stockholm: Norstedts Juridik, 2006), 357.

As stated above, special liability statutes supersede the general rules in the Tort Liability Act. However, such special statutes rarely deal with every aspect involved in tort law. For instance, the specific liability provision in the Personal Data Act does not give guidance on how to determine the compensation for violation of personal integrity. As to the calculation of damages, the courts apply the general principles set forth in the Tort Liability Act.

337. The fundamental question when determining whether a person has been negligent or not is if the person challenged with negligence has deviated in a blameworthy manner from what can be expected from her or him. Naturally, you can expect more from an expert in a certain field than from a novice. The assessment of a deviant behaviour or action is made primarily from any law or regulation that may exist governing the specific area, precedents and established customary practices. If none of the above gives guidance on how to act in a certain situation, the assessment of a deviant behaviour or action has to be made on a case-by-case basis. The test performed by the Swedish courts is similar to what is often called 'the Learned Hand formula', after a famous American judge.[660]

In short, the test is performed by assessing the likelihood that a certain conduct will injure others (including property damage), the seriousness of the injury if it happens, balanced against the interest which she or he must sacrifice to avoid the risk, taking into account the person's subjective possibility to foresee the damage. These different factors are weighed against one another in an overall assessment to determine whether the circumstances called for a different behaviour than the one that occurred. Swedish courts tend to pay regard to the likelihood of damage, for example, the bigger the likelihood of damage, and the bigger the damages that might occur, the higher the demands on the person performing the action. It should be stressed that to a large extent the meaning and scope of the notion negligence in Swedish tort law is based on case law.[661]

338. As far as the employer's liability for damages caused by her or his employees is concerned, the general starting point, see Chapter 3 section 1 Tort Liability Act, is that the employer is liable for personal injury and property damage that an employee has caused within the course of her or his employment. Damage caused by an employee unrelated to the employment are consequently not covered by this rule. Only under extraordinary circumstances is the employer free from liability for damages caused by employees through fault or negligence in the course of the employment.

660. Hellner & Radetzki, 133–134.

661. See, e.g., Decision by Supreme Court from 10 May 1984, NJA 1984 s. 323; Decision by Supreme Court from 10 May 1995, NJA 1995 s. 274; and Decision by Supreme Court from 5 Nov. 1998, NJA 1998 s. 617.

§2. Financial Loss and Property Damage

339. In the Information and Communications Technology (ICT) sector, the legal classification of the damage is essential since liability for purely financial loss typically arises only when the loss is caused by a criminal act or where a special statutory regulation extends the liability.

The distinction between purely financial loss and property damage is not always as obvious as it would seem. For example, loss of data on a hard drive without destroying the hard drive per se is often categorized as property damage.[662] Under Swedish law, this is due to the fact that the loss of data is a consequence from altering the hard drive in a negative way, but there are many examples in the ICT sector where the damage might be categorized as purely financial. For example, if valuable data on a hard drive is copied, the hard drive still is in the same condition as before. If damage is caused by the disposition the damage is to be considered to be purely financial, since it is not connected with either property damage or personal injury.

§3. Jurisdiction

340. Much can be said on the often complex legal aspects as to the rules on jurisdiction and choice of law in the ICT sector. These aspects will, however, not be covered here. Nevertheless, it should be noted that the main rule stipulated in Chapter 2 section 1 Swedish Penal Code (*Brottsbalk (1962:700)*), which is relevant in many cases concerning non-contractual liability, is that crimes committed in Sweden are to be judged in accordance with Swedish law and by a Swedish court. The same applies when it is uncertain where the crime was committed but grounds exist for assuming that it was committed in Sweden. The main rule in the Swedish Code on Judicial Procedure (*Rättegångsbalk (1942:740)*) concerning tortuous actions stipulates that action for recovery of damages may be brought to the court at the place where the tortuous act was committed or where the injury or damage occurred,[663] or in the court where the defendant resides.[664]

662. See Lindberg & Westman, 109.
663. Chapter 10 s. 8 Code on Judicial Procedure.
664. Chapter 10 s. 1 Code on Judicial Procedure.

Chapter 2. Liability of Network Operators

341. In the Electronic Communications Act (*Lag (2003:389) om elektronisk kommunikation*), which is the result of the implementation of the European Union (EU) Regulatory Framework for electronic communications into Swedish law,[665] a distinction is made between: (i) an operator of an electronic communications network; and (ii) an electronic communication service provider. An operator is defined as the owner of an electronic communications network. An electronic communications network is in brief a transmission system in the wired or wireless arena. In this Chapter, the notion 'network operator' is understood as corresponding to the notion 'operator' in the said Act. An *electronic communication service provider* is an undertaking that, normally for remuneration, conveys signals on electronic communications networks.[666]

In short, the Electronic Communications Act obliges undertakings to give notice to the PTS of activities involving the providing of public communications networks and publicly available communications services. The aim of the regulation is to assure private and public needs for electronic communication, and to ensure efficient competition. PTS is the central administrative authority with overall responsibility in the field of electronic communications.

342. Network operators, as well as most other natural or legal persons, are subject to the general rules of the Tort Liability Act and must subsequently repair personal injury and damage to property caused intentionally or through negligence. In addition, liability is in some cases extended through the Electronic Communications Act.

According to Chapter 7 section 13a Electronic Communications Act, an operator with significant influence on the market that deliberately or as a result of negligence takes a measure that is in breach of, or fails to take a measure that is necessary in order to comply with, an obligation under Chapter 4 section 4 or Chapter 5 section 13 of the said Act, shall compensate for the damage thereby incurred.

The requirements referred to in Chapter 7 section 13a have as their objective to ensure just competition, such as obligations not to apply discriminatory terms and conditions or obligations as to pricing policies. The requirements under Chapter 4 section 4 are obligations towards other operators, while the requirements under Chapter 5 section 13 are obligations towards consumers.

According to Chapter 8 section 7, a company is considered to have a significant influence on a specified market if it, alone or in cooperation with other companies, is able to act independently of its competitors, its customers and the consumers. This latter prerequisite corresponds to a large extent to the notion of dominance found in national and EU competition law. In addition, the Government or PTS gives guidance on how to evaluate whether a company is considered to have a significant

665. See Part I Ch. 1 *supra* (para. 41).
666. The liability of service providers is dealt with in Ch. 3 *infra* (paras 344 et seq.).

influence on a specified market under Chapter 8 section 7. For example, the Swedish telecom operators Telia and Tele2 have been considered to have a significant influence on the Swedish telecommunications market for interconnection.[667]

343. The liability rule stipulated in Chapter 7 section 13a covers, according to the preparatory works, not only damage caused by means of actions, but also damage caused by omission.[668] Subsequently, network operators with significant influence on a market, must actively make sure that they honour the obligations that are applicable to them. For example, if a network operator is obliged by PTS to make its technical specifications public and fails to do so, that network operator is liable for damages caused to other operators by the omission.

As have been accounted for in the previous chapter, liability for purely financial loss is limited under Swedish law and typically only arises when the loss is caused by a criminal act. As has also been mentioned in the previous chapter, liability may be extended to cover purely financial loss in certain situations. The most important consequence of Chapter 7 section 13a is that the liability, through the provision, is extended to include purely financial loss, which should be the damage most likely to be caused to competitors by unfair competition.[669]

The provision in Chapter 7 section 13a has been imposed to ensure that other operators, which do not have a contractual relationship with the operator accused of causing damage, can be compensated for purely financial losses. However, the relatively new rule has not, to the author's knowledge, yet been applied in civil proceedings against a network operator.

667. See PTS Decision of 21 Feb. 2002, no. 00-14849/23.
668. Government Bill (Proposition) 2006/07:119, 'En effektivare lag om elektronisk kommunikation', 45.
669. *Ibid.*

Chapter 3. Liability of Service Providers

§1. General Statement

344. Service providers – the notion here is understood as providers of services by electronic means – in the ICT sector are subject to the general liability rules of the Tort Liability Act. Consequently, service providers must repair personal injury and damage to property caused intentionally or through negligence. However, as stated above, it is possible for the legislator to derogate from the general rules of the Tort Liability Act by enacting specific statutory provisions. We outline in this chapter the most important special liability statutes for service providers in the ICT sector.

The Swedish rules on complicity in crime in the Penal Code should also briefly be mentioned since liability may be extended in accordance with the provision. Chapter 23 section 4 Swedish Penal Code states that a punishment in accordance with the Penal Code shall be imposed not only on the person who committed the act, but also on anyone who furthered it by advice or deed. The same applies to any other act punishable with imprisonment under another law, for example, copyright infringement in accordance with the Copyright Act. Each accomplice is judged according to the intent or the negligence attributable to her or him.

§2. Liability in Accordance with the Electronic Commerce Act

I. Background

345. The Swedish Act on Electronic Commerce and other information society services (*Lag (2002:562) om elektronisk handel och andra informationssamhällets tjänster*; hereinafter 'Electronic Commerce Act') is based on the EU Directive on Electronic Commerce.[670] The main objective of the Directive is to ensure the free movement of information society services between the Member States. The term information society service is defined in the Directive on Technical Standards and Regulations)[671] as *any service normally provided for remuneration, at a distance, by electronic means and at the individual request of a recipient of services*, for example, ISPs. As far as non-contractual liability is concerned, the Electronic Commerce Act lays down rules on freedom from liability in certain cases. However, as accounted for below, the exemptions from liability are far from absolute and are dependent on several requirements and conditions.

670. Directive 2000/31/EC of the European Parliament and of the Council of 8 Jun. 2000 on certain legal aspects of information society services, in particular e-commerce, in the Internal Market.
671. Article 1(2) of Directive 98/48/EC of the European Parliament and of the Council of 20 Jul. 1998 amending Directive 98/34/EC of the European Parliament and of the Council of 22 Jun. 1998 laying down a procedure for the provision of information in the field of technical standards and regulations.

II. Mere Conduit

346. Section 16 Electronic Commerce Act (corresponding to Article 12 Directive on Electronic Commerce), stipulates that an *information society service provider* shall not be liable for the content of the information, if the service only consists of the transmission of information, provided by a recipient of the service, in a communication network, or if the service provider only gives access to a communication network.

This exemption from liability applies only if the service provider: (i) has not initiated the transmission; (ii) does not select the receiver of the transmission; and (iii) does not select or modify the information contained in the transmission.

347. In contrast, service providers which are the sources of the information, select recipients of the transmission, or modify the information transmitted, with exception of mere technical manipulation during the transmission,[672] can be liable for the damage caused.

Further, in accordance with Recital 42 Directive on Electronic Commerce, the exemptions from liability only cover cases where the activity of the service provider is of a mere technical, automatic and passive nature. The service provider must neither have knowledge of nor control over the information which is transmitted or stored.

348. The question of an ISP's responsibility for its customers' communication has recently been discussed in two cases in Swedish courts. In both cases the plaintiffs demanded injunctions to prohibit the ISPs to provide Internet service for BitTorrent trackers – that is, servers that assist in the communication between peers using the BitTorrent protocol – accused of copyright infringement. However, one of the cases (The Portlane-Case) did not regard liability per se, but a temporary injunction.

A. *The Black Internet-Case*[673]

349. In the first case, copyright holders filed a request for an injunction to prohibit the Swedish ISP Black Internet, to provide Internet service for the well-known Pirate Bay.[674] The copyright holders also requested a temporary injunction, until the case was finally adjudicated or otherwise is decided. Such injunction and temporary injunction are provided for under section 53b Copyright Act.

The grounds for the injunction (as well as the temporary injunction) was that Black Internet, by providing Internet service for The Pirate Bay, objectively was considered aiding and abetting the copyright infringements taking place with the

672. See Recital 43 Directive of Electronic Commerce.
673. Decision of the District Court of Stockholm from 21 Aug. 2009, no. T 11712–09.
674. See s. 2 IV A *infra* (para. 354).

help of the file sharing service provided for by The Pirate Bay. Black Internet disputed the motions and held that their role as an ISP could not be considered aiding and abetting copyright infringement.

The District Court initially had to decide with regard to the request for temporary injunction. The court declared that the Electronic Commerce Act does not hinder such an injunction. Reference was made to Article 12(3) Directive of Electronic Commerce, where it is stated that the Directive shall not affect the possibility for a court or administrative authority, in accordance with the legal system of the Member State, of requiring the service provider to terminate or prevent an infringement. The Court held that, since Black Internet provided Internet service for The Pirate Bay, and that it was established in the case that Black Internet was well aware of the copyright infringement conviction in the criminal proceedings against people behind The Pirate Bay, Black Internet objectively contributed to the copyright infringement, for which the copyright holders had shown probable cause. Thus, the Court temporarily prohibited by penalty of a fine Black Internet to provide Internet services to The Pirate Bay.

The decision was appealed by Black Internet. The Court of Appeal upheld the ruling in all essential aspects.[675] After another appeal was filed by Black Internet, the Supreme Court decided to deny leave to appeal.[676]

Thereafter, the case continued in the district court, which now had to decide on the plaintiffs' request for injunction to prohibit Black Internet (which had now changed its name to Abandonner) to provide Internet service for The Pirate Bay. The court held that Black Internet objectively contributed to the copyright infringement, since it: (i) was the ISPs for The Pirate Bay, even if the service was provided via an intermediary; (ii) was well aware of the above-mentioned copyright infringement conviction; and (iii) had continued to provide Internet service after receiving notice of the infringement from the copyright holders, even though it was practically possible for Black Internet to stop providing the Internet service via the intermediary (which it had done after the preliminary injunction was issued). Thus, the court in its final judgment prohibited by penalty of a fine Black Internet to provide Internet services to The Pirate Bay.[677] Black Internet did not file an appeal and the judgment of the district court has gained legal force.

B. The Portlane-Case[678]

350. In the second case, copyright holders filed a similar temporary injunction to prohibit the Swedish ISP Portlane, to provide Internet service to one or more BitTorrent trackers connected with the domain name <tracker.openbittorrent.com>. In this case, however, the district court came to the conclusion that an ISP cannot be

675. Decision of Svea Court of Appeal from 21 May 2010, no. Ö 7131-09, Ö 8773-09.
676. Decision of Supreme Court from 13 Oct. 2010, no. Ö 2904-10.
677. Decision of the District Court of Stockholm from 16 Oct. 2012, no. T 7540-09, T 11712–09.
678. Decision of the District Court of Stockholm from 1 Dec. 2009, no. T 17127–09.

burdened with such far-reaching responsibility that they can be regarded as contributors to the copyright infringement. Hence, the petition for temporary injunction was denied.

The decision was appealed by the copyright holders. The Court of Appeal overruled that decision and held that the copyright holders had shown a probable cause that Portlane had objectively contributed to the copyright infringement. Thus, the Court of Appeal temporarily prohibited by penalty of a fine Portlane to provide Internet services to the BitTorrent trackers.[679]

Portlane thereafter went bankrupt and the parties entered into a settlement. The case was therefore dismissed.[680]

III. Caching

351. Section 17 Electronic Commerce Act, corresponding to Article 13 Directive on Electronic Commerce, provides for a rule on freedom from liability regarding caching. In brief, caching is the process where information is temporarily stored by, for example, ISPs or other intermediaries, for the purpose of reducing the amount of resources that otherwise would be involved in the transmission of data. For example, ISPs regularly store parts of popular websites on their servers, thus increasing the access speed and freeing bandwidth for its subscribers. From a legal point of view, caching primarily raises questions regarding copying under the law on copyright, but also other branches of law may be concerned.

For caching to be legally possible without infringement of copyright or other rights, section 17 Electronic Commerce Act stipulates that a Service Provider is not liable for transmissions of information provided by a recipient of the service in a communication network if the storage of information is automatic, intermediate and temporary, and the storage is made for the sole purpose of making the transmission to other recipients of the service more efficient.

Further, for freedom from liability, it is required that the provider does not modify the information, complies with conditions on access to the information, complies with rules recognized and used by the industry regarding updating of the information, does not interfere with the lawful use of technology widely recognized and used by the industry, and, finally, without delay intervenes to remove or to disable access to the information it has stored upon obtaining actual knowledge of the fact that the information at the initial source of the transmission has been removed from the network, or access to it has been disabled, or that a court or an administrative authority has ordered such removal or disablement.

---

679. Decision of Svea Court of Appeal from 21 May 2010, no. Ö 10146-09.
680. Decision of the District Court of Stockholm from 8 Mar. 2011, no. T 17127-09.

352. As far as copyright is concerned, it is necessary to mention the special limitations of reproduction rights, stipulated in section 11a Copyright Act.[681] The provision in the aforesaid section excludes from the rights of the copyright holder any temporary acts of reproduction which are an integral and essential part of a technological process, and where the reproductions only are transient or incidental. Further, the reproductions must not have any independent economic significance, the purpose of the reproduction must be to enable transmission in a network between third parties and the use must be lawful.

The consequence of the aforesaid provision in the Copyright Act is that section 17 Electronic Commerce Act regarding caching, to some extent loses its importance, at least in the area of copyright. The Electronic Commerce Act is only applicable in situations where the intermediary is liable according to the Copyright Act. Since section 11a Copyright Act excludes liability for temporary acts of reproduction, the Electronic Commerce Act is not applicable. Thus, the importance of section 17 Electronic Commerce Act has been reduced by section 11a Copyright Act.

IV. Hosting

353. The rule in the Electronic Commerce Act limiting liability for various hosting services is found in section 18, and corresponds to Article 14 Directive on Electronic Commerce. Examples of hosting services covered by the provision are web hotels, electronic bulletin boards, guest books and other interactive online services.[682] In accordance with section 18, service providers which store information provided by a recipient of the service are not liable for the information stored. However, to have the benefit of freedom from liability, the service provider must not have actual knowledge of the illegal information or activity, and must not be aware of facts or circumstances from which the illegal activity or information is apparent. As soon as the service provider obtains such knowledge or awareness, the service provider must, without delay, prevent further access to the information.

The question of freedom from liability for hosting services has recently been subject to two judgments in Svea Court of Appeal and District Court of Stockholm.

A. The Pirate Bay-Case[683]

354. In the first case, the question of freedom from liability for hosting services arose in the criminal proceedings against the people behind the Swedish file sharing website The Pirate Bay (thepiratebay.org).

681. Section 11a Copyright Act is the result of the implementation of Directive 2001/29/EC of the European Parliament and of the Council of 22 May 2001 on the harmonization of certain aspects of copyright and related rights in the information society. See Part II Ch. 1 s. 6 I *supra* (paras 162–163).

682. Government Bill (Proposition) 2001/02:150, 'Lag om elektronisk handel och andra informationssamhällets tjänster, m.m.', 21.

683. Judgment of the Svea Court of Appeal from 26 Nov. 2010, no. B 4041-09.

In the case, the prosecutor charged the defendants with complicity in copyright infringement. It was argued that copyright-protected material was made available to the general public in a way which was to be regarded as a breach of the Copyright Act. The defendants pleaded not guilty. In accordance with the Swedish Code on Judicial Procedure, civil claims of copyright holders were also addressed in the case.

Regarding liability for hosting services, the Court of Appeal confirmed the finding of the district court, and held that the file sharing service provided by The Pirate Bay was considered an information society service covered by the Electronic Commerce Act. However, referring to European Court of Justice's judgment in case C-236/08-C-238/08, the court stated that a person providing a search engine service can very well be a service provider within the meaning of the EU Directive on Electronic Commerce, without being covered by any of the provisions regarding limitations of liability. In order for a release from liability for damages according to sections 16–18 Electronic Commerce Act, the service provided must be limited to either forwarding, caching or hosting services only. The court found that although the website did not involve a pure transmission service or caching, it did in certain aspects correspond to hosting services covered by section 18 Electronic Commerce Act. However, this release of liability provision focuses on liability for the *content* of stored information. The damages claim was not based on liability for the content of the information stored on the website, but on the *functions* which were provided and that had furthered copyright exploitation by users. Therefore, the court found that the service on the website was not covered by any of the provisions set forth in sections 16–18 Electronic Commerce Act and the rules of freedom from liability could not be applied. The Court of Appeal found the defendants guilty of complicity in copyright infringement. It should be noted that, in accordance with Swedish penal law, to be convicted for complicity in crime it is not a requirement that the perpetrators behind the main crime are identified, provided that an actual crime has been committed. It should also be noted that the court found Swedish law applicable in accordance with the above-mentioned rules on jurisdiction and choice of law. The defendants were sentenced to four to twelve months imprisonment (each defendant was punished only for the act he had committed himself) and ordered to pay damages in the range of SEK 46 million (approximately EUR 5.2 million). However, the sentence has been appealed and is pending a decision in the Court of Appeal.

The sentence was appealed to the Supreme Court by the defendants, who also requested that a preliminary ruling be obtained from the European Court of Justice. The Supreme Court denied this request and also denied leave to appeal.[684]

684. Decision of Supreme Court from 1 Feb. 2012, no. B 5880-10.

B. The Matklubben.se-Case[685]

354.1. In the second case, a copyright holder claimed damages for copyright infringement from the companies behind the Swedish website Matklubben.se.[686] The website offers a database which contains thousands of recipes and photographs of each dish. All recipes and photographs are uploaded and shared by the Internet users themselves and not by any of the companies behind the website. Regarding liability for hosting services, the district court held that the file sharing services provided by Matklubben.se was considered an information society service covered by the Electronic Commerce Act. It was clear that the services were provided at a distance by electronic means and at the individual request of the recipients of the services (see the definition above).

Even though the recipients of the service did not pay for the service (see the requirement normally provided for remuneration), the court found that since it was partly funded by advertising revenue, the service was covered by the Electronic Commerce Act. Further, the court stated that since the website contained only uploaded recipes and photographs, discussion forums and adverts, and no editorial material, the service was to be regarded as a hosting service covered by section 18 Electronic Commerce Act. As stated above, for freedom from liability, the service provider must not be aware of the illegal information or activity, and is obliged to prevent further access to the information when such knowledge is obtained. In the case, it was established that Matklubben.se was used mainly for legal purposes. It was further established that the defendants had offered to immediately prevent access to files uploaded on Matklubben.se, as soon as requests had been made by copyright holders. Thus, the defendants had fulfilled its obligations under section 18 Electronic Commerce Act and were released from liability. The copyright holders did not appeal and the ruling has gained legal force.

§3. Electronic Bulletin Boards

355. An Electronic Bulletin Board is, in accordance with the legal definition in the Act on Responsibility for Electronic Bulletin Boards (*Lag (1998:112) om ansvar för elektroniska anslagstavlor*), a service for the electronic transmission of messages. According to the Act, a message is text, pictures, sound or other information. However, the law does not apply to network operators, mediation of messages within a public authority or between public authorities or within an enterprise or between a legal group of enterprises. Further, the law does not apply to services that are covered by the regulations in the Freedom of the Press Act or the Fundamental Law on Freedom of Expression, such as the rule regarding databases found in Chapter 1 section 9 Fundamental Law on Freedom of Expression, and email.[687]

Examples of Electronic Bulletin Boards are services, where users can perform functions such as uploading and downloading software and data, reading news and

685. Judgment of the District Court of Stockholm from 27 Jun. 2013, no. T 10848-09.
686. www.matklubben.se.
687. See Government Bill (Proposition) 1997/98:15, 'Ansvar för elektroniska anslagstavlor', 12.

exchanging messages with other users. There are no special liability rules in the Act of Responsibility for Electronic Bulletin Boards. The supplier of an electronic bulletin board is of course not exempted from the general principles of the Tort Liability Act. However, since electronic bulletin boards fall under the definition of hosting services in section 18 Electronic Commerce Act, the provisions on freedom from liability regarding hosting in that Act must also be taken into account.[688]

356. The main principles on liability in the Act on Responsibility for Electronic Bulletin Boards are found in sections 3–5.

First, according to section 3, the supplier of an electronic bulletin board must notify each person who connects to the service of the identity of the supplier and to what extent messages posted will be available to other users.

Second, according to section 4, the supplier has an obligation to supervise the service to an extent that is, reasonable considering the extent and objective of the service.

Third, according to section 5, the supplier must remove a message, or in some other way make it inaccessible, if it is obvious that the message is in breach of certain sections of the Swedish Penal Code. Such obligations arise if a message is inciting rebellion,[689] agitates against an ethnic group or another group of persons with allusion to race, colour, national or ethnic origin, religious belief or sexual orientation,[690] portrays or in any other way makes pornographic pictures of children available to others,[691] or is an unlawful depiction of violence.[692] Further, the supplier must also remove messages if it is obvious that the user, by submitting the message, has committed copyright infringement.

357. The obligation to remove messages concerning agitation against a group with certain sexual orientation was recently subject to a ruling of the Swedish Supreme Court.[693] Certain negative remarks concerning persons with homosexual preferences were posted on an electronic bulletin board (in this case a guestbook on a website) with reference to the Bible. The Court held that even if the messages objectively constituted agitation against an ethnic group in accordance with Chapter 16 section 8 Penal Code, this was not obvious to the supplier of the electronic bulletin board, thus the supplier was freed of all charges.

358. As stated above, there are no special rules of liability in the Act on Responsibility for Electronic Bulletin Boards. The responsibilities set forth in the Act – for example, the omission to remove certain postings – are sanctioned by fine or imprisonment. This, however, does not exclude liability in accordance with the Tort Liability Act. As accounted for in section 1, the fundamental question when determining whether a person has been negligent or not is if the person accused of being negligent has deviated in a blameworthy manner from what can be expected from

688. Government Bill (Proposition) 2001/02:150, 121.
689. Chapter 16 s. 5 Penal Code.
690. Chapter 16 s. 8 Penal Code.
691. Chapter 16 s. 10a Penal Code.
692. Chapter 16 s. 10b Penal Code.
693. Decision by Supreme Court from 7 Nov. 2007, NJA 2007 s. 805.

her or him. The assessment of a blameworthy deviant behaviour is made primarily based on any law or regulation governing a specific area. The rules in the Act on Responsibility for Electronic Bulletin Boards stipulate a certain way of conduct, for example an obligation to remove certain messages. Hence, damage caused by deviance from this way of conduct, unless the circumstances provide otherwise, is generally a basis for liability. The consequence of the fact that it is a criminal act not to remove, for instance, copyright protected material, is that the liability also covers purely financial loss.

§4. Personal Data Protection

359. Many companies in the ICT sector process personal data in the course of their business. To understand the special liability statutes in the field of personal data protection it is initially necessary to outline the fundamental features of the Personal Data Act (*Personuppgiftslag (1998:204)*).[694]

The Personal Data Act, which is a result of the implementation of the Data Protection Directive[695] into Swedish law, aims to protect people against the violation of their personal integrity by processing of personal data. According to section 5 Personal Data Act, the Act applies to all processing of personal data that is, wholly or partly, performed with the aid of computers. The Act also applies to other processing of personal data, if the data is included in or is intended to form part of a structured collection of personal data that is, available for searching or compilation according to specific criteria. Processing of personal data that a natural person performs in the course of activities of a purely private nature is, however, excluded.

Processing means, in the sense of the Personal Data Act, everything one does with personal data, whether performed through a computer or not. For example, collection, registration, storage and compilation of personal data are all considered processing in the meaning of the Personal Data Act.

Section 9 prescribes that personal data may only be processed if it is lawful. In addition, data must always be processed in a correct manner, and in accordance with good practice. Further, the data may only be collected for specific, explicitly stated and justified purposes and must not be processed for any purpose that is incompatible with the purpose for which the information is collected. No more personal data than is necessary may be processed and the personal data may not be kept for a longer period than necessary with regard to the purpose of the processing.

The processing of personal data, covered by the Personal Data Act, requires in principle notification to the Data Inspection Board (*Datainspektionen*), see section 36 Personal Data Act. However, there are extensive exceptions to this obligation.

360. As far as liability is concerned, section 48 provides a special liability statute. As previously stressed, special statutes supersede the general liability rules of

694. See also Part VI Ch. 1 *infra* (paras 370 et seq.).

695. Directive 95/46/EC of the European Parliament and of the Council of 24 Oct. 1995 on the protection of individuals with regard to the processing of personal data and on the free movement of such data (hereinafter 'Data Protection Directive').

the Tort Liability Act. However, general tort law principles apply to the extent that the special statute does not give guidance in a certain question, for instance on how to determine the compensation or how to divide liability in the event of several liable persons.

Section 48 grants registered persons a right to damages for intrusion of personal integrity caused by the processing of personal data in violation of the provisions of the Personal Data Act. Liability is strict and the right to damages therefore arises regardless of any intent or negligence attributable to the person violating the rules. All damages, including personal injury, property damage, purely financial loss and violation of personal integrity, are covered by the statute. Even processing in breach of good practice, as mentioned above, is subject to strict liability. What is to be considered good practice is up to the courts to decide in light of directions of, *inter alia*, the Data Inspection Board and other customary practices developed in the field of data protection.[696]

The compensation for violation of personal integrity shall be reasonable with regard to the circumstances of the case. Factors to be weighed in are the risk of spread of sensitive personal data and if the registered person, because of processing of personal data in conflict with the rules of the Personal Data Act, has suffered a negative decision or other measures.

However, section 48 also provides a relief from liability in some cases. If the person providing the personal data can show that the error was not caused by her or him, the compensation may to a reasonable extent be adjusted. Such an adjustment can even reduce the amount to zero. For example, this could be the case if the individual has given incorrect information resulting in the processing of personal data in breach of the Personal Data Act.

§5. Liability under the Fundamental Law on Freedom of Expression

361. In Sweden, there are two separate constitutional laws concerning freedom of speech. The Freedom of the Press Act (*Tryckfrihetsförordning (1949:105)*) regulates the printed word, such as books and newspapers, whereas the Fundamental Law on Freedom of Expression (*Yttrandefrihetsgrundlag (1991:1469)*) regulates certain other types of mass media, such as television, certain web sites, radio, and films. This chapter will briefly deal with the Fundamental Law on Freedom of Expression and the special liability statutes provided therein.

In accordance with Chapter 1 Article 1 Fundamental Law on Freedom of Expression, every Swedish citizen is guaranteed the right, vis-à-vis the public institutions, to publicly express thoughts, opinions and sentiments, and in general to communicate information on any subject whatsoever on sound radio, television and certain like transmissions, films and video recordings. The only restrictions permitted are the ones stated in the Fundamental Law on Freedom of Expression. For example, the general rule in Chapter 1 Article 3, stating that censorship prior to publication is not allowed, is restricted in the same Article for movies intended for public showing.

696. Government Bill (Proposition) 1997/98:15, 142.

The purpose of the Fundamental Law on Freedom of Expression is to protect the freedom of expression in the media forms covered by the law. However, when the freedom of expression in such media is abused, the law points out who may be held responsible. In Chapter 4 Fundamental Law on Freedom of Expression, it is stipulated that all radio programmes and technical recordings shall have a responsible editor empowered to supervise the publication. In Chapter 6 of the aforesaid Law, the liability for freedom of expression offences (e.g., defamation) rests with the responsible editor, or if a deputy is acting in place of the editor, liability rests with the deputy. If none of those persons are traceable, someone else steps in, in a kind of chain of responsible persons. Hence, in these situations undertakings involved in the provision of information society services, such as ISPs, are exempted from liability by statutory provisions in the Swedish constitution.

Chapter 4. Product Liability

§1. General Statement

362. The primary regulation of product liability in Sweden is found in the Product Liability Act (*Produktansvarslag (1992:18)*). The Act is a result of the implementation of the EU Directive on Liability for Defective Products[697] in Swedish law. However, liability may also follow from principles developed in Swedish case law.[698] The existence of the Product Safety Act (*Produktsäkerhetslag (2004:451)*) concerning the safety of products should also be noted. However, the Act will not be dealt with further in this chapter, since it does not concern liability per se.

In accordance with section 1 Product Liability Act, the main rule is that personal injury caused due to a defect in a product shall be compensated. This also applies to property damage, if the damage is caused by a defect in the product and the product is of a type that is intended for private purposes, provided the damage was caused when the product was used mainly for the purpose intended for such products. Hence, property damage caused by products in the course of business is not covered by the Product Liability Act. Liability for such damages may, however, follow from general principles developed in Swedish case law.[699] Furthermore, the Swedish Supreme Court has established that the notion property damage shall have the same meaning as in the Tort Liability Act.[700]

There is no requirement of intent or negligence, consequently the liability is strict.

To be compensated, damages must exceed SEK 3,500 (approximately EUR 350). This unusual regime is due to a general deduction from any compensation to be paid under the Act.[701] Even though the Directive on Liability for Defective Products provides the possibility to set a threshold for the producer's total liability, such a limitation has not been implemented in the Swedish Product Liability Act. It should be noted that damages that must be compensated under the Product Liability Act do not cover purely financial losses.

697. Council Directive 85/374/EEC of 25 Jul. 1985 on the approximation of the laws, regulations and administrative provisions of the Member States concerning liability for defective products (hereinafter 'Directive on Liability for Defective Products'). The Directive 1999/34/EC of the European Parliament and of the Council of 10 May 1999 amending Council Directive 85/374/EEC on the approximation of the laws, regulations and administrative provisions of the Member States concerning liability for defective products did not give rise to any changes of the Product Liability Act.

698. Lindberg & Westman, 125.

699. Government Bill (Proposition) 1990/91:197, 'Regeringens proposition om produktskadelag', 76–78.

700. See Decision by Supreme Court from 20 Feb. 1996, NJA 1996 s. 68.

701. Section 9 Product Liability Act.

§2. MOVABLES, HARDWARE AND SOFTWARE

363. In accordance with section 2 Product Liability Act, the notion product includes all movables. It also includes movables that are incorporated into or in some other way have become a component part of another movable or an immovable. If damage has occurred due to a defect in a product that has become a component part of another movable or an immovable, both products shall be deemed to have caused the damage. However, in contrast to the Directive on Liability for Defective Products, the Product Liability Act does not include electricity. The discrepancy is explained in the Government Bill.[702] According to Swedish law electricity is not recognized as a movable. Instead, the provisions on strict liability in relation to electricity were included in the Electricity Act (*Ellag (1997:857)*).[703]

It is evident that hardware, such as a computer, is covered by the notion product, and thus falls under the Product Liability Act. In contrast, software is in principle not considered a product under the Product Liability Act. In accordance with the preparatory works, software is merely considered to be a series of instructions that make hardware perform certain actions.[704]

If damage is caused by a product, in the sense of the Product Liability Act, and the damage is due to a defect in software integrated in the product, it is still the product that shall be deemed to have caused the damage. However, the legislator provides some openings for the courts to make other interpretations of the notion product with account to technical development.[705] It has been argued that software should fall under the notion product, and thus the strict liability in the Product Liability Act.[706] The uncertainty is noteworthy considering how common it is that software controls important occurrences and defects may cause a great deal of damage. However, it should also be noted that liability for software still may follow from the general principles of the Tort Liability Act.

§3. DEFECTIVE PRODUCTS

364. The notion defect is defined in section 3 Product Liability Act. A product is considered defective when it does not provide the safety that a person is entitled to expect. When determining the safety of the product, account must be taken to the use to which it could reasonably be expected that the product would be put and how it was marketed. Furthermore, account must be taken to the directions for use, the time when the product was put into circulation and all other circumstances. In Article 6(2) Directive on Liability for Defective Products, it is stated that a product shall not be considered defective for the sole reason that a better product is subsequently put into circulation. No such provision is included in the Product Liability

702. Government Bill (Proposition) 1990/91:197, 14.
703. Chapter 10 ss 2 and 3 Electricity Act.
704. Government Bill (Proposition) 1990/91:197, 93.
705. *Ibid.*, 94.
706. Lindberg, Westman, 125.

Act. Nevertheless, the preparatory works state that a rule with the same meaning may be applicable under the Product Liability Act.[707]

§4. Persons Liable for Damages

365. With the given definition of the notion product,[708] it is also evident that services are excluded from the strict liability of the Product Liability Act. For example, ISPs are not liable under the Product Liability Act for damages caused to a computer in connection with the service. However, they may be liable for providing hardware causing damage.

According to sections 6 and 7 Product Liability Act, liability is vested with the manufacturer, the creator or the collector of the tortuous product, the importer of the product into the European Union, or any person who has marketed the product as her or his own by putting her or his trademark or other distinguishing feature on the product. When none of the above can be identified, each supplier of the product will be liable in accordance with the Product Liability Act.

The supplier may escape liability if she or he, within one month from a claim of compensation or request for information about the producer of the product, informs the claimant of the identity of the producer or of the person who supplied her or him with the product.

Contractual derogation from liability is declared null and void according to section 5 Product Liability Act.

366. The persons liable for damages in accordance with sections 6 and 7 Product Liability Act may, however, escape liability under certain circumstances as specified in section 8 of the Act. No liability is inflicted to the person normally liable in accordance with the above, if that person:

(i) shows that she or he did not put the product into circulation in the course of business; or
(ii) makes it probable that the defect which caused the damage did not exist at the time when the product was put into circulation; or
(iii) shows that the defect is due to compliance of the product with mandatory regulations issued by the public authorities; or
(iv) shows that the state of scientific and technical knowledge at the time when the product was put into circulation was not such as to enable the existence of the defect to be discovered.

Section 8 Product Liability Act corresponds to a large extent to Article 7 Directive on Liability for Defective Products. However, section 8 Product Liability Act does

707. Government Bill (Proposition) 1990/91:197, 108.
708. See s. 2 *supra* (para. 363).

not include a defence for manufacturers of a component. According to the preparatory works, no divergence is intended.[709] The situation is considered to be covered by the above-mentioned rule in section 2 Product Liability Act, which states that the component manufacturer as well as the manufacturer of the finished product shall be liable for damages caused by a defect in the component part.

367. When two or more are liable for the same damage, the general principle in the Tort Liability Act is joint and several liability.[710] Since the principle is generally applicable, the legislator did not find it necessary to include an explicit provision on this in the Product Liability Act, even though such provision is found in Article 5 Directive on Liability for Defective Products.

§5. Reduction of Liability, Limitation of Actions

368. Under section 10 Product Liability Act, the liability may be reduced having regard to what is reasonable, when negligence on the part of the injured person has contributed to the damage. Compared to the general rules of the Tort Liability Act, under which liability may only be mitigated due to gross negligence or intent on the part of the injured person, the Product Liability Act provides a less consumer friendly approach in this respect. Nevertheless, in accordance with the preparatory works, the injured person still has the possibility to claim damages under the Tort Liability Act, provided that the injured person can establish that the producer was negligent. Thus the person liable for the tortuous product has to show gross negligence on the part of the injured person for the liability to be mitigated.[711]

369. Section 12 Product Liability Act provides a statutory rule limiting the time within which proceedings can be brought. Actions must be launched within three years from the day on which the plaintiff became aware, or should reasonably have become aware, of the relevant circumstances. Furthermore, section 12 Product Liability Act states that the right to compensation in accordance with the Act is extinguished after the expiry of a period of ten years from the date on which the producer put the product which caused the damage into circulation.

709. Government Bill (Proposition) 1990/91:197, 96.
710. Chapter 6 s. 4 Tort Liability Act.
711. Government Bill (Proposition) 1992/93:38, 'Proposition om ändring i produktansvarslagen (1992:18) m.m.', 15.

Part VI. Privacy Protection

Chapter 1. Regulation of Personal Data Processing

§1. General Statement

370. The Swedish Instrument of Government (*Regeringsform (1974:152)*) is one of the four constitutional laws in Sweden. Its Chapter 2 Article 6 paragraph 2 protects privacy as a fundamental right. While privacy was previously regulated in Chapter 2 Article 3, the constitution now states in Chapter 2 Article 6:

> [e]veryone shall be protected in their relations with the public institutions against significant invasions of their personal privacy, if these occur without their consent and involve the surveillance or systematic monitoring of the individual's personal circumstances.

Though privacy is not defined as such in the constitution, Article 6 mentions surveillance and monitoring, which seems to indicate that the focus remains to be processing of personal data.

Sweden implemented the European Parliament and Council Directive 95/46/EC of 24 October 1995 on the protection of individuals with regard to the processing of personal data and on the free movement of such data (hereinafter 'Data Protection Directive') in 1998 by enacting the Personal Data Act (*Personuppgiftslag (1998:204)*). The Personal Data Act replaced the previously in force Swedish Data Act (*Datalag (1973:289)*) from 1973, which had mainly focused on computer registers and not data processing in general.

371. The Swedish legislative framework protects privacy in many different aspects.[712] Starting from criminal provisions protecting against kidnapping or unlawful deprivation of liberty,[713] defamation,[714] breach of postal or telecommunication secrecy[715] or eavesdropping,[716] privacy-related provisions can also be found within tax law (exchange of personal data between public authorities), credit information and debt collection, court proceedings and criminal procedural coercive

712. See for a complete analysis of privacy-related legislation: Government Official Report SOU 2007:22, 'Skyddet för den personliga integriteten, Kartläggning och analys Del 1'.
713. Chapter 4 s. 1 and 2 Penal Code.
714. Chapter 5 s. 1 Penal Code.
715. Chapter 4 s. 8 Penal Code.
716. Chapter 4 s. 9a Penal Code.

measures, as well as police investigations (surveillance and databases with criminal records), within health and social care and in the rules relating to processing of employee personal data. In the following, focus will be placed on the general legal framework for automated data processing, along with the mention of a few special statutory provisions.

§2. Swedish Personal Data Act

372. In accordance with Article 1 Data Protection Directive, the Swedish Personal Data Act protects individuals against violations of their personal integrity. As stipulated in the constitution,[717] the protection covers data processing and not privacy in general.

The Swedish Act applies to processing that is done by controllers who are established in Sweden or who use equipment that is situated in Sweden.[718]

The Act regulates the processing of personal data and the requirements such processing has to fulfil, in particular sections 9 and 10, in order to be allowed. As these rules might complicate everyday processing of personal information in electronic communications as well as ordinary composing of texts, the Swedish Personal Data Act was amended in 2007, and special rules for unstructured processing were implemented.[719]

Besides this specific provision on unstructured processing, the Personal Data Act follows the setup of the Data Protection Directive, covering requirements for processing of personal data, rules on sensitive personal information, information to the individual as well as the transfer of personal data to third countries.

I. Definitions

373. In compliance with Article 2 Data Protection Directive, the Swedish Personal Data Act defines, *inter alia*, the following terms in section 3.

A. Personal Data

> Personal data: All kinds of information that directly or indirectly may be attributed to a natural person who is alive.

374. The restriction to a natural person excludes data on legal persons, unless the company is a sole trader. As the registration number of a sole trader consists of the personal number of the owner of the company, it is considered personal data.[720]

---

717. See s. 1 *supra* (para. 370).
718. Section 4 Personal Data Act.
719. Government Bill (Proposition) 2005/06:173, 'Översyn av personuppgiftslagen'.
720. See decision by the Court of Appeal Svea hovrätt from 31 Aug. 2004, nr B 4151–04.

Any information that can be attributed to an individual is personal data, regardless of whether it concerns that person's private, work or social life.[721] Examples of personal data therefore include name, address, telephone number, personal number and car registration number. Images or sounds can constitute personal data if an individual can be directly or indirectly identified in them.[722] Biometric data, such as fingerprints, retinal patterns, facial structure and DNA, also falls within the category of personal data.[723]

In accordance with Recital 26 Data Protection Directive, in determining 'whether a person is identifiable account should be taken of all the means likely reasonably to be used either by the controller or by any other person to identify the said person'. This means that as long as somebody, not necessarily the controller, can link a piece of information to a natural person, it is considered personal data. Therefore also encrypted data, as well as anonymous details such as IP-numbers or other eIDs that require a key or access to the database of the ISP, fall within the scope of data protection.[724] In a decision in 2005, the Swedish Data Inspection Board (*Datainspektionen*), as well as the Stockholm Administrative Court of Appeal (*Kammarrätt*) considered IP-numbers being used by a Swedish anti-pirate organization as personal data.[725]

Examples that do not fall within the definition of personal data are generic names of cities or streets, general descriptions of people concerning hair or eye colour, as well as the history list on a computer that contains all previously visited web pages.[726]

The requirement of 'who is alive' excludes dead or unborn people such as embryos. Information about relatives of the deceased or parents of an unborn child are, however, considered to be personal data.

B. Sensitive Personal Data

375. Though not stipulated in section 3 Personal Data Act, section 13 states certain rules for sensitive data, which is defined as personal data that reveals or concerns:

- race or ethnic origin;
- political opinions;
- religious or philosophical beliefs;
- membership of a trade union; or

---

721. See Art. 29 Data Protection Working Party, 'Opinion N° 4/2007 on the concept of personal data', 01248/07/EN – WP 136, 6–7.

722. Sören Öman & Hans-Olof Lindblom, *Personuppgiftslagen – En kommentar*, 4th edn (Stockholm: Norstedts, 2009), s. 3.

723. See Art. 29 Data Protection Working Party, 'Opinion N° 4/2007 on the concept of personal data', 8.

724. Öman & Lindblom, *Personuppgiftslagen*, s. 3.

725. Decision by the Data Inspection Board from 8 Jun. 2005, nr 593–2005; and Decision by the Administrative Court of Appeal (*Kammarrätt*) in Stockholm from 8 Jun. 2007, nr 285–07.

726. See Decision by the Swedish Supreme Administrative Court from 11 Oct. 1999, RÅ 1999 ref. 18 II.

– health or sex life.

Several governmental reports have considered details about a name and language skills being able to indirectly reveal a persons ethnic origin.[727]

Details regarding health life include all types of data concerning physical as well as psychological health of an individual, including indications of drug abuse, pregnancy, prescriptions for medicine, and possibly even information about sick leave. In accordance with a decision by the European Court of Justice, information about somebody injuring their foot and being on sick leave constitutes sensitive data on a person's health.[728] This was also the case for details on an employee having difficulties to cooperate and being on sick leave.[729]

For obvious reasons, genetic data can reveal both health as well as ethnic origin and therefore constitutes sensitive data according to section 13.[730]

A question that is being discussed is to what extent photographs reveal a person's ethnic origin, health or religious beliefs. The Government considered that pictures of individuals in typical contexts generally do not reveal any sensitive data. If the photographs display people in a religious or political context, however, they typically will constitute sensitive data.[731]

The Personal Data Act also contains rules for specific types of information, including data concerning legal offences in section 21, as well as an individual's personal identity number or classification number in section 22. In this context, these types of details could also be considered sensitive data.

C. Processing

> Processing: Any operation or set of operations which is taken as regards personal data, whether or not it occurs by automatic means, for example, collection, recording, organization, storage, adaptation or alteration, retrieval, gathering, use, disclosure by transmission, dissemination or otherwise making information available, alignment or combination, blocking, erasure or destruction.

376. Read in conjunction with section 5 Personal Data Act, processing includes any use of personal information by automated or semi-automated means.[732] Once

727. Government Official Report SOU 2001:32, 'Domstolarnas register och personuppgiftslagen – En rättslig anpassning', 124; Government Official Report SOU 2001:100, 'Informationshantering och behandling av uppgifter vid domstolar – En rättslig översyn', 93 et seq.; and Government Official Report SOU 2003:40, 'Utlänningsdatalag', 180.
728. See Case C-101/01 Bodil Lindqvist [2003] ECR I-12971.
729. Decision by the Swedish Supreme Court from 26 May 2005, NJA 2005 s. 361.
730. Government Bill (Proposition) 2005/06:64, 'Genetisk integritet m.m.', 63. See also the Swedish Genetic Integrity Act (*Lag (2006:351) om genetisk integritet m.m.*).
731. Government Official Report SOU 1997:39, 'Integritet – Offentlighet – Informationsteknik'.
732. This is also in line with Recital 15 Data Protection Directive: 'Whereas the processing of such data is covered by this Directive only if it is automated.'

personal information is digitalized, all types of rendering this information fall within the Act.[733] There is no general requirement, with the exception of section 5a, that the data is structured; any type of automated processing is included in the definition.

Typical examples of processing would be collecting personal information in connection with the registration of customers or in applying for membership, storing personal information about patients in hospital, transferring details about one's employees to the tax authority, as well as publication of personal information in text or images on a website.[734]

Section 5 complies with Article 3(1) and (2) point c Data Protection Directive. Compared to the previously in force Data Act which only applied to personal data in registers, the Personal Data Act has a rather broad scope.

377. According to section 5, only processing that is wholly or partly automated falls under the scope of the data protection legislation. Manual processing is also covered to some extent, if the data 'is included in or is intended to form part of a structured collection of personal data that is available for searching or compilation according to specific criteria'.

Automated processing covers any use of personal data on a computer or network. The Swedish Data Inspection Board has in several of its decision advanced a view that any recording or collecting of personal data, even if the data is only available temporarily, falls under the definition of processing. For example, publishing pictures, taken with a digital camera, on a website without saving them, constitutes processing.[735]

Recording of personal data on analogue devices such as audio or video tapes, or mechanical time clock or cash registers, is not covered by automated processing.[736]

Processing which is partly automated also falls within the application of the Personal Data Act, according to section 5. This is the case, for example, if personal data is collected manually, but is intended to be transferred to a digital medium at a later point, or if digital personal information is printed out or shared via the telephone.

Manual processing is covered to the extent the data is or is intended to become part of a register. In order to qualify as a register, the data has to be structured and searchable by personal details.[737] The prevalent view in Sweden has been that the register has to be searchable by more than one criterion.[738] A manual file system with cards sorted by last name or personal number does, therefore, not fall under the scope of the Personal Data Act.

733. Government Official Report SOU 2003:40, 190–191.
734. See, e.g., Case C-101/01 Bodil Lindqvist [2003] ECR I-12971.
735. Decision by the Data Inspection Board from 20 Sep. 2005, no. 763–2005.
736. Government Official Report SOU 1997:39, 347.
737. See also Recital 15 Data Protection Directive: 'a filing system structured according to specific criteria relating to individuals, so as to permit easy access to the personal data in question'.
738. See Government Official Report SOU 1997:39, 342; Decision by the Administrative Supreme Court from 25 Jun. 2001, RÅ 2001 ref. 35; and Government Bill (Proposition) 2005/06:64, 47.

D. Unstructured Processing

378. The term unstructured processing is not defined in section 3 Personal Data Act but section 5a deals with special rules concerning unstructured processing and exempts most provisions of the Personal Data Act from their application to unstructured processing.

Section 5a Personal Data Act was introduced in 2007 in an attempt to facilitate everyday processing of personal data in electronic communications and ordinary composing of texts.[739] The idea was to shift from the traditional model of regulating the processing of data to a more abuse-centred regulatory approach.[740]

Section 5a defines unstructured processing as personal data that does not or is not intended to become part of a collection of personal data which has been structured in a way that clearly facilitates searching or compiling of the data. As the definition and name indicate, the important factor is the structure of the material, not the type or format of the information.[741]

Examples of unstructured processing include the following:[742]

- mentioning personal information in any continuous text;
- sending emails containing personal details;
- publishing personal information on a website;
- individuals' images or sound recordings.

Important is that the structure is not built upon personal data, that is the data can be indexed or organized, but it may not be organized by name, personal number, or any other personal information. In addition, this structure should not have a certain level or quality. In other words, not any structure related to personal data falls outside the scope of section 5a, only a structure that facilitates search and compilation of personal information.

For example, publishing a list of names sorted by last name on a webpage might meet the criteria of structured, but is not obviously enabling searching or compiling of names, and therefore falls under the definition of unstructured processing. The same applies for saving files on a computer under a personal name or number. Even a typical email programme does not reach the quality of a structure based on personal data and is therefore considered unstructured processing. Only if the email programme consists of a larger document management system or customer relations database can it fulfil the requirement of structured and therefore fall outside the scope of section 5a.[743]

739. Government Bill (Proposition) 2005/06:173, 'Översyn av personuppgiftslagen'.
740. See Sören Öman, *Implementing Data Protection in Law*, Scandinavian Studies in Law, vol. 47 (IT Law) (Stockholm: Stockholm Institute for Scandinavian Law, 2004), 392; and Sören Öman, 'Protection of Personal Data: But How?', in *Law and Information Technology -Swedish Views (SOU 2002:112)*, ed. Peter Seipel (Stockholm: IT Law Observatory, 2002), 177–184.
741. Government Bill (Proposition) 2005/06:173, 58.
742. *Ibid.*, 21 et seq.
743. *Ibid.*, 21–22.

E. Controller, Personal Data Assistant, and Personal Data Representative

> Controller of personal data: A person who alone or together with others decides the purpose and means of processing personal data.

379. Controller (*personuppgiftsansvarig*) is the natural or legal person that de facto decides on the processing, with or without legal grounds. It is the controller who is responsible for the processing being in compliance with the Personal Data Act. In a few cases of registers held by public authorities, the controller is appointed by law.

Where the controller is a legal person, it can, of course, appoint its employees responsible for the actual processing. This does, however, not exempt the company, organization or public authority from its civil liability according to the Personal Data Act.

Deciding the purpose of processing is not the same as having access to the data. Only the person being able to independently change, amend or delete the personal data will be considered the controller.[744] The Swedish Data Inspection Board declared that by linking to another website which contains personal data one does not become the controller for the site that is referred to. Only to the extent the links as such contain personal information is the website owner the controller in regard to this data.[745] This is also in line with Recital 47 Data Protection Directive, which states that the controller of personal data contained in a message transmitted by electronic communications 'will normally be considered to be the person from whom the message originates, rather than the person offering the transmission services':

> Personal data assistant: A person who processes personal data on behalf of the controller of personal data.

380. A personal data assistant (*personuppgiftsbiträde*) is a natural or legal person to whom the data controller outsourced the personal data processing. Employees of the controller do not fall within this definition.[746]

In accordance with section 30 paragraph 2 Personal Data Act, which transposes Article 17(3) Data Protection Directive, the contract between the data controller and the personal data assistant has to be in writing and specifically include a provision that 'the personal data assistant may only process personal data in accordance with instructions from the controller' and 'that the personal data assistant is liable to take' appropriate security measures referred to in section 31:

744. See Swedish Data Inspection Board, 'Datainspektionens informationsblad om personuppgiftsansvar'.
745. Answer of the Swedish Data Inspection Board in case no. 785–2000.
746. See Swedish Data Inspection Board, 'Datainspektionens informationsblad om personuppgiftsansvar'.

Personal data representative: A natural person, appointed by the controller of personal data, who shall independently assure that the personal data is processed in a correct and lawful manner.

381. A personal data representative (*personuppgiftsombud*) can only be a natural person, so companies and organizations cannot be considered. The function of the data representative as such is not stated in Article 2 Data Protection Directive, but mentioned in Article 18(2).[747] Sections 38–40 Swedish Personal Data Act regulate the obligations of a personal data representative, including 'ensuring that the controller processes personal data in a lawful and correct manner and in accordance with good practice', pointing out any inadequacies to the controller, as well as maintaining 'a register of the processing that the controller of personal data implements'.

F. The Registered Person

The registered person: A person to whom the personal data relates.

382. In accordance with the definition of personal data[748] the registered person has to be a living individual; legal persons are therefore excluded from the definition.

II. Requirements When Processing Personal Data

383. Section 9, transposing Article 6 Data Protection Directive, stipulates several requirements which have to be met when personal data is being processed. Most of these requirements refer to the purpose of processing and all of them are applicable regardless of whether the data is personal or even sensitive. In particular, the controller has to ensure that:

(a) personal data is processed only if it is lawful;
(b) personal data is always processed in a correct manner and in accordance with good practice;
(c) personal data is only collected for specific, explicitly stated and justified purposes;
(d) personal data is not processed for any purpose that is incompatible with that for which the information is collected;

747. Article 18(2) Data Protection Directive: '[W]here the controller, in compliance with the national law which governs him, appoints a personal data protection official, responsible in particular: – for ensuring in an independent manner the internal application of the national provisions taken pursuant to this Directive; – for keeping the register of processing operations carried out by the controller, containing the items of information referred to in Art. 21(2).'
748. See A *supra* (para. 374).

(e) the personal data that is processed is adequate and relevant in relation to the purposes of the processing;
(f) no more personal data is processed than is necessary having regard to the purposes of the processing;
(g) the personal data that is processed is correct and, if it is necessary, up-to-date;
(h) all reasonable measures are taken to correct, block or erase such personal data as is incorrect or incomplete having regard to the purposes of the processing; and
(i) personal data is not kept for a longer period than that as is necessary having regard to the purpose of the processing.

A. Lawful Processing (Points A and B)

384. The assessment of whether processing is lawful according to point a is made with reference to the provisions of the Personal Data Act in general, as well as other related legislation such as the Swedish Penal Code (e.g., intrusion into a safe depository[749]); as well as eavesdropping,[750] breach of data secrecy[751] and the Marketing Act (e.g., provisions on unsolicited commercial communication). Sending of emails to teachers at a certain school, without prior consent, was not considered as unsolicited communication according to the Marketing Act and therefore the processing of personal data complied with section 9 Personal Data Act.[752]

Good practice according to point b will, as is usual, be determined by guidelines, recommendations and decisions by the Swedish Data Inspection Board, by common rules within the industry developed by established branch associations, and by common practices of data controllers.

B. Collection for Specific Purposes (Point C)

385. Section 9 paragraph 1 point c requires specific, explicitly stated and justified purposes for any collecting of personal data. Though there is no provision of this statement being in writing, section 36 stipulating registration with the supervisory authority and sections 23–25 and 42 obliging the controller to render information to the individual, indirectly lead to such a requirement.

The purposes of processing have to be specified at the time of collecting the personal data. The word specific presumes a certain level of explicitness and precision in the purposes, which is also necessary for determining if the information is adequate and relevant (point e). The Swedish Data Inspection Board did not consider control a specific enough purpose for logging and surveillance, but also

749. Chapter 4 s. 9 Penal Code.
750. Chapter 4 s. 9a Penal Code.
751. Chapter 4 s. 9c Penal Code.
752. See Decision by the Administrative Court of Appeal (*Kammarrätt*) in Stockholm from 8 Feb. 2006, no. 6624–05; and Decision by the Administrative Court of Appeal (*Kammarrätt*) in Jönköping from 20 Jan. 2006, no. 3162–05.

demanded the intention behind the control, for example, to follow up on compliance with internal technical and security measures.[753]

C. Processing Compatible with Purpose at Collection (Point D)

386. The requirement of point d (personal data is not processed for any purpose that is incompatible with that for which the information is collected) has to be assessed with regard to case law and supplementing regulations. An example where the purpose is not compatible with the original collecting is evaluating employee performance by using data collected in the context of control of compliance with security measures in the workplace.[754] Neither is collecting information on employees for human resources administration and later using it to assess employee performance compatible with section 9 point d Personal Data Act.[755] Last, but not least, registering the personal number of children at a school for administration purposes and subsequently using it to publish the pupils' individual schedules on the Internet is not compatible with section 9 point d.[756]

D. Adequate and Relevant Processing (Points E and F)

387. The general assessment of adequate and relevant is, at first, left for the controller. In some cases, however, processing of certain data is not deemed adequate or relevant. Registering the birth date of all customers buying alcoholic drinks in order to ensure that they are above 18 years old was not considered adequate in regard to section 9 point e.[757]

In a decision from 2008, the Supreme Administrative Court held that using children's fingerprints in a school's lunch room was adequate and relevant in relation to the purpose of ensuring that only pupils who had paid for the meals could receive food.[758] The fact that the information concerned biometric data did not constitute inadequate processing as such, but had to be viewed in relation to the purpose and type of processing adopted.

E. Processing of Correct Data (Points G and H)

388. The term correct can be interpreted in different ways. The general assumption is that correct means accurate with regard to reality. The actual circumstances

753. Swedish Data Inspection Board, 'Monitoring in working life', Report 2005:3.
754. Government Official Report SOU 2002:18, 'Personlig integritet i arbetslivet', 136 and 297.
755. Swedish Data Inspection Board, 'Behandling av personuppgifter för kontroll av anställda', Report 2003:3, 9.
756. Decision by the Swedish Data Inspection Board from 1 Oct. 2008, no. 898–2008.
757. Decision by the Swedish Data Inspection Board from 9 Mar. 2005, no. 1978–2004; see also Decision of the District Administrative Court (*Länsrätten*) in Stockholm from 9 Jun. 2006, no. 7055–2005.
758. Decision by Supreme Administrative Court from 16 Dec. 2008, RÅ 2008 ref. 83.

might, however, not always be easily determined. Therefore, correct can also be understood as the processed data corresponding to the collected data.[759]

The controller has an active duty to adjust incorrect and out-of-date information, as well as to rectify, block or erase such personal data at the request of the individual.[760] The obligation includes informing any third party to whom the data has been disclosed.

F. Limited Storing of Personal Data (Point I)

389. The time for storing personal information depends on the purpose of the processing. The Swedish Data Inspection Board has published guidelines and recommendations on the period of time necessary for different purposes.[761]

For direct marketing purposes, information about previous customers may be kept for a period of one year after the client relationship has ceased, that is the product or service has been delivered. Personal details of members in a club or association, after they terminated their membership, should be erased immediately but may be kept for up to one year in order to encourage them to rejoin the organization. In the event of dismissal of employees, any personal data should be deleted immediately unless necessary for purposes stipulated by the law, for example, rules on taxes or pensions.

Personal data collected in the context of control of employee email or Internet use should be anonymized or erased as soon as it is not of value for the control anymore. In the event of camera surveillance or alike, information should be deleted daily or weekly.[762]

According to the Swedish Data Inspection Board, a public transport company storing data on its customers' travel may keep the information for up to sixty days.[763] The Swedish Rail Administration SJ (*Statens järnvägars*) was allowed to keep information about its passengers for three months as this corresponded to the recommended objection period.[764]

G. General Rules

390. Paragraphs 2, 3, and 4 of section 9 Personal Data Act state specific rules regarding personal information, which is processed for historical, statistical or scientific purposes. Historical purposes mainly relate to archiving of information.

759. Öman & Lindblom, *Personuppgiftslagen*, s. 9.
760. Section 28 Personal Data Act.
761. Swedish Data Inspection Board, 'Hur länge får personuppgifter bevaras?', Datainspektionen informerar, No. 10, Nov. 2008.
762. Swedish Data Inspection Board, 'Monitoring in working life', 19 and 24.
763. Decisions by Swedish Data Inspection Board from 30 Oct. 2007, nos 183–2007, 550–2007 and 1356–2007.
764. Decision by the Swedish Data Inspection Board from 22 Dec. 2008, no. 711–2008.

According to this provision, 'historical, statistical or scientific purposes' shall not be regarded as incompatible with the original purposes for collection. In addition, the time necessary for storing of personal data can be extended.

Personal data that is processed for historical, statistical or scientific purposes may only be used if the person has given consent or there is extraordinary reason with regard to the vital interests of the registered person.

Consent from the individual cannot exempt the applicability of section 9. Collecting data that the registered person agreed to, but which is inadequate and irrelevant in relation to the purpose of the processing, will still be in conflict with section 9 Personal Data Act.

III. When Processing is Allowed

391. Section 10 Personal Data Act, which transposes Article 7 Data Protection Directive, stipulates the conditions under which processing is allowed. Besides consent of the individual, processing can be permitted if it is necessary for one of the stated six reasons. The list in section 10 is exhaustive, that is processing cannot be allowed for other reasons than specified in this provision. Section 10 is, however, not applicable for unstructured processing.[765]

The consent of the individual always leads to the processing being allowed. Consent is defined in section 3 Personal Data Act as:

> Every kind of voluntary, specific and unambiguous expression of will by which the registered person, after having received information, accepts processing of personal data concerning her or him.

This definition contains four conditions for an act of consent to be accepted by the law: voluntary, specific, unambiguous and informed. With regards to unambiguous, the consent does not have to be in writing, though the burden of proof is on the controller. The law can, however, stipulate form requirements and demand a written consent, as is the case, for example, in section 15 Personal Data Act.

Unambiguous does not cover tacit or hypothetical consent, that is, the controller cannot presume (hypothetical) or interpret failure to respond to a request to process personal data (tacit) as consent. Acceptance by action is, however, generally recognized, that is, where the individual fills out a form with personal details.

The condition of voluntary typically means that the individual agreed to the processing without being forced or in fear of certain consequences. In employment relationships this has been considered a difficult question, as consent by an employee to certain data processing involving control and surveillance might not be completely optional.[766] The consent of flight passengers to use their fingerprints for check-in was considered voluntary, as it was also possible to use manual identity controls.[767]

---

765. See for a definition I D *supra* (para. 386); and for s. 5a IV *infra* (paras 402–404).
766. Government Official Report SOU 2009:44, 'Integritetsskydd i arbetslivet', 237 et seq.
767. See Decision by the Swedish Data Inspection Board from 30 Mar. 2006, no. 84–2006.

Specific expression of acceptance concerns the type of processing and is therefore also related to section 9, requesting explicit purposes for the use of personal data. Last, but not least, informed consent requires the controller to inform the individual of the purpose and type of processing before any valid consent is possible. Even though not explicitly stipulated in section 3, the registered person has to accept processing before it starts, consent cannot be given in retrospect.[768]

392. Without consent, and even against the wishes of an individual, personal data may be processed if this is necessary in order:

(a) to enable the performance of a contract with the registered person or to enable measures that the registered person has requested to be taken before a contract is entered into;
(b) that the controller of personal data should be able to comply with a legal obligation;
(c) that the vital interests of the registered person should be protected;
(d) that a work task of public interest should be performed;
(e) that the controller of personal data or a third party to whom the personal data is provided should be able to perform a work task in conjunction with the exercise of official authority; or
(f) that a purpose that concerns a legitimate interest of the controller of personal data or of such a third party to whom personal data is provided should be able to be satisfied, if this interest is of greater weight than the interest of the registered person in protection against violation of personal integrity.

The first requirement is that processing is necessary. In a judgment[769] the European Court of Justice held that 'the concept of necessity laid down by Article 7(e) of the [Data Protection] Directive cannot have a meaning which varies between the Member States. It follows that what is at issue is a concept which has its own independent meaning in Community law'. The Court did, however, not particularly define the term 'necessity' in general. The common perception in Sweden is that the requirement of 'necessary' is met if the processing obviously facilitates a task or legal obligation.[770]

Point a is commonly considered to cover any type of contract, including sales of goods, employment, rental or service contracts.

A legal obligation pursuant to point b is usually presumed if the duty stems from a statutory provision or decision by a public authority. To what extent obligations based on foreign national law are covered is currently not completely clear.[771] Processing of personal data in the context of public administration is covered by point e.

768. See Decision by the Supreme Court from 26 May 2005, NJA 2005 s. 361.
769. Case C-524/06 Huber [2008] ECR I-0000.
770. Öman & Lindblom, *Personuppgiftslagen*, s. 10.
771. *Ibid.*; see also Art. 29 Data Protection Working Party, 'Opinion 1/2006 on the application of EU data protection rules to internal whistleblowing schemes in the fields of accounting, internal accounting controls, auditing matters, fight against bribery, banking and financial crime', 00195/

Though 'vital interests' of point c obviously includes use of personal data which is 'essential for the data subject's life',[772] its application might have a wider scope. Examples of 'work tasks of public interest' include archiving for historical purposes, research, compilation of statistics, surveys concerning questions of interest for society, and statistics of salaries in certain industries.[773]

393. The balance of interest argument is an omnibus clause for allowing processing of personal data in accordance with the Personal Data Act. The legitimate interest of the controller or the third party is weighed against the interest of the registered person to be protected against privacy violation. Again, the requirements of section 9 have to be met here too.

This means that a legitimate interest of the controller or third party first has to be established, and then weighed against the privacy interest of the individuals. The question on the legitimacy of the interest has to be decided on a case-by-case basis. The Swedish Data Inspection Board confirmed a legitimate interest to archive data in a system of identification and attendance control for a period of two years in order to allow the handover of the data to the Tax Authority.[774] It was also considered legitimate to hand over data collected in an electronic access control system to the police in the context of filing a report.[775] The Data Inspection Board did, however, not recognize as legitimate an interest of a private company providing an online service where electronic police reports could be filed by individuals, which were automatically passed on to the police.[776]

In general, legitimate purposes concerning security measures have been considered as weighing more heavily than economic interests.[777] When balancing economic interests against privacy of an individual, the former have to weigh considerably more in order for processing to be allowed according to section 10 point f Personal Data Act.

A statement by an individual not to agree to data processing will not automatically exclude a balance of interest argument, but has to be weighed accordingly and will therefore raise the bar for a legitimate interest of the controller or third party.[778]

06/EN WP 117, 8: 'By contrast, an obligation imposed by a foreign legal statute or regulation which would require the establishment of reporting systems may not qualify as a legal obligation by virtue of which data processing in the EU would be made legitimate. Any other interpretation would make it easy for foreign rules to circumvent the EU rules laid down in Directive 95/46/EC. As a result, SOX whistleblowing provisions may not be considered as a legitimate basis for processing on the basis of Art. 7(c).'

772. Recital 31 Data Protection Directive.

773. Government Official Report SOU 1997:39, 305, 355 and 36.1.

774. Decision by the Data Inspection Board from 25 Jul. 2007, no. 1036–2006.

775. Decision by the Data Inspection Board from 6 Nov. 2007, no. 276–2007.

776. Decision by the Data Inspection Board from 10 Jul. 2006, no. 706–2006.

777. Swedish Data Inspection Board, 'Monitoring in working life', 22.

778. Compare s. 12 that allows individuals to revoke their consent. The provision is, however, not applicable if the processing is necessary. Section 11, on the other hand, allows the individual to oppose any processing for direct marketing purposes and therefore will weigh stronger than any economic interest of the controller or third party.

394. When it comes to sensitive data,[779] the Personal Data Act stipulates special requirements in addition to the general provisions of sections 9 and 10. Section 13 stipulates a general prohibition for processing of sensitive data. According to section 14, however, controllers may process sensitive data if the individual has consented to it or if it is necessary for certain specific reasons.

A valid consent has to fulfil all the requirements stipulated in section 3 and in addition be explicit, according to section 15, which usually excludes acceptance by action alone.[780] Publication of the sensitive data by the individual also allows processing of that data, pursuant to section 15.

Sensitive personal data may also be processed if it is necessary, according to section 16, in order that:

(a) the controller of personal data should be able to comply with her or his duties or exercise her or his rights within employment law;
(b) the vital interests of the registered person or some other person should be able to be protected and the registered person cannot provide a consent; or
(c) legal claims should be able to be established, exercised or defended.

Non-profit organizations may process sensitive data within their administration, pursuant to section 17. Sensitive data may, furthermore, under certain conditions, be processed for health care, pursuant to section 18, as well as for research or statistical purposes according to section 19.

IV. Legitimate Processing and Misuse

395. Since the amendment of the Personal Data Act in 2007, Swedish law has protected privacy through two different models, one focused on requirements regarding processing, the other approach allowing processing unless it involves a violation of somebody's privacy. The first model has been described in Chapters II and III, dealing mainly with general principles of processing and requirements for its permissiveness. The second model is incorporated in section 5a Personal Data Act and will be described in more detail below.

Section 5a Personal Data Act allows unstructured processing of personal data to the extent it does not violate somebody's privacy. In other words, unstructured processing of personal data is allowed, even if sections 9 and 10 are not complied with. The law in this case only punishes misuse, but does not regulate processing as such.

396. In order for section 5a to apply, the data first has to be processed in an unstructured way. As mentioned above,[781] this is the case if the personal data does not, or is not intended to, become part of a collection of personal data which has been structured in a way that clearly facilitates searching or compiling of the data.

---

779. For a definition see I B *supra* (para. 375).
780. See Swedish Data Inspection Board, 'Samtycke enligt personuppgiftslagen', 10 Oct. 2007.
781. See I D *supra* (para. 378).

If these conditions are met, the processing is allowed and certain provisions of the Personal Data Act do not have to be followed. The sections that do not apply with regard to unstructured processing are:

- Section 9 (Fundamental requirements for processing of personal data).
- Section 10 (When processing of personal data is permitted).
- Sections 13–19 (Prohibition and exemptions from prohibition to process sensitive personal data).
- Sections 21–22 (Processing of information concerning legal offences and of personal identity numbers).
- Sections 23–26 (Information to the registered person).
- Section 28 (Rectification).
- Sections 33–34 (Prohibition and exemptions from prohibition to transfer personal data to a third country).
- Section 42 (Information to the public about processing that has not been notified).

In other words, unstructured processing does not lead to the Personal Data Act not being applicable at all, but only to its partial application. Several sections of the Act are still mandatory, especially sections 31 and 32 dealing with security measures that the controller has to implement, as well as sections 48 and 49 stipulating rules on damages and penalties.

For example, publishing personal information on a website, sending an email containing personal details, or recording images of an individual is allowed without the consent of the individual as long as the privacy of that individual is not infringed. As sections 13–19 are not applicable, even details on ethnic origin or health may be processed without the consent of the registered person or without any other exemption in the Personal Data Act being applicable. Neither does the individual have to be informed about the processing.

397. Unstructured processing is, however, only allowed to the extent it does not infringe somebody's privacy. The factors that should be taken into account for this decision are the following:[782]

- for which purpose the data has been processed;
- the extent of dissemination (including potential dissemination) of the information;
- the potential result of the processing.

The type of personal information is therefore not the only relevant factor, but all these parameters should be looked at collectively. For example, somebody spreading personal data in order to harm somebody's reputation would be considered harming the integrity of that person. In addition, collecting large amounts of data

782. Government Bill (Proposition) 2005/06:173, 59.

on one single person might qualify as a violation. Lastly, intentional use of false or misleading personal data can constitute abuse.[783]

In the event of an unstructured processing harming an individual's privacy the controller can be liable for damages, according to section 48. Under certain circumstances violation of someone's personal integrity can also lead to criminal liability and penalties, pursuant to section 49. This does not, however, exclude any potential criminal liability for defamation according to Chapter 5 section 1 Penal Code.[784]

In order to ensure compliance with the Personal Data Act, a controller can choose to follow the provisions of the complete Act, including sections 9 and 10, also for unstructured processing. In this case the controller can never be considered having violated the individual's privacy.[785]

V. Information to the Registered

398. Sections 23–26 Personal Data Act stipulate information obligations for the controller. Certain information about the identity of the controller and the purposes of processing has to be provided to the registered person without any prior request by the individual.

Upon written application by the registered person, the controller shall provide, free of charge and once per year, information on:[786]

(a) what information about the applicant that has been processed;
(b) where this information has been collected;
(c) the purpose of the processing; and
(d) to which recipients or categories of recipients the information has been disclosed.

VI. Transfer to a Third Country

399. Sections 33–35 Personal Data Act stipulate specific rules for transfer of personal data to a country outside of the European Union or the EEA, that is third country.

As for sensitive data, section 33 establishes a prohibition for transferring personal information to a third country unless certain conditions are met. In general, a transfer is allowed to third countries with an adequate level of protection or with the consent of the registered person, according to sections 33 and 34.

783. *Ibid.*, 27.
784. Chapter 5 s. 1 Penal Code: 'A person who points out someone as being a criminal or as having a reprehensible way of living or otherwise furnishes information intended to cause exposure to the disrespect of others, shall be sentenced for defamation to a fine.
785. Government Bill (Proposition) 2005/06:173, 59.
786. Section 26 Personal Data Act.

Unstructured processing does not fall within the scope of sections 33–35. As is the case for all provisions in the Personal Data Act, only automated processing is covered by these rules. In other words, sending a paper document with personal information to a country outside of the EEA does not have to abide by the regulations of section 33.

The question on what constitutes a transfer had been unclear after the adoption of the Data Protection Directive. The Swedish view was that uploading personal data on a website allowed others to access this information, which therefore was transferred to countries outside the EEA.[787]

A judgment by the European Court of Justice from 2003 now provides some clarity in this regard.[788] Since this decision, typical publication of information on a website has not been considered a transfer to a third country, unless the organization hosting the website is established outside the EEA. In particular the Court of Justice held that:

> there is no transfer [of data] to a third country [. . .] where an individual in a Member State loads personal data onto an Internet page which is stored with his hosting provider which is established in that State or in another Member State, thereby making those data accessible to anyone who connects to the Internet, including people in a third country.[789]

VII. Sanctions and Supervision

400. In case the controller does not comply with the provisions of the Personal Data Act, the individual shall be compensated for damages caused by the unlawful processing, according to section 48.

Certain processing can also lead to criminal liability according to section 49. A person can be sentenced to a fine or imprisonment of up to six months in case of non-compliance with sections 13–21. Other acts leading to criminal liability include omission of notification under section 36 paragraph 1 and transfer to personal data to a third country contrary to sections 33–35. Minor offences are exempted from criminal liability.

401. The Swedish Data Inspection Board (*Datainspektionen*)[790] is the appointed supervisory authority for privacy-related issues.[791] It issues directives and guidelines and also carries out inspections and handles complaints.

787. Government Official Report SOU 1997:39, 413.
788. Case C-101/01 *Bodil Lindqvist* [2003] ECR I-12971.
789. *Ibid.*, point 71.
790. <www.datainspektionen.se>.
791. Section 2 Personal Data Ordinance (*Personuppgiftsförordning (1998:1191)*).

The controller has to notify the Data Inspection Board of any processing of personal data, according to section 36 Personal Data Act. This has to be done in writing before the processing is initiated. This notification does not lead to an approval by the Board whether the processing complies with the Personal Data Act.

The notification duty does, however, not apply if:

- the controller has appointed a personal data representative (and notified the Data Inspection Board thereof);[792]
- another statute provides otherwise;
- the personal data is processed in linear text, for example, on websites;[793]
- the personal information is processed by a non-profit organization;[794]
- the registered person has consented to the processing.[795]

§3. Other Legislation Dealing with Personal Data Protection

402. According to its section 2, the Personal Data Act is subsidiary to other legislation dealing with privacy and data protection.

One such example is the Swedish Camera Surveillance Act (*Kameraövervakningslag (2013:460)*)[796] that stipulates rules for the use of camera surveillance in public and non-public places. With regards to public places the Act requires a permit by the (*Länsstyrelsen*) to use camera surveillance, for non-public places the Act stipulates consent by the surveilled person or a balance of interest in order to be able to use camera surveillance.

There is also a Swedish Act on Covert Camera Surveillance (*Lag (1995:1506) om hemlig kameraövervakning*) which deals with the requirements of using camera surveillance in the context of police investigations.

The Swedish Credit Information Act (*Kreditupplysningslag (1973:1173)*) stipulates requirements for credit-rating agencies regarding their processing of information on the financial details of individuals. Companies intending to provide such services have to apply for a permit with the Data Inspection Board, which is also the supervisory authority in these cases. Several online services that allow private individuals to access other people's financial records have emerged in the past years and the Act was adapted in 2011 to meet this challenge. The Act builds now on two principles: the one requesting access to the financial records has to have a legitimate interest in the records and the data subject has to receive a copy of the

792. Section 37 Personal Data Act.
793. Section 4 Personal Data Ordinance.
794. Section 5 Personal Data Ordinance.
795. Section 2 Regulation 2001:1 Data Inspection Board Statute Book (*Datainspektionens författningssamling (DIFS)*).
796. The 2013 Act replaced the previously in force Act on Public Camera Surveillance (*Lag (1998:150) om allmän kameraövervakning*).

information that was accessed. In order to ensure compliance with the rules, the Data Inspection Board has initiated several supervisory measures in the past years and threatened a few companies with fines up to 1 million Swedish crowns (about EUR 1 million).

403. The majority of public authorities process personal data about citizens to some extent. In these cases, the Personal Data Act normally does not apply; instead special statutes dealing with specific databases held by the different authorities are applicable. For example, the Patient Data Act (*Patientdatalag (2008:355)*) deals with processing of personal information within the health sector, the Act on the National Address Register (*Lag (1998:527) om det statliga personadressregistret (SPAR)*) covers provisions on access to the national register of individuals' addresses, the Police Data Act (*Polisdatalag (2010:361)*) regulates the processing of personal data by the Swedish police, and the Act on Processing of Data by the Tax Agency for Taxation Purposes (*Lag (2001:181) om behandling av uppgifter i Skatteverkets beskattningsverksamhet*) states rules on the use of data by the tax authorities.[797]

§4. Processing That Is Exempted from the Personal Data Act

I. Processing by Non-automated Means

404. As mentioned[798] processing of personal data which is not wholly or partly automated does not fall within the scope of the Personal Data Act, according to section 5. In other words, all manual processing is exempted from the application of the Act.

II. Processing for Private Purposes

405. In addition, section 6 Personal Data Act, transposing Article 3(2) Data Protection Directive, exempts processing for purely private purposes. Examples for private use of personal information include private address books, writing of texts by individuals, and diaries on a computer.

Publication of private data on a website can never be regarded as private purposes even if the website is operated as a hobby. The European Court of Justice held in the Lindqvist judgment that the:

> exception must [. . .] be interpreted as relating only to activities which are carried out in the course of private or family life of individuals, which is clearly not the case with the processing of personal data consisting in publication on

797. For more examples see Öman, *Implementing Data Protection*, 392.
798. See I C *supra* (paras 376–377).

the Internet so that those data are made accessible to an indefinite number of people.[799]

III. Processing for Journalistic Purposes

406. Section 7 paragraph 2 Personal Data Act stipulates a specific provision for 'such processing of personal data as occurs exclusively for journalistic purposes or artistic or literary expression'.

Journalistic purposes have been defined in case law as 'to inform, criticize or foster a debate on questions for society which are of interest for the general public'.[800] The European Court of Justice has also used a broad interpretation of the words 'journalistic purposes'. In a decision in 2008, the Court held that processing is carried out 'solely for journalistic purposes . . . if the sole object of those activities is the disclosure to the public of information, opinions or ideas'.[801] In other words, it is not necessary that the author of the publication is a journalist, the relevant factor is if the purpose of the processing, for example, publication of certain personal information on a website, is to inform the public or raise discussion on issues of society.

Section 7 makes a difference between publications that fall completely outside of the scope of the Personal Data Act[802] and processing for journalistic purposes. In the latter case, certain parts of the Personal Data Act are still applicable, mainly sections 30–32 on the security of processing. Requirements such as stipulated in sections 9 and 10 or 13–19, and sections 47–49 concerning civil and criminal liability, are, however, exempted.

IV. Processing versus Freedom of the Press

407. Section 7 paragraph 1, transposing Article 9 Data Protection Directive, exempts use of personal information in the context of freedom of the press and freedom of expression from the application of the Personal Data Act. In other words, newspapers and other protected media that fall within the scope of either the Freedom of the Press Act (*Tryckfrihetsförordning (1949:105)*) or the Fundamental Law on Freedom of Expression (*Yttrandefrihetsgrundlag (1991:1469)*) do not have to follow the data protection rules.

There are several possibilities for a publication to fall within the scope of the Freedom of the Press Act or the Fundamental Law on Freedom of Expression, *inter alia*:

799. Case C-101/01 *Bodil Lindqvist* [2003] ECR I-12971, point 47.

800. Decision by Supreme Court from 12 Jun. 2001, NJA 2001 s. 409.

801. Case C-73/07 *Tietosuojavaltuutettu v. Satakunnan Markkinapörssi Oy and Satamedia Oy* [2008] ECR I-09831.

802. See IV *infra* (paras 407–408).

- written matters in the printing press;[803]
- radio programmes which are directed to the general public;[804]
- technical recordings;[805]
- database rule for newspapers and other media;[806]
- certificate by the Swedish Radio and TV Authority (*Radio- och TV-verket*).

408. The *database rule* is especially important for publications on the Internet. Newspapers publishing their content on a website are covered by Chapter 1 section 9 Fundamental Law on Freedom of Expression.

A 'certificate of no legal impediment to publication' (*utgivningsbevis*) issued by the Radio and TV Authority can be obtained by a website, under the following conditions:

(a) a legally responsible editor (*utgivare*) is appointed and the Radio and TV Authority is notified thereof;
(b) the website has a common presentation;
(c) the website is not interactive, that is only the website owner can make changes to the content;
(d) the website is available to the public;
(e) there has to be a link to Sweden, for example, the editorial office is in Sweden; and
(f) the name of the website cannot be confused with another activity registered with the Radio and TV Authority.

The certificate gives constitutional protection but also stipulates certain obligations for the website owner: The editor is solely criminally liable for the content of the publications. The published information has to be documented and archived for six months.

Unmoderated online discussion forums, guest books or blogs cannot receive a 'certificate of no legal impediment to publication', unless every comment or entry is approved by the editorial staff prior to publication on the website.[807]

408.1. In the past years many organizations and websites have obtained such a certificate[808] and are therefore exempted from the Personal Data Act. A recent example is an online service that collected decisions by the lower courts and structured the data according to the address of the accused, in the original version with a map function. The site was met by a lot of criticism,[809] but the Swedish Data

803. Chapter 1 Art. 5 Freedom of the Press Act.
804. Chapter 1 Art. 6 Fundamental Law on Freedom of Expression.
805. Chapter 1 Art. 10 Fundamental Law on Freedom of Expression.
806. Chapter 1 Art. 9 Fundamental Law on Freedom of Expression.
807. Chapter 1 s. 9 para. 1 point 1 Fundamental Law on Freedom of Expression.
808. According to the register of the Radio and TV Authority, there are 884 companies in Sweden that have a certificate, see <www.radioochtv.se/Tillstand-och-registrering/Sok-i-registret/> (accessed 31 Mar. 2014).
809. A short news report in English, published 28 Jan. 2014, by the Swedish Public Radio Broadcaster is available at <sverigesradio.se/sida/artikel.aspx?programid=2054&artikel=5768451>.

Inspection Board could not intervene as the site was exempted from the Personal Data Act due to its 'certificate of no legal impediment to publication'. Even an investigation by the Chancellor of Justice (*Justitiekanslern*/JK)[810] looking into a possible prosecution for defamation did not lead to any charges.[811] This is just one example of the challenges with regards to a balance of interest between privacy and freedom of expression in Sweden and illuminates the risks connected with the wide application of exemptions.

V. Processing versus Freedom of Information

409. Sweden has a very strong principle of openness, which is enshrined in Chapter 2 Freedom of the Press Act. In general, all records held by authorities are public unless otherwise stated in the Public Access to Information and Secrecy Act (*Offentlighets- och sekretesslag (2009:400)*).

Section 8 Swedish Personal Data Act exempts the data protection rules for any data processing by public authorities within the principle of openness. The Public Access to Information and Secrecy Act refers in Chapter 21 Article 7 back to the Personal Data Act, which in practice means that documents held by a public administration can be kept secret if the transfer of the personal data would violate the Personal Data Act.

Although section 8 leads to the non-applicability of the Personal Data Act, Chapter 21 Article 7 Public Access to Information and Secrecy Act does allow for privacy concerns to be taken into consideration.

810. JK is the responsible supervisory authority in cases of freedom of expression; see para. 10.
811. Read the decision in Swedish at <jk.se/Beslut/Tryck-OchYttrandefrihetsarenden/699-14-31.aspx>.

Chapter 2. Protection of Telecommunications Privacy

§1. Legislative Framework

410. In 2002, the European Union enacted Directive 2002/58/EC of the European Parliament and the Council of 12 July 2002 concerning the Processing of Personal Data and the Protection of Privacy in the Electronic Communications Sector (hereinafter 'Directive on Privacy and Electronic Communications'). The Directive aimed to harmonize the provisions regarding privacy 'with respect to the processing of personal data in the electronic communication sector', according to Article 1.

Sweden transposed the Directive on Privacy and Electronic Communications, together with the other Directives concerning the regulatory framework for electronic communications[812] into Swedish national law in 2003 by enacting the Electronic Communications Act (*Lag (2003:389) om elektronisk kommunikation*). The 2009 amendments[813] to the Directive were implemented into Swedish law in 2011.

Though the Electronic Communications Act is not applicable to the content being transmitted in electronic communication networks, it contains several provisions regarding privacy.[814] In particular, the Act stipulates several obligations for operators and rights for their subscribers in Chapter 6.

In addition, some provisions of the Swedish Penal Code (*Brottsbalk (1962:700)*) can be applicable to protection of privacy in telecommunication, especially Chapter 4 section 8 dealing with breach of postal or telecommunication secrecy.

§2. Object of Protection

I. Content of a Message

411. Chapter 4 section 8 Swedish Penal Code protects the content of a message and stipulates:

> A person who unlawfully obtains access to a communication which a postal or telecommunications firm delivers or transmits in the form of mail or as a telecommunication, shall be sentenced for breach of postal or telecommunication secrecy to a fine or imprisonment for a maximum of two years.

The provision protects messages that are being transmitted. The term message does not include books or newspapers, though packages containing a message fall within the scope. Typically, the definition would cover telephone conversations, as well as

812. See Part I Ch. 1 s. 1 *supra* (paras 38 et seq.).
813. Directive 2009/136/EC of the European Parliament and of the Council of 25 Nov. 2009 amending Directive 2002/22/EC on universal service and users' rights relating to electronic communications networks and services, Directive 2002/58/EC concerning the processing of personal data and the protection of privacy in the electronic communications sector and Regulation (EC) No. 2006/2004 on cooperation between national authorities responsible for the enforcement of consumer protection laws.
814. Government Bill (Proposition) 2002/03:110, 'Lag om elektronisk kommunikation, m.m.', 1.

sound, text, images, or data transmitted through radio, light or electro magnetic waves.[815]

The sender or receiver does not have to be specified; even messages from anonymous addressors or to an undefined group of people are covered by Chapter 4 section 8. The message has to be in transit in order to be protected. Once the message has reached the sender, Chapter 4 section 8 Penal Code will therefore no longer apply. Other provisions in the Penal Code might, however, come into play.

412. Unlawful access implies that the offender does not have any authorization to open or read the message. Consent by the sender or receiver therefore prevents any criminal liability. The offender does, however, not necessarily have to read the message; already accessing it can lead to committing a 'breach of telecommunication secrecy'.

In addition to Chapter 4 section 8 (*brytande av post- eller telehemlighet*), several other provisions of the Penal Code can be of interest. In particular:[816]

- Chapter 4 section 9: intrusion into a safe depository (*intrång i förvar*), for example, unauthorized opening of a letter.[817]
- Chapter 4 section 9a: eavesdropping (*olovlig avlyssning*).[818]
- Chapter 4 section 9b: preparation of a breach of telecommunication secrecy or of eavesdropping.[819]
- Chapter 4 section 9c: breach of data secrecy (*dataintrång*).[820]

Chapter 4 section 8 Swedish Penal Code, as well as the other crimes just mentioned, do not stipulate any obligations for the postal or telecommunication companies. Instead, they criminalize unauthorized access to messages or data as such and state a punishment for the offender in this respect.

815. In accordance with the earlier definition of telemessage in the previously in force Tele Act (*Telelag (1993:597)*).
816. See for more detail Part VII Ch. 2 s. 1 I A *infra* (paras 429 et seq.).
817. The provision is subsidiary to Ch. 4 s. 8 Penal Code.
818. Chapter 4 s. 9a Penal code: 'A person who, in a case other than as stated in s. 8, unlawfully and secretly listens to or records by technical means for sound reproduction, speech in a room, a conversation between others or discussions at a conference or other meeting to which the public is not admitted and in which he himself does not participate, or to which he has improperly obtained access, shall be sentenced for eavesdropping to a fine or imprisonment for a maximum of two years.'
819. Chapter 4 s. 9b Penal code: 'A person who employs technical means with the intention of committing a breach of telecommunication secrecy . . . or to commit a crime as defined in s. 9a, shall be sentenced for preparation of such a crime to a fine or imprisonment for a maximum of two years.'
820. Chapter 4 s. 9c Penal code: 'A person who . . . unlawfully obtains access to a recording for automatic data processing or unlawfully alters or erases or inserts such a recording in a register, shall be sentenced for breach of data secrecy to a fine or imprisonment for a maximum of two years.'

II. Other Data Concerning the Message

413. The Swedish Electronic Communications Act defines the terms electronic message and traffic data. According to Chapter 6 section 1, an electronic message is all information that is exchanged or transferred between a finite group in a public electronic network. Transmissions via radio or on TV are not covered unless the information can be linked to a specific user.

Traffic data is information that is processed in order to transmit an electronic message in an electronic communications network or in order to bill this message. Commonly, traffic data includes information on which numbers or addresses have been used for communication and the date and time of the message. Traffic data can also include location data, which indicates the geographical position of the terminal equipment, such as a mobile phone or computer, of a user.

Network operators traditionally also process information about a subscription, including the name and address of the subscriber.

§3. Obligations for Network Operators

I. Security of Communications

414. According to Chapter 6 section 3 and 3a Electronic Communications Act, the provider of a publicly available electronic communications service must take appropriate measures to protect the processed data. Having regard to the available technology and the costs of their implementation, these measures shall ensure a level of security appropriate to the risk of privacy intrusion.

These two provisions transpose Article 4(1) Directive on Privacy and Electronic Communications and are not to be confused with the operational reliability and security in the service stipulated by the Access Directive and the Universal Service Directive.

414.1. In accordance with the new Article 4(3) of the Directive on Privacy and Electronic Communications the Swedish Electronic Communications Act was amended to include the obligation to notify the supervisory authority in cases of personal data breaches. A personal data breach is defined as an 'event that leads to accidental or unlawful destruction, loss or alteration, or unauthorised disclosure of, or unauthorised access to, data processed in connection with the provision of a publicly available electronic communications service'.[821]

According to Chapter 6 section 4a network operators have to notify the supervisory authority, PTS, in case of a personal data breach (*integritetsincident*). In addition, according to Chapter 6 section 4b, network operators have to keep lists on such breaches. PTS has issued guidelines that specify more in detail how network

821. Chapter 6 s. 1 point 3 Electronic Communications Act.

operators should notify the authority.[822] The guidelines stipulate, for example, that the notification has to occur within twenty-four hours of the breach, and that it should, *inter alia*, describe the causes and consequences of the breach, the type and content of the data and the initiated measures to remedy the weakness and to avoid similar incidents in the future. In its guidelines, PTS explicitly refers to Commission Regulation (EU) No 611/2013 of 24 June 2013 on the measures applicable to the notification of personal data breaches under Directive 2002/58/EC of the European Parliament and of the Council on privacy and electronic communications.

II. Confidentiality of Communications

415. The providers of a publicly available electronic communications service are obliged to keep confidential personal information concerning a subscription or the content or other related data of an electronic message. Chapter 6 section 20 Electronic Communications Act, transposing Article 5 Directive on Privacy and Electronic Communications, stipulates a principle of confidentiality of communications. The principle does not apply to the subscribers themselves or any other party taking part in the message.

Confidentiality (*tystnadsplikt*) applies to:

- information about a subscription (name and address of the subscriber, telephone number, IP-number);[823]
- the content of an electronic message; or
- any other data concerning a particular electronic message (traffic and location data, such as telephone number/IP address of the sender and receiver, the date and time of a communication, the identification number of the terminal equipment (IMEI-number)).

416. Chapter 6 sections 21–23 Electronic Communications Act stipulate several exemptions from the principle of confidentiality. Providers can, in certain cases, even be obliged to release personal data. For example, the police can request access to certain personal information in accordance with Chapter 6 section 22 Electronic Communications Act.

Operators are obliged to release personal data based on a court order for secret wiretapping (*hemlig avlyssning av elektronisk kommunikation*) or surveillance (*hemlig övervakning av elektronisk kommunikation*) in accordance with Chapter 27 section 18 or 19 Swedish Code of Judicial Procedure (*Rättegångsbalk (1942:740)*). Secret wiretapping concerns the content of an electronic message and can only be ordered by the court for offences with a punishment of a minimum of two years

822. Swedish Post and Telecom Agency (PTS), 'Vägledning om skyldigheten att rapportera integritetsincidenter', 26 Aug. 2013; a summary in Swedish is available at <pts.se/sv/Bransch/Internet/Integritet/Regler/Rapportera-integritetsincidenter/>.

823. The information has to be directly or indirectly linked to a subscriber. Therefore the PUK-code, for example, though processed by the operator, does not fall within this category, which means that the principle of confidentiality (Ch. 6 s. 20) does not apply. In this case, however, the information cannot be released to the police either.

imprisonment or if the crime is expected to lead to a two years imprisonment.[824] Secret surveillance regarding traffic data and location data can be ordered for offences with a minimum of six months imprisonment and also for data intrusion according to Chapter 4 section 9c Swedish Penal Code. Chapter 27 sections 18 and 19 Code of Judicial Procedure were amended in 2012 and according to the new paragraph 3 in section 18 an order for secret wiretapping now also gives the right for surveillance.

Apart from the provisions in the procedural Code, which concern pre-trial cases, the Act on Retrieval of Data on Electronic Communication by Law Enforcement Agencies (*Lag (2012:278) om inhämtning av uppgifter om elektronisk kommunikation i de brottsbekämpande myndigheternas underrättelseverksamhet*) allows the police and customs to request traffic data, including location data, under certain circumstances with regards to their intelligence activities. Any such request has to be reported, however, to a specific supervisory authority, the Swedish Commission on Security and Integrity Protection (*Säkerhets- och integritetsskyddsnämnden*).[825]

The supervisory authority for network operators, PTS, has published information about the obligations of network operators[826] and has issued a Regulation with regards to the compensation for operators.[827]

417. In addition, Chapter 6 section 17 Electronic Communications Act prohibits wiretapping and stipulates that anybody other than the user may not access or in any other way process information in an electronic message without the consent of the user. This provision not only applies to telecom operators but to any third party who accesses electronic messages.

III. Processing of Data

A. Obligation to Delete Personal Data

418. Chapter 6 section 5 Electronic Communications Act stipulates an obligation for network operators to erase or anonymize traffic data. The provision transposes Article 6 Directive on Privacy and Electronic Communications and only allows telecom operators to process personal data to the extent this is necessary for the transmission of the message.

824. Chapter 27 s. 18 Code of Judicial Procedure.
825. The Commission on Security and Integrity Protection (<www.sakint.se/>) supervises the activities of crime-fighting agencies (e.g. secret surveillance) the processing of personal data by the Swedish Police, including the Swedish Security Service.
826. In Swedish at <www.pts.se/sv/Bransch/Internet/Integritet/Regler/Utlamning-av-teleuppgifter/>.
827. Swedish Post and Telecom Agency's Regulation on Compensation for Disclosure of Stored Data for Crime-Fighting Purposes (*PTSFS 2013:5 Post- och telestyrelsens föreskrifter om ersättning vid utlämnande av lagrade uppgifter för brottsbekämpande ändamål*), 11 Dec. 2013.

Providers of an electronic communication service may only process traffic data for billing purposes or with the consent of the subscriber.[828] Such processing is permissible only up to the end of the period during which the bill may lawfully be challenged or payment pursued.

Location data, which is not traffic data, may be processed with regards to value added services.[829] The data either has to be anonymized or may otherwise only be processed with the consent of the user to the extent and for the duration necessary for the provision of the value added service.

419. Chapter 6 section 7 Electronic Communications Act, transposing Article 6(5) Directive on Privacy and Electronic Communications, stipulates that only certain people may access personal data. The group includes employees given the task of billing, customer inquiries or marketing of electronic communication services.

The general principle to delete personal data does not apply if a court or the police need access to the information, or if messages are covered by a court order for surveillance of the communication.[830] The data should, however, never be stored for longer than one year, unless justified for a specific reason, such as police investigations or court proceedings.[831]

B. Obligation to Store Personal Data

420. In transposing Directive 2006/24/EC of the European Parliament and of the Council of 15 March 2006 on the retention of data generated or processed in connection with the provision of publicly available electronic communications services or of public communications networks and amending Directive 2002/58/EC (hereinafter 'Data Retention Directive') the Electronic Communications Act was amended to include an obligation to store personal data.[832]

The new section 16a–16f in Chapter 6 Electronic Communications Act introduce and specify network operators' obligation to store traffic data for crime-fighting purposes. According to Chapter 6 section 16a network operators have to retain data that is necessary to track and identify the source and the target for the communication, the date, time and duration, the type of communication, the equipment and the localization of the mobile communication equipment at the beginning and the end of the communication. The provisions are further specified by sections 37–44 Ordinance on Electronic Communication (*Förordning (2003:396) om elektronisk kommunikation*). With regards to internet access section 43 Ordinance on Electronic Communication specifies, for example, that the following data has to be stored: IP address, information about the subscription, date and time for logging on and off from the

828. Chapter 6 s. 6 Electronic Communications Act.
829. Chapter 6 s. 9 Electronic Communications Act.
830. Chapter 6 s. 8 Electronic Communications Act.
831. Government Bill (Proposition) 2002/03:110, 'Lag om elektronisk kommunikation', 392.
832. Sweden was late in transposing the Directive. The European Court of Justice ruled on 4 Feb. 2010 that Sweden failed to adopt, within the prescribed period, the provisions necessary to comply with the Data Retention Directive. Case C-185/09, *European Commission v. Kingdom of Sweden*, Judgment of the Court of 4 Feb. 2010.

internet access, capacity that was used, information that identifies the equipment that was used. The supervisory authority, PTS, has also issued Guidelines on which data has to be retained.[833]

The maximum retention period is six months counted from the day the communication ended (Chapter 6 section 16d Electronic Communications Act). Chapter 6 section 16c states that processing of the retained data is only allowed for the purposes of releasing the data to certain authorities according to the previously stated legislation.[834]

421. The obligation to store data has lead to a challenging balance of interest between protection of privacy and copyright regulation. As stated earlier, the 'order to provide information' (*informationsföreläggande*) according to the Swedish Copyright Act[835] can only force telecom operators to release personal data about their subscribers in the event this information is still stored in their systems. In a Supreme Court judgment from 2012[836] this argument was confirmed and the interest of the copyright holders was considered outweighing the interest of privacy of the subscribers. The Supreme Court also stated, however, that data that is being stored due to the network operators' data retention obligation (Chapter 6 section 16a–16f Electronic Communications Act) cannot fall under the 'order to provide information' and can therefore not be released to copyright holders.

C. Cookies

422. Chapter 6 section 18 Electronic Communications Act deals explicitly with cookies and transposes Article 5(3) Directive on Privacy and Electronic Communications. Electronic communication networks may be used to store or gain access to information stored in the terminal equipment of a subscriber or user only if the subscriber or user is provided with information about the purpose of the processing and has consented to the processing by the data controller.

The 2009 amendment to the Directive on Privacy and Electronic Communications was implemented into the Swedish Electronic Communications Act in 2011 and exchanged the earlier 'right to refuse' with the requirement of consent. The requirement has, however, not been interpreted in a clear manner in practice. The Swedish Interactive Advertising Bureau (IAB Sweden),[837] for example, together with some other industry organizations has produced a Recommendation for the use of cookies by market players.[838] IAB's recommendation builds upon the OBA-Framework (Online Behavioural Advertising) by IAB Europe. With regards to consent, the Recommendation states that certain browser settings can be regarded as

833. Swedish Post and Telecom Agency (PTS), Uppgifter som ska lagras för brottsbekämpande ändamål – en vägledning, 23 May 2012.
834. See s. 3 II *supra* (para. 416).
835. See Part II Ch. 1 s. 8 *supra* (para. 171).
836. Decision by Supreme Court from 21 Dec. 2012, NJA 2012 s. 975.
837. <iabsverige.se/>.
838. The recommendation is available to the public at < www.minacookies.se> and <iabsverige.se/standards-och-guidelines/oba-framework/>.

consent by the user, which would entail no change in practice from the previous legal wording. The supervisory authority, PTS, is looking into the legal compliance at the moment and might issue clearer guidelines on the requirements of consent in the next year.

The information and consent requirement does not apply in the event the storage or access are necessary in order to carry out the transmission of an electronic message over an electronic communication network,[839] or is otherwise required to provide an information society service explicitly requested by the subscriber or user. For example, if the user wishes to access a banking service that requires cookies to be stored or accessed on the user's computer, the data controller is allowed to employ cookies in the technical process. Caching necessary for a transmission for technical reasons is also permitted according to Chapter 6 section 18 Electronic Communications Act.

423. Furthermore, the Electronic Communications Act stipulates specific provisions on criminal liability with regards to non-compliance with Chapter 6 section 18. Unless liability is not covered by the Swedish Penal Code, violation of Chapter 6 section 18, intentionally or with gross negligence, can lead to a fine.[840]

IV. Directories of Subscribers

424. Chapter 6 sections 15 and 16 Electronic Communications Act, transposing Article 12 Directive on Privacy and Electronic Communications, stipulate some requirements for operators with regard to data processing in relation to directories of subscribers. A subscriber who is a natural person shall receive information about the purposes of a printed or electronic directory, free of charge and before the personal data is included in the directory. With regards to electronic directories, the subscriber shall also be informed about the search possibilities in the service.[841]

Personal data may only be processed in these directories with the consent of the subscriber. In addition, the user has to be able to request verification, correction or deletion of the data.[842]

§4. Sanctions and Supervision

425. In accordance with Article 15(2) Directive on Privacy and Electronic Communications, Chapter 6 section 2 Electronic Communications Act refers to the Personal Data Act. In particular, questions of civil liability are to be answered according to the Personal Data Act.

---

839. The wording 'or facilitate' the transmission was deleted in the 2011 amendment of the section, thereby restricting the allowed use of cookies to cases where cookies are necessary for the transmission and not just facilitate it.
840. Chapter 7 s. 15 Electronic Communications Act.
841. Chapter 6 s. 15 Electronic Communications Act.
842. *Ibid.*

Chapter 7 Electronic Communications Act contains provisions on criminal liability for, *inter alia*, breach of confidentiality.

426. According to section 2 Ordinance on Electronic Communications (*Förordning (2003:396) om elektronisk kommunikation*), the PTS is the responsible supervisory authority for data protection within the electronic communications sector. PTS monitors providers of electronic communications networks and also ensures compliance with the privacy rules of the Electronic Communications Act. In its supervisory capacity PTS also published guidelines on data protection within electronic communications.

Part VII. Computer-Related Crime

Chapter 1. General Legal Development

427. Sweden's long history of criminalizing computer-specific crime stretches back to the Data Act (*Datalag (1973:289)*) of 1973 which *inter alia* criminalized data intrusion. At the time, the legislature obviously did not have Internet-based hacking in mind, but intended instead to penalize persons who physically broke into offices housing computers (or terminals) in order to change information in registers. The Swedish Penal Code does not refer to 'computer-crimes' as a stand-alone category of crimes, but nevertheless criminalizes acts where computers and technology are involved. Most computer-related crimes were present in criminal law long before the advent of information technology, and will have their names and places in the traditional criminal law structure. Computer-specific crimes, however, are unique in the sense that they do not have their offline equivalents, they have a shorter history and they have been attributed places in the criminal law structure that may appear to be tentative, or even randomly chosen.

For want of a given structure for computer-crimes and computer-related crimes in national law, this chapter will follow the structure of the European Council Convention on Cybercrime. Sweden signed the Treaty on 23 November 2001 in Budapest, but has not ratified it yet, although most provisions in the Convention are covered by Swedish law.[843] Following the structure of the Cybercrime Convention,[844] there are four main categories of computer-related crimes. The first include the core of computer-based offences, that is offences against the confidentiality, integrity and availability of computer data, and systems as well as those 'where computer and telecommunication systems are used as a means to attack certain legal interests which mostly are protected already by criminal law against attacks using

843. A Government-appointed Public Inquiry presented its proposal SOU 2013:39 'Europarådets konvention om it-relaterad brottslighet' in May 2013, presenting the remaining legislative amendments necessary to permit ratification uf the convention and its additional protocol by Sweden. The Inquiry was also tasked with analysing the need and making proposals for the legislative amendments needed to implement the draft (not yet formally adopted). Directive of the European Parliament and of the Council on attacks against information systems, repealing Council Framework Decision 2005/222/JHA, as well as considering the need for tougher penalties for breaches of postal or telecommunication secrecy, or data security, in order to allow greater scope to take more nuanced account of the seriousness of large-scale attacks on information systems.

844. European Treaty Series (ETS) No. 185.

traditional means'.[845] The second category relates to ordinary crimes that are frequently committed using a computer system, but its traditional scope was not broad enough to cover situations involving new technologies. The third covers content-related offences regarding child pornography, whereas the fourth category covers infringement of intellectual property rights.

428. The Swedish Penal Code (*Brottsbalk (1962:700)*) entered into force on 21 December 1962, that is well before the advent of information technology, as we know it today. Although the code has been amended extensively, its main structure has remained intact. One of the crimes described in the code from the outset is *breach of postal or telecommunications secrecy*, Chapter 4 section 8.[846] This has traditionally been seen as an infringement on the liberty and privacy of the individual, and consequently we find the provision in Chapter 4 of the Code, where crimes against the peace and freedom of the individual are gathered. The traditional place of this crime in the Penal Code is the main reason why more contemporary amendments that include hacking are located in conjunction to this provision. Thus, the Swedish legislature has used Chapter 4 section 9 of the Penal Code as the section to deal with computer/technology-based crimes. Chapter 4 section 9a deals with illicit eavesdropping (bugging) using electronic means, section 9b deals with the illicit accessing of messages through electronic means and section 9c deals with illicit data intrusion.

Other criminalized acts, that can be applicable to computer-related crimes, can be found in other sections of the Penal Code and in other laws.

845. See Explanatory Report to ETS No. 185, para. 35.
846. In its current form, since 1993 (SFS *1993:601*).

Chapter 2. Application of Substantive Criminal Law in the Area of ICT

§1. Offences against the Confidentiality, Integrity, and Availability of Computer Data and Systems

I. Illegal Access and Illegal Interception

A. *Illegal Access*

429. 'Illegal access' as described by section 1 Article 2 Cybercrime Convention has its equivalent in Chapter 4 section 9c of the Swedish Penal Code. The provision in section 9c describes 'data intrusion' (*dataintrång*). This is an act, which the Cybercrime Convention would refer to as 'illegal access' and is the equivalent of 'hacking' in the vernacular. The crime itself consists of accessing information aimed to be processed through an automated process without permission. It also includes the illicit alteration, deletion or insertion of such data as well as the blocking or disruption of such data.

It is interesting to note that already back in the seventies, when the act was first introduced, the Swedish legislature tried to implement a technologically neutral phrasing so that the law would keep up with future technical developments. So, instead of criminalizing illegal access to computer systems (which is the path chosen by the Cybercrime Convention and which may be conceptually easier to understand for the general public but more difficult to define and is constantly changing), the legislators criminalized illegal access to computer data. This is why section 9c is phrased as the illicit accessing of information (i.e., computer data). Although this may seem as a major difference at first, the reality is that the Swedish interpretation of the phrasing encompasses both illicit access to computer systems and illicit access to computer data. The way in which this is achieved is two-fold.

First, the definition of 'information' is interpreted in its widest form. Much like the definition of the term 'computer data' in the Convention, the Swedish interpretation of 'information' in section 9c defines *not only what* 'kind' of data that is encompassed by section 9c, but also where the data can be in order for it to be encompassed by the section. Thus, the Swedish interpretation is such that the section encompasses all forms of data that can be processed by a computer. This includes data 'permanently' stored on a computer (a document or picture on the hard drive, for example), temporarily stored for processing (ones and zeros in the Random Access Memory of a computer) or actual programs/applications which process the previously mentioned forms of data along with data that is under transmission in wires.[847]

Second, the phrasing of section 9c is such that it also includes situations where a perpetrator *may* be able to illicitly gain access to information even if she or he did in fact not do so. In other words, any illicit access to a computer device/system is

847. If the data is part of an electronic message or transmitted through the air, then illicit accessing of it is covered through other sections of the Penal Code, such as Ch. 4 s. 8.

illegal because any such access would entail the possibility to also access data/information without permission. As a matter of fact, since there is no requirement for the illicit accessing to entail the circumvention of any security measures, the key factor becomes whether the person had 'authorization'[848] to access the information or not.

In summary, by using a wide definition of data/information and setting the penalization point to the possibility of gaining access to unauthorized data/information, the Swedish Penal Code criminalizes both the illicit accessing of computer data and of computer systems.[849]

430. The rule on data intrusion is subsidiary to the rules in Chapter 4 sections 8 and 9 Penal Code which define illicit *breaking of postal or telecommunications secrecy* and *intrusion into a safe depository* for such purposes respectively. While section 9b deals with conspiracy to such crimes, section 9 criminalizes illicit wiretaps and will be discussed in the next section.

Anyone who unlawfully obtains access to a message that a postal or telecommunications company conveys, may under section 8 be convicted of breaking the secrecy of the message to a fine or imprisonment for up to two years. The provision protects messages both in the traditional form and in the form of electronic messages, meaning messages conveyed through telecommunication. Messages conveyed by radio or data systems, however, fall outside the criminal area. The criminal law protection applies regardless if the content of the message (i.e., the contents of the envelope) consists of audio, video, text or otherwise, from the time the message was delivered for transmission until it is received by the intended recipient.[850]

Chapter 4 section 9 extends the reach of section 8, which only encompasses messages from the time they are sent/transmitted to the time they are received, thus protecting messages before and after they are sent/transmitted. Through section 9, illicitly opening a letter or telegram or illicitly accessing a message that is stored in a sealed manner, locked in or otherwise inaccessible is penalized as well.

Originally designed to protect postal delivery and storage of letters, the provision was later updated to cover telegrams, telephony and, more recently, other forms of telecommunication, including messages conveyed through information technology (through the previously discussed section 9c).[851] The penalty for acts that fall under sections 8 and 9 is fines or imprisonment for up to two years. Attempt and preparation for an intrusion, that if completed would not have been insignificant, is also punishable under section 10. Private transmission, that is, not relying on third parties for the transmission is, however, not protected by the criminal provision.

---

848. It is worth noting that 'authorization' does not only refer to a technical access through a user account on a system, but to a generic concept of whether the person had consent to gain access to a specific information by someone who can be considered the 'owner' of the information or not. Thus, data intrusion can be committed on a completely unprotected system as long as the 'owner' of the system did not authorize entry. See Government Bill (Proposition) 2006/07:66, 'Angrepp mot informationssystem', 34 et seq.
849. Government Bill (Proposition) 2006/07:66, 49–51.
850. Government Bill (Proposition) 2006/07:66, 49–51.
851. See Government Bill (Proposition) 2006/07:66; and Government Bill (Proposition) 1997/98:44, 'Personuppgiftslag'.

While unsuccessful attempt in this case is not criminalized, preparation for the commission of the crime is, through a specific provision in section 9b. Affixing a technical aid with the intent to break confidentiality in the manner described in section 8, is regarded as conspiracy to commit the offence, and the penalty is fines or imprisonment for up to two years.

B. Illegal Interception

431. As stated above, the illegal interception of communication during transmission or storage is covered by Chapter 4 sections 8, 9, 9b, and 9c. The provision in Chapter 4 section 9a covers the illegal interceptions or recordings of a private conversation, through any technical means, which neither the listener nor the public is meant to be privy to. In other words, this provision forbids illicit eavesdropping or bugging of a room to protect personal privacy as well as the privacy of boardrooms and the like.

The rule is subsidiary to the criminal provision on breach of postal or telecommunications secrecy (section 8). The punishment is fines or imprisonment for up to two years. Attempt is not punishable, while preparations fall within an ancillary provision in section 9b.

In addition, if the criminal act causes injury, it may lead to criminal liability for damages, provided that the act caused injury to a physical object and that the damage was covered by the offender's criminal intent. If such harmful acts are directed against vital interests of society (critical infrastructure) liability under the criminal law provisions regarding sabotage and serious sabotage may come into play.[852]

C. Common Provisions for Illegal Access and Illegal Interception, and the Confidentiality of Collected Traffic Data

432. Current Swedish legal provisions on confidentiality and disclosure of operators, comply with the provisions of the Cybercrime Convention's Articles 20 and 21. These national provisions are not, however, found in the Penal Code. Rules on disclosure of telecommunications carriers and providers are found in the Electronic Communications Act (*Lag (2003:389) om elektronisk kommunikation*), notably Chapter 6. According to Chapter 6 section 21 operators have to respect the confidentiality of the use of secret measures of compulsion, namely secret surveillance (bugging), covert remote surveillance and the detention of deliveries or shipments. Such secrecy also applies to the subscriber of services concerned.[853] These measures ensure that service providers *inter alia* keep information about official

852. In this context, it should be pointed out that serious criminal damage, sabotage and serious sabotage are punishable as terrorist offences, under the conditions set out in the Act on Sanctions for Terrorist Offences (*Lag (2003:148) om straff för terroristbrott*). For an overview of EU activities in this field, see <www.ec.europa.eu/justice_home/funding/2004_2007/epcip/funding_epcip_en.htm>, 15 Mar. 2010.

853. The rules on disclosure, in the same Chapter of the Electronic Communications Act, meet the Convention requirements of Art. 20 paras 3 and 21, para. 3.

police investigations carried out with their assistance and the result of these confidential.

433. The penalty for the criminal acts that the Convention refers to as 'illegal access' and 'illegal interception' – in Swedish law mainly constituting the singular crime data intrusion, Chapter 4 section 9c – is fines or imprisonment for a maximum of two years. For damaging property and seriously damaging property, the penalties are a fine or imprisonment for a maximum of one year and four years respectively. The penalty for sabotage is imprisonment for a maximum of years and for serious sabotage imprisonment for a minimum of two and a maximum of ten or lifetime imprisonment.

The penalty for attempt generally holds the same maximum as the completed form of the same crime[854] and may not go below imprisonment if the minimum penalty for the completed crime is imprisonment for two years or more. For instigation and accessory crimes, the same penalties apply as for the main crime. Certain latitude exists for reduction concerning accessories to crime.[855] Aggravating circumstances are described in Chapter 29 section 2 Penal Code, for example, if the crime forms part of criminal activities that has been carefully planned or carried out in organized proportions in which the perpetrator has played a significant role.

Swedish provisions on penalties for legal persons, stipulated in Chapter 36 sections 7–10 Penal Code, make companies liable for crimes that have been carried out in the conduct of business. A condition for this is that the crime has constituted a serious disregard of the particular obligations that the business entails or that the crime is of a particularly serious kind. An additional requirement is that the company has been negligent, that is, not done what could reasonably have been expected of it, in order to prevent the crime. The calculation of the size of the fine follows from the provisions in Chapter 36 section 8 Penal Code, that is not less than SEK 5,000 and not more than SEK 10,000,000.

434. Computer data, as defined by Chapter 4 section 9c Penal Code, that is illicitly changed, can be deemed as forgery if it involves the changing of a document or a record. Forgery of computer data will be discussed in a later section.[856] If, on the other hand, the change is made in a data process that does not qualify as such a record, the illegal changing of the data would fall under Chapter 4 section 9 c Penal Code. As mentioned above, the illicit changing, deleting, blocking or inserting into a register of computer data is considered as data intrusion. Thereby any alteration of computer data (as defined and interpreted by Chapter 4 section 9 c is considered to be 'hacking' if carried out without consent.

Chapter 4 section 9c was expanded in 2007 with a second sentence aimed at capturing Denial Of Service (DOS) attacks.[857] Following this amendment, any action that seriously disrupts or obstructs the use of computer data is also considered as

854. Chapter 23 s. 1 Penal Code.
855. Chapter 23 s. 5 Penal Code.
856. See s. 2 I *infra* (paras 439–440).
857. Amendment of Ch. 4 s. 9c through Act 2007:213, proposed in Government Bill (Proposition) 2006/07:66, 49–51. DoS-attacks as well as dDOS-attacks (distributed DOS-attacks) are intentionally launched against a computer system in order to prevent the proper operation of the system, thereby

data intrusion. It is important to note here that accidental or minor disruptions do not fall under the provision. The reasoning behind this follows Chapter II Article 4 paragraph 2 Cybercrime Convention whereby Member States can reserve the right to only criminalize serious forms of interception. Thus, the Swedish legislation requires both intent and the occurrence of serious damage as a result of DOS-attacks in order for these to be considered data intrusions.

Besides the section of the Penal Code that deals with computer-related offences, other sections of the Penal Code may also be applicable to DOS-attacks and the like. To destroy or damage property, movable or immovable, to the detriment of another person's right to the property, falls under the criminal offence of *inflicting damage*.[858] If the act entailed serious danger to someone's life or health – for example, if the act results in the malfunctioning of medical equipment – or if damage was inflicted on property of great cultural or economic significance or was otherwise serious, the act may be considered as *gross infliction of damage*.[859] These provisions primarily refer to physical life situations, such as when, a car or a house is damaged, but can also be applied to when computer data or computer systems are damaged. Since the provisions are not limited to physical damages, damage originating from 'cyber attacks' (i.e., data intrusion) also falls under the provision, for example, when a DOS-attack results in economic damages for the victim of the attack.

The destruction or damaging of property that has considerable significance for national defence, public security, justice or the administration or for maintaining public order and security, or by other measures that seriously interferes with or prevents the use of such property may be considered as sabotage.[860] This also applies if a person through criminal damage or other acts seriously interferes with or prevents public intercourse or use of telegraph, telephone, radio or similar public facilities *inter alia* for the supply of water, light, heat or power. If danger has been caused to national security, to several human lives or to property of particular importance by the offence, the perpetrator may be sentenced for aggravated sabotage.[861]

Once again, these provisions do not require the source of the damage to be physical and they do not even require the result of the damage to be physical. For example, the hacking or DOS-attack on the systems controlling traffic lights would fall under the provisions of Chapter 13 section 4.

---

denying users of its services. The most common attack type is saturation attacks, in which the system will use a scarce function or resource almost exclusively in order to manage data generated by the attack. For more information, see, e.g., <www.crime-research.org/articles/network-security-dos-ddos-attacks>, 15 Mar. 2010.

858. Chapter 12 s. 1 Penal Code.
859. Chapter 12 s. 3 Penal Code.
860. Chapter 13 s. 4 Penal Code.
861. Chapter 13 s. 5 Penal Code.

II. Data Interference and System Interference

435. Although these acts are described in the Cybercrime Convention as separate acts from illegal access and illegal interception, they are not separately criminalized under Swedish law. Data and system interferences are subsumed under the hacking offence described above.

III. Misuse of Devices

436. The Cybercrime Convention has a specific provision on 'misuse of devices', a concept borrowed from US Federal criminal law that finds few equivalents in European law.[862] The Convention thus calls not only for the criminalization of using devices for committing crimes under the Convention but also for the criminalization of possession and 'the production, sale, procurement for use, import, distribution or otherwise making available of'[863] such devices. For Sweden and several other signatories to the Convention, there are no specific provisions or offences for these forms of 'preparatory' acts/measures. They are, instead, subsumed under general rules on attempt and preparation of crimes. Using this technique, current legislation complies in all substantial aspects with the requirements of the Convention on criminal liability for non-independent forms of crime – all steps taken in preparing the execution of the crimes concerned are covered – although attempted ancillary forms of petty offences are not always punishable. The rules regarding preparation to commit crime do, therefore, make specific criminal provisions on abuse of tools or devices superfluous.

The general rule on criminal attempts specifies that if anyone has commenced the execution of a crime, the person shall, in cases where there is a specific provision to that effect linked to the crime in question, be sentenced for attempt to commit the offence.[864] A prerequisite for liability is, however, that there was clear danger of completion of the crime or that this danger was excluded only due to accidental circumstances. No liability will exist if the offender voluntarily suspended the act, before reaching the point of completion. The penalty for attempt will be determined on the same basis as the completed crime.[865]

437. Chapter 23 section 2 Penal Code stipulates criminal responsibility for preparation to commit a crime, for any person that:

862. Compare Title 18 Part I Ch. 47 s. 1029 US Code on 'Fraud and related activity in connection with access devices'.
863. Chapter II Art. 6 para. 1a Cybercrime Convention.
864. Chapter 23 s. 1 Penal Code.
865. In relation to the obligations under the Convention, non-independent liability exists in Swedish law for crimes under Arts 3 (illegal interception), 4 (data interference), 5 (system disturbance), 7 (data falsification) 8 (computer fraud) and 9 (child pornography). From pre-IT case law, it is worth noting that a person caught with a main key to a residence or hotel, or with keys to premises or housing to which the person has no connection, can incur responsibility for preparation of theft. See, e.g., Decision by Supreme Court from 18 Oct. 1960, NJA 1960 s. 442.

(1) receives or gives money or other items as payment for a crime or to cover the costs of carrying out a crime; or
(2) acquires, manufactures, supplies, receives, stores, transports, prepares or procures something particularly designed or well-adapted to be used as an aid in a crime.

When these conditions are met, the person shall be charged for the preparation of the offence in question whether it was completed or not.

For certain explicitly specified crimes in the Penal Code, the act of conspiracy can also result in criminal liability, covering situations where a person, in consultation with other persons, agrees to carry out a criminal act or otherwise conspires to bring it about. Criminal responsibility for preparation is excluded if the prospects for success of the attempt were small.

The rules on preparation were amended in 2001, when criminal responsibility was extended, and the provision on preparation of crimes was given its current, more general phrasing.[866] The introduction of a reference to procuring 'something particularly designed . . . to be used as an aid in crime' in Chapter 23 section 2 was motivated by necessary modernization, as such aids could be physical items but also more arbitrary items such as computer viruses and other software produced solely for hacking purposes or other types of criminal activities such as counterfeiting.[867] The penalty for preparing or conspiring cannot be higher than the highest level of penalty for the offence itself, but may be lower than the lowest level of penalty for the offence.[868]

According to Chapter 23 section 4 Penal Code, criminal liability shall be imposed not only on anyone who carries out a prohibited act, but also on other persons that have given advice or assisted in the criminal act. This responsibility includes all crimes in the penal code and penal provisions of other laws and regulations, provided that imprisonment is prescribed for the offence.

438. Using devices or programs that gain unauthorized access to closed services or to telecommunication equipment can be punishable as fraud.[869]

---

866. See SFS 2001:348.
867. See Government Bill (Proposition) 2000/01:85, 'Förberedelse till brott m.m.', 41.
868. Article 6 of the Convention requires the extensive criminalization of functions with different types of tools, from technical tools and software that are particularly suited for use in the crimes covered by the Convention to computer passwords, access codes and similar information. The latter are intended to only have a legal purpose, but may, if they come into the wrong hands, be used to commit crimes. As far as tools of the former kind are concerned, the amendment in 2001 was intended to include them and make the provision more technologically neutral. It is at first more doubtful whether passwords, access codes and the like can be seen as something that is particularly likely or designed to be used as a tool in crime. Because they are part of the security arrangements around the computer facility or computer system, they have a very important role and can best be compared with keys. The possession of illicitly obtained keys can, on the other hand, constitute a typical step-in the preparation of a crime.
869. See II *infra* (para. 441).

§2. Other Computer-Related Offences

I. Computer-Related Forgery

439. Chapter 14 section 1 Penal Code stipulates that a person who by writing another person's – real or fictitious – name, or by deceit obtains another person's signature, or by other means produces a false document of proof or fraudulently alters or adds to a genuine document, shall be deemed guilty of forgery or falsification of a document, which is the term reserved for this crime in Swedish law. A condition for such an act to be punishable is that the measure jeopardizes the verification or proof value of the document.[870]

Falsification of electronic documents that have not been transferred to paper does not constitute forgery according to a precedent from the Svea Court of Appeal.[871]

Section 17 Act on Qualified Electronic Signatures (*Lag (2000:832) om kvalificerade elektroniska signaturer*), the Swedish implementation of the EU Directive on Electronic Signatures[872] stipulates that advanced electronic signatures shall have the same legal status as handwritten signatures on documents where handwritten signatures are required through legislation (such as signing of a person's last will and testament or the transfer of real estate). Although the current legislation does not explicitly state that electronic documents signed with advanced electronic signatures can be subject to forgery, nor has this been affirmed by any court, it is widely assumed that such documents can indeed be subject to forgery.[873] The reason for this being, that electronically signed documents do indeed have an original copy – the copy which was signed. Any such document cannot be altered or tampered with (on a hard drive or in a print-out) without it becoming apparent once the electronic signature is verified.

The vast majority of electronic documents, however, such as saved documents of a word-processor, would not meet the fundamental requirement for forgery. Before the contents have been compiled and materialized into a physical document, any manipulation of the information in question may meet the requirements for criminal liability for data intrusion (if there is a case of illicit access), but would not constitute forgery as the information is not (yet) part of an object that can be forged. For the same reason the rules on counterfeiting can rarely be applied to information in electronic form.

The penalty for falsification of a document is prison up to two years. For *gross falsification of a document* the penalty is prison of not less than six months, and not more than six years.[874] In considering whether the crime is serious or not, particular

870. From the original Act introducing the Penal Code 1962:700.

871. See for extensive reasoning Government Official Report SOU 2007:92, 'Urkunden i tiden – en straffrättslig anpassning'. A decision from Svea Court of Appeal (Svea Hovrätt) states that documents that only exist in a format created by a word-processor are more like transcripts or copies and thus lack the level of originality that is required under Ch. 14 Penal Code; Decision by Svea Court of Appeal from 31 May 2002, no. B 5358–01, 67.

872. Directive 1999/93/EC of the European Parliament and of the Council of 13 Dec. 1999 on a Community framework for electronic signatures.

873. See Government Official Report SOU 2007:92.

874. Chapter 14 s. 3 Penal Code.

regard needs to be given to whether the forgery pertains to documents archived by public authorities or documents of proof of particular importance in general commerce, such as bonds, stocks or instruments of real estate mortgage.[875] Another reason for considering an act serious can be that the act has been of a particularly dangerous nature. If the act of forgery is considered to be of minor gravity, the sentence may concern alteration of documents of proof and amount to a fine or prison up to six months.[876]

440. Attempt and preparation of forgery and aggravated forgery are also punishable.[877] This does not apply if the crime, had it been completed, would have been considered to be minor, in which case it would be labelled rendering a document of proof inaccurate.

The sections about forgery and counterfeiting only encompass situations where a perpetrator changes a genuine document. A closely related offence occurs when a person destroys, renders useless or disposes of a genuine document without permission. A person found guilty of such an act will be convicted for the suppression of a document.[878] The penalty is imprisonment for up to two years. If the offence is minor, the penalty is a fine or imprisonment up to six months. If aggravating circumstances are demonstrated, the penalty is imprisonment of between six months and a maximum of four years. Attempt and preparation for the suppression of documents is punishable.[879] This does not apply if the crime, had it been completed, would have been considered to be minor.

II. Computer-Related Fraud

441. Under Swedish criminal law, fraud is regulated in a general manner, Chapter 9 section 1 (with a petty form of the crime described in Chapter 9 section 2, and a aggravated form in Chapter 9 section 3) covering all situations where a person 'by deception induces someone to commit or omit to commit some act which involves gain for the accused and loss for the deceived or someone represented by the latter'. The same applies for 'a person who, by delivering incorrect or incomplete information, or by making alterations to a programme or recording or by other means, unlawfully affects the result of automatic data processing or any other similar automatic process so that gain accrues to the offender and loss is entailed by any other person'. The penalty for fraud is imprisonment for at most two years. Should the gain/loss be negligible, the minor form of the crime would be applicable, Chapter 9 section 2. If no gain or loss results from the act, but the victim nevertheless is harmed, Chapter 9 section 8 holds liability for dishonest conduct when a person acts dishonestly by misleading someone and inducing her or him to do or omit to do something, thereby harming her or him or someone she or he represents.

875. From the original Act introducing the Penal Code, 1962:700.
876. Chapter 14 s. 2 Penal Code.
877. Chapter 14 s. 2 Penal Code.
878. Chapter 14 s. 4 Penal Code.
879. Chapter 14 s. 12 Penal Code.

Liability for fraud, as defined in the above-mentioned provision, also follows from the act of providing inaccurate or incomplete information for example, by altering a computer program or recording, or otherwise illicitly affects the outcome of an automated information process or a similar automated process, so that the offender benefits to the detriment of someone else. This provision thus encompasses computer system or data manipulation which is done for financial profit such as 'hacking' ATM's or the copying of the magnetic stripes on credit cards ('skimming'). The provision would, however, also encompass 'phishing' attacks where, for example, copies of banks' web pages would be set up in order to steal the bank customers' login details.[880]

Under aggravating circumstances, the offender may be sentenced for serious fraud to imprisonment of not less than six months and a maximum of six years.[881] In determining the seriousness of the offence, consideration will be given to whether the offender has misused public confidence or used a forged document or misleading accounting or if the act otherwise was of a particularly dangerous nature, pertained to a substantial value or entailed considerable damage.

If the crime, in view of the extent of damage and other circumstances, is considered to be of a minor nature – for instance with regard to the amounts involved – the sentence may refer to fraudulent behaviour instead of fraud, and the penalty set to a fine or imprisonment of up to six months.[882]

Attempt and conspiracy to commit fraud and serious fraud is a criminal offence, according to Chapter 9 section 11 Penal Code, while petty offences are not punishable at these preliminary stages.

§3. Content-Related Offences

442. The Act on Child Pornography[883] came into force on 1 January 1999, as Criminal Code Chapter 16 section 10a. According to this Section, all forms of handling child pornography are prohibited. It is thus prohibited to depict children in pornographic images, to transfer or make available images of child pornography, to broker contacts between buyers and sellers of child pornography, etc. Images in electronic form are covered by the provision. The responsibility is not limited to photos where children are involved in acts which clearly have a sexual meaning. Pornographic images involving children that occur in conjunction with one or more adults engaged in sexual acts are also subject to criminalization. Any person that through commercial activities or otherwise for gain negligently distributes child

880. This section was added to the Penal Code in 1986 through SFS 1986:123, and although the expression 'the outcome of an automated information process' may seem alien today, it is the result of the earliest attempts to create a wide and technology-neutral definition for digitized data stored on various mediums, such as magnetic tapes. For developments in the EU related to credit card fraud, see <www.ec.europa.eu/internal_market/payments/fraud/index_en.htm>, 15 Mar. 2010. For links to articles and research on this topic, see, e.g., <www.crime-research.org/articles/1562>, 15 Mar. 2010.

881. Chapter 9 s. 3 Penal Code.

882. Chapter 9 s. 2 Penal Code.

883. SFS 2005:90.

pornographic images may also sentenced for child pornography crimes. The law does not, however, prohibit the viewing of child pornography on the Internet, although the Act is currently under review, *inter alia* in this respect.

443. Current criminal responsibility for child pornography in Swedish law, is in many respects more stringent than required by the Convention. In principle, any handling of child pornographic material is prohibited.

A person found guilty of child pornography related crimes may be sentenced to imprisonment for up to two years. If the crime is considered to be a minor offence, the applicable penalty is a fine or imprisonment for up to six months. Under aggravating circumstances, child pornography related crimes may result in penalties between six months and six years of imprisonment. Aggravating circumstances include situations where the crime is committed professionally or for profit, as a part of criminal activities perpetrated systematically or on a large-scale. Further aggravating circumstances are situations where a particularly large number of images are used or situations where the images depict children exposed to particularly ruthless treatment.

Criminal responsibility includes attempt and preparation of the crime, provided that it would not, if completed, have been considered minor.[884]

§4. Offences Related to Infringements of Copyright and Related Rights

444. Swedish copyright rules include both criminal penalties and other sanctions for crimes infringing on intellectual property. According to section 53 Act on Copyright in Literary and Artistic Work (Lag *(1960:729) om upphovsrätt till litterära och konstnärliga verk*; hereinafter 'Copyright Act') liability applies to anyone who, with intent or negligence, commits an act that infringes on the copyrights of literary or artistic works.

Section 26g and h Copyright Act regulate the use of software and computer programs. A person who has obtained the right to use a computer program (i.e., bought it) can copy it and even modify it in order to ensure that it functions as intended. To this end, the rightful owner of a program may even correct errors in the program itself to ensure that it works as intended. The rightful owner may also create security-backups of the program if this is necessary for the intended use of the program. These copies may, however, not be used once the owner no longer has the right to use the original program (e.g., if the original CD with the program on it was sold to a third party).

Decompilation of a computer program is allowed in situations where the computer program is being examined with the intent to make it compatible with another computer program. Such decompilation is only allowed if it is carried out by a person that has a right to use the program being decompiled, if the information is not readily available elsewhere and if only the relevant sections of the program are decompiled. The information thus gained cannot be used for purposes other than to

884. Chapter 16 s. 17 Penal Code.

make the program compatible with another program. Nor can it be handed over to third parties unless the purpose of the handover is to ensure the compatibility measures in question.

Copying computer programs for private use is allowed as long as the copy is not used in business or public activities and the perpetrator does not make use of the copies for anything other than personal use.[885]

Penalties for copyright infringement are a fine or imprisonment for up to two years. Attempt and preparations for copyright infringement lead to the same penalties, section 53 paragraph 5 Copyright Act. A restriction in the general prosecution principle applies for this crime, to the extent that a copyright violation may only be prosecuted by the prosecutor if the plaintiff brings charges to that effect, or if prosecution is warranted from a general point of view.[886]

According to section 5 Act on Responsibility for Electronic Bulletin Boards (*Lag (1998:112) om ansvar för elektroniska anslagstavlor*; hereinafter 'BBS Act'), the owner of the BBS[887] or a similar forum is obliged to delete or otherwise prevent the circulation of certain messages, including messages whereby a user of the BBS is obviously committing copyright violations. The liability provision in the Act on Liability for Electronic Bulletin Boards is subsidiary to the rules of the Copyright Act, according to section 7.

885. Section 53 para. 2 Copyright Act.
886. Section 59 Copyright Act.
887. Section 1 BBS Act defines BBS as a service for the electronic conveying of messages.

Chapter 3. Application of the Criminal Procedure Law in the Area of ICT

§1. Search and Seizure of Stored Computer Data

445. Search and seizure are criminal procedural measures of coercion – in some jurisdictions appearing jointly, in others separately – through which law enforcement authorities, investigating a suspected crime, may search a property (search), belonging to one or more persons, and confiscate (seizure) objects that could be relevant to the investigation, and later serve as evidence to the crime. Seizure may, according to Chapter 27 Section 1 Swedish Code of Judicial Procedure (*Rättegångsbalk (1942:740)*), include objects, which could reasonably be expected to have significance for the investigation of a crime or that could be the product of criminal activity. Seizure therefore does not require a suspect, nor is there a requirement that the crime must be of a certain degree of gravity, with some exceptions. Seizures can be decided following any type of crime and against both suspects and others, pursuant to Chapter 27 section 1 Code of Judicial Procedure. Seizure may be ordered only if the reasons for the action outweigh the interference and personal interests of the suspect. Seizures often include written documents[888] and through the development of case law, electronic documents (i.e., a separate compilation of electronic data) are equated with written documents.[889]

For seizure of electronic data, it is crucial that the data has been transferred to a physical medium – the Code of Judicial Procedure assumes physical form and would not permit seizing intangible objects, should such objects be possible to seize.[890] It is uncertain whether data in electronic form, which has not been compiled, can be considered equivalent to a written document and therefore possible to seize. The log files demonstrating the albeit temporal existence of such data, do, however, qualify as objects that can be searched and 'seized' in the sense, that for example, an ISP may be coerced, using the same or similar mechanisms, to provide printouts of relevant log files. Data stored with a telephone operator may not be seized as a substitute measure for covert remote surveillance, an instrument defining exclusive possibilities for obliging a telecom operator through coercive powers in order to obtain information on telecommunications and other electronic communications. There are, however, other provisions in the Electronic Communications Act with obligations for telecommunications carriers to provide certain information to law enforcement authorities.[891]

888. Chapter 27 s. 2 Code of Judicial Procedure.

889. See, e.g., Government Bill (Proposition) 1998/99:11, 'Ny skyddsåtgärd vid immaterialrättsintrång', 54 et seq., Ministry Publications Series (Ds) 2003:29, 'FORMEL – Formkrav och elektronisk kommunikation', 95 et seq., as well as Government Official Report SOU 1992:110, 'Datastraffrättsutredningen'.

890. See Ministry Publications Series (Ds) 2005:6, 'Brott och brottsutredning i IT-miljö, Europarådets konvention om IT-relaterad brottslighet med tilläggsprotokoll', 126 et seq.

891. See Directive 2006/24/EC of the European Parliament and of the Council of 15 Mar. 2006 on the retention of data generated or processed in connection with the provision of publicly available electronic communications services or of public communications networks and amending Directive 2002/58/EC.

446. A search warrant gives authorities a legal title to search premises for objects that may be seized. The preconditions for a search warrant, however, are stricter than the conditions for seizure – Chapter 28 section 1 Code of Judicial Procedure provides a positive permission for searches in the premises of the suspect of a crime, but defines the scope for searches in other premises more negatively. An electronic message, transferred to paper or materialized in another physical form is, with the exceptions listed below, accessible to seizure under the normal rules. Similarly, an electronic message that is stored in a computer by someone other than a telecom operator, for example, by the subscriber, may be seized, if the conditions are otherwise satisfied.[892]

Searches may be carried out, if there are grounds for assuming that a criminal offence, for which imprisonment may follow, has been committed. Searches may be carried out in houses, rooms or enclosed storage facilities, either to search for objects that are subject to seizure or to determine other factors that may have importance for the investigation of the offence, pursuant to Chapter 28 section 1 Code of Judicial Procedure.

447. A search of the premises or property of a suspect requires that she or he is reasonably suspected of a crime, pursuant to Chapter 28 section 1 Code of Judicial Procedure. Searches may still be carried out, at lower levels of suspicion, but only when there is strong reason to believe that the search will produce objects to be seized or that other investigative advantages can be won. Search of the property of other persons than the suspect may be undertaken if the premises were the scene of the crime, or the scene of arrest of the suspect. A search (in this context, reference is made to a so-called real search, that is, pertaining to objects, rather than personal search, pertaining to anything related to a specific individual) may, according to Chapter 28 section 1 Code of Judicial Procedure, be undertaken in order to search for items that may later be subject to seizure – a decision to seize an object can only be made once the object has been found – or to discover evidence that may be relevant to the investigation of a crime. Using a search warrant for the detection of crimes is not consistent with these requirements. Nor may the purpose of the search be to provide information on other crimes than the crime, the investigation of which was the basis for issuing the search warrant, or in order to ascertain whether the suspect may have committed crimes to a greater extent (i.e., in greater volumes or frequency) than expected initially.[893]

The conditions for searches follow the same general restriction as seizure, namely that the search can be permitted only if the grounds of the measure outweigh the interference.[894] There are no specific rules concerning the examination of computers in relation to searches and seizures. When a search warrant is issued in order to gain access to digitally stored information, the object of the search can be either the data carrier (usually a computer), or data stored in the data carrier or the code (the

---

892. See Ministry Publications Series (Ds) 2005:6, 278 et seq. See also Gunnel Lindberg, *Straffprocessuella tvångsmedel – När och hur får de användas*, 2nd edn (Stockholm: Thomson Förlag, 2005).

893. See Government Bill (Proposition) to the original Code of Judicial Procedure, published in NJA II 1933, 97 et seq., as well as the Decision by the Parliamentary Ombudsman JO 1988/89 53.

894. Chapter 28 s. 3a Code of Judicial Procedure.

pattern of ones and zeros, not linked to specific data) that represents the stored information. If the carrier is the object for the action, the specific rules restricting later seizure of written documents in Chapter 27 Code of Judicial Procedure are not applicable, although the carrier may contain sensitive material, and vice versa.[895]

448. Searches can be carried out without any limitations on the type of premises to be searched, and can therefore, if conditions in Chapter 28 Code of Judicial Procedure are met, be made wherever there is a computer or other equipment likely to have been used in a crime. The prohibition of seizures in Chapter 27 section 2 Code of Judicial Procedure may however be indirectly relevant here. If there are legal obstacles to the seizure of an object, then a search for the same object is not permissible.[896]

Facilities open to the public may be searched for the purpose stated above, even if there is no suspect.[897] This includes shops, restaurants, cafes, theatres, cinemas, and – arguably – Internet cafés open to the public. Facilities usually used by persons likely to engage in criminal activity may also be searched for these purposes and under the same conditions.[898]

§2. Interception

449. Communication between computers may be intercepted under the rules in Chapter 27 Code of Judicial Procedure, which also regulate secret telecommunications interception. This measure means that messages sent to or from a telecommunication address may be secretly intercepted and listened in on in real time or recorded by technical means in order to reproduce the content of a message at a later time. The term 'telecommunication' in this context is defined in Chapter 6 section 19 paragraph 3 Act on Electronic Communications as sound, text, images, data or other forms of information conveyed by means of radio or light or electromagnetic oscillations.[899]

Secret telecommunications interception may be used in investigations concerning offences with a lower penalty threshold of two years imprisonment. It may also be used in situations dealing with attempt, preparation or conspiracy to commit such crimes, if these independent forms of crime are specifically criminalized.[900]

Covert remote surveillance is a different instrument that may not be used to obtain the content of messages but only the traffic that conveys the message, its source and destination. Covert remote surveillance may be used in the investigation

895. See Government Official Report SOU 1992:110, 344 and 350.
896. See Decision by Supreme Court from 28 Jun. 1977, NJA 1977 s. 403.
897. Chapter 28 s. 3 first paragraph Code of Judicial Procedure.
898. For an interesting contribution to the discourse related to this issue, and useful references to relevant case law, see Henrik Bengtsson & Emil Dicksved, 'Dataintrång', *Ny Juridik* 4 (2009).
899. See Government Bill (Proposition) 2002/03:110, 'Lag om elektronisk kommunikation, m.m.'
900. Chapter 27 s. 18 Code of Judicial Procedure. This threshold was established by amendments proposed in Government Bill (Proposition) 2002/03:74, 'Hemliga tvångsmedel – offentliga ombud och en mer ändamålsenlig reglering'.

concerning criminal offences for which the minimum penalty is six months in prison, as well as for two specific crimes: hacking and child pornography crimes.[901]

§3. Jurisdiction

450. Chapter 2 section 1 Penal Code establishes Swedish jurisdiction over all crimes committed on Swedish territory, as well as over offences believed to have been committed on Swedish territory. Jurisdiction also extends to all Swedish citizens and foreigners resident in Sweden, and for crimes committed abroad, under the dual criminality condition.[902] Exceptions in the latter case are made for crimes committed on territory not belonging to any state, and for crimes that do not carry more than fines as a penalty under Swedish law.

451. For purposes of determining criminal jurisdiction, a crime is considered to have been committed, for purposes of jurisdiction, where the criminal act was carried out, where the commission of the crime was completed or, concerning attempts, where it would have been completed.[903] In addition to this, Swedish courts also have formal jurisdiction over crimes committed abroad, *inter alia* for crimes committed against Sweden, a Swedish municipality or other constituency, or against a Swedish public facility. Moreover, Swedish courts have formal jurisdiction over crimes that carry a minimum penalty of four years imprisonment[904] even if they were committed outside of Swedish territory and even if the actions are not criminalized in the country where they were committed. In order to launch prosecution of crimes committed abroad, however, Chapter 2 section 5 Penal Code requires the prosecution service to obtain a government authorization to prosecute (*åtalsförordnande*), as a restraining measure on the exercise of universal jurisdiction.[905]

§4. Extradiction and Judicial Cooperation

452. Following the Act on Surrendering of Persons from Sweden in Accordance with a European Arrest Warrant (*Lag (2003:1156) om överlämnande från Sverige enligt en europeisk arresteringsorder*), surrendering may not be denied on the sole ground that the subject of the warrant is a citizen of the requested state. The Act, implementing an EU Framework Decision,[906] is applied in relation to other EU Member States instead of extradition procedures.

901. These provisions in the Code of Judicial Procedure were introduced through SFS 2003:1146, resulting from Government Bill (Proposition) 2002/03:74.
902. Chapter 2 s. 2 Penal Code.
903. Chapter 2 s. 4 Penal Code.
904. Chapter 2 s. 3 Penal Code.
905. See also Government Official Report SOU 2002:98, 'Internationella brott och svensk jurisdiktion'.
906. Council Framework Decision of 13 Jun. 2002 on the European arrest warrant and the surrender procedures between Member States (2002/584/JHA).

453. Swedish law contains several mechanisms to ensure proper cooperation between different jurisdictions, based upon international treaties, conventions and agreements. The central instruments that outline Sweden's obligations in this regard are the European Convention on Mutual Assistance in Criminal Matters ratified by Sweden on 1 February 1968, the Convention Implementing the Schengen Agreement, signed on 19 June 1990, as well as the EUROPOL and EUROJUST systems established under the European Union for cooperation between police authorities and prosecution services respectively.[907]

§5. Electronic Evidence

454. The Swedish criminal procedure is mainly oral and there is considerable freedom for the court to accept any type of evidence. The Code of Judicial Procedure contains no definition of, nor any specific provisions concerning evidence in digital form. This is a consequence of the fact that Swedish procedural law does not distinguish between different types of evidence that may be presented before a court. Chapter 35 section 1 stipulates that the court shall try everything that has been presented in the case before it and then decide what has been proven, a procedural principle of free trial of evidence in the sense that any evidence may be presented and the court given wide latitude in evaluating the evidence presented.[908] Taking this principle into the digital environment, electronic evidence may consist of any kind of information derived from digital technology environments, as well as information processed and presented by means of electronic equipment.[909]

Aggregated presentations covering all relevant evidence – seized computers, individual files, log files from service providers, results from covert account monitoring, etc. – are frequently made by the prosecution, in order to make technically complex operations judicially manageable. Indirect transcriptions are therefore the norm rather than an exception, when it comes to technical evidence. The possibility of introducing evidence through witnesses, such as the authorities or law enforcement agents that had access to the evidence, is frequently used.[910]

907. For more information on the cooperation of these agencies see <www.europol.europa.eu/> and <www.eurojust.europa.eu>.

908. Naturally, there *are* certain limitations, cf. Ch. 35 s. 14 and 36 s. 3 Code of Judicial Procedure.

909. See Kronkvist, Stefan, *Brott och digitala bevis – En handledning*, 2nd edn (Stockholm: Norstedts Juridik, 2007), 15 et seq.

910. *Ibid.*

Part VIII. Conclusions

Chapter 1. Conclusions

455. Various areas of cyber law have been harmonized within the European Union in recent years. Sweden has transposed Directives and Regulations in the fields of intellectual property law, data protection and telecommunications. Contract and procedural law have remained in the sovereignty of the national states, which may lead to minor legal differences in the various countries.

Though both the Swedish Contracts Act (*Lag (1915:218) om avtal och andra rättshandlingar på förmögenhetsrättens område*) and the Swedish Code of Judicial Procedure (*Rättegångsbalk (1942:740)*) are not specifically adapted to any technological development, the principle of freedom of contract and the non-existence of any exclusionary rules regarding evidence have opened up for a technology-neutral interpretation of the provisions. The Acts have proven to be flexible enough to allow electronic means in contracting and electronic messages as evidence in court.

In general, Swedish law is well prepared to deal with new developments in ICT to the extent that the laws are kept technology-neutral. The tendency to amend legislation to suit specific technologies can, however, be noticed in a few areas, even within the fields that are harmonized within the European Union, which has lead to difficulties regarding interpretation of the existing law on a few occasions.

Selected Bibliography

§1. Books

I. English

Carlson, Laura. *The Fundamentals of Swedish Law*. Lund: Studentlitteratur, 2009.
Magnusson Sjöberg, Cecilia (ed.). *IT Law for IT Professionals: An introduction*. Lund: Studentlitteratur, 2005.
Magnusson Sjöberg, Cecilia (ed.). *Legal Management of Information Systems: Incorporating Law in E-solutions*. 2nd edn. Lund: Studentlitteratur, 2005.
Seipel, Peter (ed.). *Law and Information Technology: Swedish Views (SOU 2002:112)*. Stockholm: IT Law Observatory, 2002.
Wahlgren, Peter (ed.). *IT Law*. Scandinavian Studies in Law, vol. 47. Stockholm: Stockholm Institute for Scandinavian Law, 2004.
Wolk, Sanna (ed.). *Ownership of the Copyright in Works and the Patent Right in Inventions Created by Employees in Finland, Sweden, Germany, Austria, the United Kingdom, Estonia and Argentina*, Gröna Serien, No. 120. Stockholm: Institute of Intellectual Property Law and Marketing Law: Institutet för Immaterialrätt och Marknadsrätt (IFIM), 2002.

II. Swedish

Hellner, Jan, Richard Hager & Annina H Persson. Speciell avtalsrätt II, Kontraktsrätt: Särskilda avtal. 4th edn. Stockholm: Norstedts Juridik, 2005.
Hultmark, Christina. *Elektronisk handel och avtalsrätt*. Stockholm: Norstedts Juridik, 1997.
Koktvedgaards, Mogens & Marianne Levin. *Lärobok i immaterialrätt*. Stockholm: Norstedts Juridik, 2007.
Kronkvist, Stefan. *Brott och digitala bevis: En handledning*. 2nd edn. Stockholm: Norstedts Juridik, 2007.
Lindberg, Gunnel. *Straffprocessuella tvångsmedel: När och hur får de användas*. 2nd edn. Stockholm: Thomson Förlag, 2005.
Lindberg, Agne, Johan Kahn & Björn Krouthén. *IT-avtal: Särskilt om outsourcing*. Stockholm: Norstedts Juridik, 2009.
Lindberg, Agne & Daniel Westman. *Praktisk IT-rätt*. 3rd edn. Stockholm: Norstedts Juridik, 2002.

Olsson, Henry. *Upphovsrättslagstiftningen: En kommentar.* 2nd edn. Stockholm: Norstedts Juridik, 2009.
Öman, Sören & Hans-Olof Lindblom. *Personuppgiftslagen: En kommentar.* 4th edn. Stockholm: Norstedts Juridik, 2009.
Pedersen, Kristian. *Upphandlingens Grunder*. Stockholm: Jure, 2008.
Ramberg, Jan & Christina Ramberg. *Allmän avtalsrätt.* 6th edn. Stockholm: Nordstedts Juridik, 2002.
Seipel, Peter. *Juridik och IT: Introduktion till Rättsinformatiken*. 8th edn. Stockholm: Nordstedts Juridik, 2004.

§2. ARTICLES

I. English

Edstrom, Jerker & Henrik Nillson. 'The Pirate Bay Verdict: Predictable, and Yet . . .'. *European Intellectual Property Review* 31, no. 9 (2009): 483–487.
Magnusson Sjöberg, Cecilia & Anna Nordén. *Managing Electronic Signatures: Current Challenges*, Scandinavian Studies in Law, vol. 47 (IT Law). Stockholm: Stockholm Institute for Scandinavian Law, 2004.
Öman, Sören. *Implementing Data Protection in Law.* Scandinavian Studies in Law, vol. 47 (IT Law). Stockholm: Stockholm Institute for Scandinavian Law, 2004.
Öman, Sören. 'Protection of Personal Data: But How?'. In *Law and Information Technology-Swedish Views (SOU 2002:112)*, edited by Peter Seipel. Stockholm: IT Law Observatory, 2002.
Ramberg, Christina Hultmark. 'The E-commerce Directive and Formation of Contract in a Comparative Perspective'. *European Law Review* 26, no. 5 (2001): 429–450.
Wennerström, Erik. *EU-legislation and Cybercrime: A Decade of European Legal Developments*. Scandinavian Studies in Law vol. 47 (IT Law). Stockholm: Stockholm Institute for Scandinavian Law, 2004.
Wistam, Henrik & Therese Andersson. 'The Pirate Bay Trial'. *Computer and Telecommunications Law Review* 15, no. 6 (2009): 129–130.

II. Swedish

Bengtsson, Henrik. 'Marknadsföring med hjälp av elektroniska meddelanden'. *Ny Juridik* 3 (2009): 35–51.
Bengtsson, Henrik. 'Svenska domännamnstvister: Praxis enligt den s.k. II-stiftelsens systems för alternativ tvistelösning'. *Nordiskt Immateriellt Rättskydd* 3 (2005): 256–277.
Bengtsson, Henrik & Emil Dicksved. 'Dataintrång'. *Ny Juridik* 4 (2009): 40–61.
Hübner, Johan. 'Analog tillämpning av lagen om handelsagentur på återförsäljare av datorprogram'. *Lov & Data* 93 (2008): 14–15.

§3. ONLINE PUBLICATIONS

I. English

Government Official Report SOU 2009:44. 'Integritetsskydd i arbetslivet', English summary at <www.regeringen.se/sb/d/108/a/125763>.

Swedish Data Inspection Board, 'Monitoring in working life', Report 2005:3, <www.datainspektionen.se/in-english/publications/>.

Personal Data Act (*Personuppgiftslag (1998:204)*), in English at <www.datainspektionen.se/in-english/legislation>.

Act on Qualified Electronic Signatures (*Lag (2000:832) om kvalificerade elektroniska signaturer*), in English at <www.pts.se/en-gb/Industry/Internet/Electronic-signatures>.

Translations to Swedish Acts are partly available at <www.sweden.gov.se/sb/d/3288>.

II. Swedish

All decisions and reports by the Swedish Data Inspection Board are available at <www.datainspektionen.se>.

All decisions and reports by the Swedish Post and Telecom Agency (PTS) are available at <www.pts.se>.

All Government Bills (Proposition), Government Official Reports (SOU) and Ministry Publications Series (Ds) can be searched by their number at <www.regeringen.se/sb/d/108>.

Selected Bibliography

Index

The numbers here refer to paragraph numbers.

Index

www.ingramcontent.com/pod-product-compliance
Lightning Source LLC
Chambersburg PA
CBHW071433230926
51846CB00001B/212
9789041156679